YOUR SUPERVISED PRACTICUM AND INTERNSHIP

Your Supervised Practicum and Internship is a complete, up-to-date guide to everything a graduate student in the helping professions needs for a successful practicum, internship, or field experience. This helpful resource takes students through the necessary fundamentals of field experience, helping them understand the supervision process and their place in it. The authors fully prepare students for the more advanced or challenging scenarios they are likely to face as helping professionals. The new edition also interweaves both CACREP and NASW standards, incorporates changes brought by the DSM-5, and places special focus on brain-based treatments and neurocounseling. *Your Supervised Practicum and Internship* takes the practical and holistic approach that students need to understand what really goes on in agencies and schools, providing evidence-based advice and solutions for the many challenges the field experience presents.

Lori A. Russell-Chapin, PhD, is professor and associate dean of the College of Education and Health Sciences at Bradley University. She is also codirector for the Center for Collaborative Brain Research (CCBR), a partnership between OSF Saint Francis Medical Center and the Illinois Neurological Institute, and was recently named AMHCA's national counselor educator of the year.

Nancy E. Sherman, PhD, is professor in the department of leadership in education, nonprofits, and counseling at Bradley University, where she is also clinical coordinator for the master of arts in counseling program.

Allen E. Ivey, PhD, is Distinguished University Professor (emeritus) at the University of Massachusetts–Amherst and president of Microtraining Associates, an educational publishing firm. He is a diplomate of the American Board of Professional Psychology, past president and fellow of the Society of Counseling Psychology of the American Psychological Association, and an elected fellow of the American Counseling Association, Society for the Psychological Study of Ethnic Minority Issues, and the Asian American Psychological Association.

YOUR SUPERVISED PRACTICUM AND INTERNSHIP

Field Resources for Turning Theory into Action

Second Edition

Lori A. Russell-Chapin
Nancy E. Sherman
Allen E. Ivey

Routledge
Taylor & Francis Group

NEW YORK AND LONDON

Second edition published 2016
by Routledge
711 Third Avenue, New York, NY 10017

and by Routledge
2 Park Square, Milton Park, Abingdon, Oxon, OX14 4RN

Routledge is an imprint of the Taylor & Francis Group, an informa business

First Edition published by Cengage 2003

Library of Congress Cataloging-in-Publication Data
Russell-Chapin, Lori A.
  Your supervised practicum and internship : field resources for turning theory into action / Lori A. Russell-Chapin, Bradley University, Nancy E. Sherman, Bradley University, Allen E. Ivey, University of Massachusetts, Amherst (emeritus). — 2nd edition.
     pages cm
  Includes bibliographical references and indexes.
  1. Client-centered psychotherapy. 2. Counseling. 3. Psychotherapy.
I. Sherman, Nancy Elizabeth, 1953– II. Ivey, Allen E. III. Title.
  RC481.R875 2016
  616.89'14—dc23
  2015025513

ISBN: 978-1-138-93580-8 (hbk)
ISBN: 978-1-138-93581-5 (pbk)
ISBN: 978-1-315-67288-5 (ebk)

Typeset in Baskerville
by Apex CoVantage, LLC

CONTENTS

ACKNOWLEDGMENTS

Lori

This book continues to be a labor of love. Being a member of the helping profession is a calling for me! As I have developed and grown as a person and clinician, it has been fun to share many of my observations and ideas with others in the profession. But even more importantly are the people who have influenced me by their generosity, compassion, and dedication not only to the field of counseling but to life in general. This book is dedicated to all those people in my life who are mentors and role models to me. These people epitomize the concept of "richly living" by taking risks and generating new options.

Thank you to:

My husband, Ted, whose love and friendship have provided me with support but challenged me towards mastery

Our children, Elissa and Jaimeson, who keep me mindful of the moment

My client, Chris, who lost her life but faced her fears

Our editor, Anna, whose wisdom, foresight, and clarity have been so appreciated

My mentor, Allen Ivey, who has inspired me and countless others to be passionate about the counseling field and especially the area of neuroscience and neurocounseling

My colleague, Nancy Sherman, who has taught and presented with me for the past 22 years

My parents, Helen and Bill, who modeled for me that life is about constant growth

My students whose dedicated quest for knowledge, skills, and self-growth is a tribute to the helping professions!

Nancy

I would like to acknowledge and thank just a few of the people who have inspired and nurtured my personal and professional growth.

Lori Russell-Chapin, who hired me, mentored me, inspired me, and befriended me for life.

Evan Sherman-Hayes, who gave me the opportunity to live my most important role, that of mother to him.

Patrick Hayes, my husband, who has supported me all the way!

Section I

GETTING STARTED

You, Supervision, and the Settings

By the time you have completed Section I and the first five chapters you can expect to:

- IDENTIFY YOUR STRENGTHS AND AREAS FOR IMPROVEMENT TO ENSURE A SUCCESSFUL FIELD EXPERIENCE.
- PRESENT AND ANALYZE YOUR COUNSELING SESSIONS USING THE COUNSELING INTERVIEW RATING FORM AND MICROCOUNSELING SUPERVISION.
- UNDERSTAND THE DIMENSIONS OF EFFECTIVE SUPERVISION AND THE INFLUENCE YOUR PLACEMENT SETTING MAY HAVE ON SUPERVISION.
- LEARN ABOUT THE MAJOR SUPERVISION MODEL CATEGORIES AND THE IMPORTANCE OF A SUPERVISION QUESTION.
- CONCEPTUALIZE YOUR CASE STUDIES USING THREE STAGES OF THE COUNSELING INTERVIEW, FORMAL DIAGNOSIS, AND DEVELOPMENTAL ASSESSMENT.

1

TURNING THEORY INTO PRACTICE

Abilities Needed to Grow

The field experience takes courage—it facilitates growth most effectively if you allow yourself to become the person whom you truly are and want to be!

Overview

This first chapter introduces you, the student, to the style and format of the entire book. Each chapter focuses on the concept of "praxis," turning theory into practical skills. You will address eight abilities that you must practice in order to get the most out of your field experience. Those necessary abilities are understanding and working on the following: neurocounseling/self-regulation, risk-taking, goal-setting, feedback, respect, power, multicultural issues, and available resources.

Goals

1. Learn about the text format and function from the authors' viewpoints.
2. Analyze how neurocounseling and self-regulation skills may be integrated into your field experience.
3. Focus on personal and professional issues that you will encounter frequently throughout your field experience.
4. Discover and list fears and concerns that may interfere with effectively completing your field experience.
5. Understand the dynamics of power throughout the field experience.
6. Identify at least four goals that need to be accomplished by the end of the field experience.

Before You Start

We welcome you to one of the most exciting and, certainly, most personally involving courses in the helping field. Working with clients, their families, and the community is what it is all about. The field experience, practicum, or internship all give you a chance to show what you can do. It is a place you can test out those theories and see if they really work.

Feedback is said to be the breakfast of champions. We recommend that you use the many resources available to you to gain as much information about yourself and your work as you possibly can. We provide a large number of resources in this book. But seek feedback from your colleagues and supervisors. Having others look at your work can be challenging, but it is here that you can grow the most. We suggest that you use your practicum, internship, or field experience as a foundation for your entire professional life. It is vital that you listen carefully to clients so that you can help them grow; you, too, will grow if you listen equally carefully to those supporting your development.

Each of us would like to share some thoughts about how to use this book and the importance of the field experience, internship, and practicum.

Why was This Text Created?

Lori

I have been teaching graduate level practicum and internship courses for the past 28 years. These field experience courses are my very favorite classes, as I have the great pleasure of watching all of you, the novice counseling trainees, transform into skilled helping professionals. It is a time of immense personal change and growth.

The difficulty of this class for me was that I have never found the exact textbook that could assist you and me through this exciting but scary experience. I often used supplemental texts and individual monographs, but again there was no book that focused on all the essential areas of the field experience.

As I began creating many of my own tools, I became aware that so much of what I believe about the helping profession came from the work of Dr. Allen Ivey. I bravely decided to ask Dr. Ivey and his wife, Dr. Mary Ivey, to travel to Bradley University to be guest speakers at one of our alumni events. That was the beginning of this textbook, as Allen and I began to brainstorm enthusiastically about the needs of a field experience book that would integrate all aspects of the field experience from developmental concerns to ethics to conceptualization to supervision!

Of course discovering colleagues with whom I work directly that have complementary counseling beliefs and skills is also a blessing. Dr. Nancy Sherman and I have worked together for the past 21 years, and it is exciting and energizing to collaborate with Nancy on this project as well.

The most amazing experience for me is how much my counseling skills have continued to improve since the first edition of this book. In 2010 a colleague and I began the development and implementation of a new Center for Collaborative Brain Research among my institution, Bradley University, a large local

hospital, OSF Saint Francis Medical Center, and the Illinois Neurological Institute. Since that time seven cutting edge brain research projects have been completed and disseminated. At the same time I became trained in neurofeedback
(NFB), a noninvasive brain-based intervention using a computerized software
system and an electroencephalogram (EEG) to modulate dysregulated brain
waves. I decided I needed to know much more about the brain and the body,
so I took an anatomy and physiology course. That was very helpful, and then
I began studying for my board certification in neurofeedback (BCN).

All of these experiences truly changed how I conduct counseling today.
I want to share much of that with you readers in this book.

Nancy

As a colleague of Lori's also teaching Practicum/Internship courses at Bradley University, I have used the original version of this book since it was published. Students always comment on the usefulness, practicality, and wisdom
of the text.

It could almost be a self-guided journey through practicum and internship!
I say *almost* because the most important relationships I have had in my professional counseling career have been those with my various supervisors, the good,
the bad, and the ugly. I am honored to share some of the wisdom I have gained
from the past 25 years as a doctoral intern, counselor, and counselor educator
with you through this revised text.

Unlike Allen and Lori, I saw my first client without the benefit of a counseling
degree. I had completed a master's degree in College Student Personnel and,
after a successful career in student affairs, moved to a small town in Ohio to
help bolster my partner's career. Without a job of my own, I volunteered as an
advocate for a women's help center for victims of domestic violence and sexual
assault. When funding became available for a professional counselor position,
the director of the agency asked me to apply even though I explained my lack
of training in counseling.

Regardless, I was hired and with supervision from my social worker supervisor I saw my first client. As I was listening to her horrific story of domestic violence and sexual assault the only way I could think to respond was to share some
of my family's experiences! My intention was to let her know she was not alone
and that others have survived these crimes, to instill some hope. I don't remember if it helped as I had intended, but I do remember going to my supervisor
and processing the experience. I learned valuable lessons about how to help
clients experiencing extreme emotions as well as not making the session about
me. I have since learned the value of appropriate counselor self-disclosure!
I think I did many things "wrong" in that position but with the help of a skilled,

experienced supervisor my clients did get better. That job also led me to the decision to pursue a PhD in counselor education realizing that counseling and not student affairs was my future.

As part of my doctoral education, I completed a yearlong internship in clinical psychology at a children's hospital and a community mental health center. Besides an intense learning experience in psychological testing and diagnosing and treating people with mental disorders, I also learned that my place was in professional counseling with a developmental, wellness focus and not the medical model I was using at the time. That experience was, however, very helpful for teaching courses in assessment, DSM diagnoses, and similar aspects of clinical mental health counseling.

Allen

I'll just share one personal story as we begin. My first practical experience in counseling was as an intern in the counseling center at Tufts University under the wise guidance of Alvin Schmidt, director. I certainly was inexperienced in a professional role and felt more than a bit awkward. How would I survive my first interview?

Luckily for me, Schmidt had a ready smile and was completely supportive and confident that I would be up to the job, even though he had no evidence for that fact. That first interview was neither particularly good, nor particularly bad, but reviewing it with him made an immediate difference.

I learned that it was okay to make mistakes and that I could learn and grow from them. I learned from Alvin Schmidt, the person, that relationship is key and the nature of the person who is the counselor or therapist is as important as book knowledge. Not all of you will have the patient mentor that I enjoyed, but there is something to learn from the feedback offered by all supervisors.

Theory is vital, but it is people like you and me who take it into practice.

Growing as a person and as a therapist is one of the goals of this text.

We are going to share some ideas, but it is you who will use some of them and make them work.

Schmidt also taught me something the books at that time did not cover. I found it critical that I learn the ways of his agency, the counseling center, as quickly as possible. Forms, reports, and ethical standards were an important part of the job. I also discovered it was important to meet and know faculty members and administrators in the Tufts community. We tend to learn counseling and therapy in isolation, but it is practiced in a community context. If we are to be effective, we need to be community members and tailor our work to community needs.

Multicultural issues are an important part of the context of counseling.

We define culture broadly to include race and ethnicity, gender, socioeconomic status, sexual orientation, ability/disability, age, spirituality, and other relevant factors such as language (bilingual ability is an asset not a liability) or experience of trauma (a person who experienced rape, AIDS, cancer, loss of parent, or war has entered a special culture). Each community agency exists within a cultural setting, unique to itself. I suggest that you spend some time going beyond the immediate agency setting and learning about the community within which you work.

Let us now turn to what we have to share with you. We've enjoyed and profited from being supervised and supervising others. After you have completed work with this text, we'd enjoy hearing from you and obtaining your feedback. Please note the feedback form at the close of this book. Keep in touch and let us grow together. We welcome your feedback and suggestions, letting us know how you experienced this book.

The Need for This Text: Lori's First Client Memory

It was my first day as a new counselor working in a mental health clinic in western United States. I was 25 years old, and I was ready! Now I could truly make a difference in the world! Trying to remember all the skills I was supposed to do was intimidating, but I felt confident. I had dressed professionally. I still remember what I was wearing, a brown shirtdress and matching shoes! I arrived early to work and I was just waiting patiently. Finally it was nine o'clock in the morning.

My client's intake form had been placed in her file. In walked Rachel. She was a tall woman and from her information she was 71 years old. Before I could say "hello," before I could attempt to talk about confidentiality, and before I could speak of the counseling process, Rachel began to pace in the room and silently stare at me. She would not sit down in any of the available chairs in my office. She continued to walk around the office, carefully observing me from top to bottom. Finally Rachel snorted, "Honey, what could you possibly have to offer me? You are a child with very little life experience, and you will never be able to help or understand my problems!"

I was stunned, of course. I do remember thinking: did any of my professors or supervisors tell me what to do when this happens? I decided to be silent, not as an intentional skill, but because I did not know what else to do! Then I recalled some concept called resistance. I decided to just go with it. Rachel continued to rant, and finally there was a small lull, so I responded, "Rachel, you are probably correct. I have not lived as long as you, and I don't have as much life experience as you. All I can do is listen to you and see if a counseling relationship develops. How does that sound to you?" Fortunately for Rachel and me, that intentional response was one that worked! That was 32 years ago, and I remember it like yesterday.

For You, the Student

Your Field Experience Resource Guide: Turning Knowledge into Action will be about you and your first clients too. The primary focus of this book is to offer you a comprehensive foundation and guide for your practicum and internship field experiences. It will be about your personal student journey as you progress and evolve through the final aspects of your graduate education.

Goal of This Text

The teaching philosophy of the entire book uses the concept of "praxis," turning theory into practice. You will be able to integrate all aspects of the field experience through practical application of the two book case studies, exercises, practical reflections, individual assessments, goal-setting, and other available online resources through Routledge.

Praxis: A teaching approach allowing theoretical material to integrate into practical and relevant skill and techniques.

Book Features

First, and foremost, this book is filled with resources to guide you through your field experience. Each chapter has practical reflections and examples of resources you can utilize from instruments assessing your supervision style to forms assisting you in analyzing your interviewing skills. In addition, each chapter will offer a necessary self-regulation skill for you and your clients. Throughout the textbook, there will be a special emphasis and focus on neurocounseling, bridging brain and behavior, and brain-based concepts and techniques. We will discuss more on neurocounseling later in the chapter.

The book has been developed into two modules. Section I, Getting Started: You, Supervision, and the Settings, has five chapters that address vital areas of supervision, the need for feedback, and the essentials of client conceptualization, diagnosis, and treatment. You will learn more about Rachel throughout Section I, as Rachel and her story will be the first of the two case studies presented in this book.

Section II, Knowledge Needed to Grow: Issues in Professional Practice, has five chapters, and in these chapters you will concentrate on areas that concern all helping professionals such as multicultural competencies and ethics and the law. Additionally this section will help you focus on your well-being as a helping professional, learn about the importance of outcome-based research on super-vision, and evaluate your counseling skills.

The second case study you will work with in Section II is about a young man named Darryl. He was referred to Lori years later in her counseling career, as he was having difficulty keeping his job, his marriage was failing, and he stated that he just could not keep it together. The following is Lori's memory:

By that time, I was teaching in a university setting and counseling in a private practice one day a week. I had just terminated with one client, so an opening was available. Once again I was prepared to conduct an initial intake session when Darryl took one look at me and began talking in tongues. I had little idea of what to do, so I listened respectfully. When Darryl finished, he curled up into a fetal position on my floor. Once more, I thought did any of my professors prepare me for this?! One of my first instincts was to call security for help, but I calmed myself down and moved to the floor with him! Darryl remained in that dissociative position for 45 minutes. When he finally sat up, I was still sit-ting on the floor with him. He inquired about the session, and I told him what I observed. We processed our first session. Darryl asked to leave but wanted to set up another appointment! I set up another appointment for Darryl, and then I called my supervisor for an appointment that was sooner than a week away! You will learn more about Darryl throughout Section II.

Chapter Topics

Each book chapter will take a topic that is critical to your success in field expe-rience and supervision and present material that can have direct and practical application to your practicum and internship. In Chapter 1, Turning Theory into Practice: Abilities Needed to Grow, you are introduced to eight practical abilities necessary for a successful field experience. These abilities allow you as a novice helping professional to address fears and concerns of beginning a field experience and the chapter provides a frank discussion of self-regulation, risk-taking, goal-setting, feedback, respect, power, multicultural issues, and available resources.

Chapter 2, Reviewing and Analyzing Cases: Microcounseling Supervision, provides a basic supervision model that teaches you a general vocabulary for reviewing microcounseling skills with intention, classifying those same skills with mastery, and summarizing your counseling interview style with an individ-ualized supervision session. The Microcounseling Supervision Model teaches you the needed information to actively listen to counseling tapes and provide the corrective feedback needed to grow in your field experience.

Chapter 3, Becoming Effective as a Supervisee: The Influence of Placement Setting, introduces you to dimensions of effective supervision and the influ-ences that your chosen placement setting may have in your field experiences.

In Chapter 4, Continuing Self-Improvement: Major Supervision Model Categories, you will be introduced to additional supervision models that will help you continue to grow in your field experience. The final chapter in Section I is Chapter 5, Conceptualizing the Client: Diagnosis and Related Issues. This chapter assists you in conceptualizing your client's case and diagnosing using the DSM-5 if necessary.

Chapter 6, Becoming a Culturally Competent Helping Professional: Appreciation of Diversity in Action, focuses on issues surrounding diversity and the manner in which your racial identity has developed. In Chapter 7, Working with Ethics, Laws, and Professionalism: Best Practice Standards, ethics are differentiated from professionalism, and landmark case laws are presented. Chapter 8, Counseling Research Outcomes: Discovering What Works, outlines the effectiveness of counseling with outcome research and your evaluation of your progress to date. The final two chapters, Chapter 9, Staying Well: Guidelines for Responsible Living, and Chapter 10, Becoming a Professional Helper: Advocacy for Clients, Self, and the Profession, bring closure to your field experience by helping you assess your personal wellness and any areas of impairment and emphasizing the importance of advocacy efforts for your clients, self, and the profession.

A Guide

Please use this book as a resource guide to assist you on the adventures of becoming a skilled helping professional. Your efforts will not go unnoticed, and you will be rewarded with added confidence, wisdom, and continued curiosity about counseling and personal growth! Drs. Nancy Sherman, Allen Ivey and I will assist you through this exciting journey! The following poem by Rumi sets the stage perfectly for your challenges and growth to come.

The Guest House

This being human is a guest house.
Every morning is a new arrival.
A joy, a depression, a meanness,
some momentary awareness comes
as an unexpected visitor.
Welcome and entertain them all!
Even if they're a crowd of sorrows,
who violently sweep your house
empty of its furniture,
still, treat each guest honorably.
He may be clearing you out
for some new delight.
The dark thought, the shame, the malice,

meet them at the door laughing,
and invite them in.
Be grateful for whoever comes,
because each has been sent
as a guide from beyond.

(Barks, 1995)

Key Concepts: Needed Abilities for a Successful Field Experience

Educators are always looking for methods that assist you to "realize more and memorize less" (Albertson, profiled in Bailey, 1986). The following sections emphasize just that. If you focus on each of the presented abilities, you will more easily realize and internalize what you need to gain from your field experience.

There are eight essential abilities that will be examined to assist you in getting started in your field experience. A successful beginning to your field experience rests in your ability to self-regulate, take risks, set goals, and examine yourself openly. After classes and theory, you will find yourself facing clients. And, your counseling practice will be reviewed by others—this itself is risk-taking and requires a solid self-concept.

Feedback from others on your performance will prove invaluable, but is often challenging. Respect for yourself and others will enable you to hear supportive and corrective feedback. Power differentials underlie all classroom and agency work. Understanding how power issues play out will likely be helpful in your comfort in your field experiences. Also, multicultural issues are present in all field experiences and your awareness and ability to consider these constantly is essential. Finally, discovering available resources that can assist you in staying healthy is crucial to the overall success of your field experience.

Neurocounseling and Self-regulation Skills

The emphasis on self-regulation and the understanding of how neurocounseling impacts your work as a counselor will be the first skills and abilities discussed. Neurocounseling is a relatively new concept that has emerged in the counseling field (Russell-Chapin & Jones, 2014). A definition of neurocounseling is traditional counseling that integrates physiology and the brain into its tenets and understanding that many mental health symptoms have physiological and brain-based underpinnings. Even the number of neuroscience related presentations at the American Counseling Association (ACA) Conferences has tripled from 2008 to 2013 (Russell-Chapin & Jones, 2014). At the 2015 ACA Conference there were a record number of 15 neurocounseling and Neuroscience Learning Institutes and educational sessions. A new Neuro-counseling Interest Network was approved by ACA's Governing Council and in September of 2014 a monthly column was created for the *Counseling Today* magazine called Neurocounseling: Bridging Brain and Behavior (Russell-Chapin & Jones, 2014). A new movement in the counseling world has begun!

This exponential, almost daily, new information gained about the brain and its functions is overwhelming and abundant. Neuroimaging capabilities have allowed access to the innermost regions of the brain. We know the brain is a three-pound organ with 100 billion neurons, is plastic, and has neurogenerative functions. The brain loves challenges, and those challenges help build new neuronal pathways.

We have known for years that counseling helps people because counselors can hear new beliefs and thoughts and see changes in behaviors. Now through neuroimaging and neurocounseling research, we know that counseling changes the brain through positive plasticity (Russell-Chapin & Jones, 2015).

Neurocounseling: Integrates physiology and the brain into counseling tenets and understanding that many mental health symptoms have physiological and brain-based underpinnings.

Self-regulation

Our brain functions on electrical and chemical processes. The entire electrical output is between 30 and 40 watts. That is about the same wattage that is needed for one light bulb in our home. The cortex, thalamus, and brain stem create the electrical activity. The cortex contains 97% of the brain's 100 billion neurons. The thalamus, a subcortical structure, is the mechanism responsible for the rhythm of neuronal firing and generation of the brainwave frequencies (Thompson & Thompson, 2003). We will talk about the different brainwave categories in another chapter.

Self-regulation: An individual's ability to intrinsically alter and control many physiological functions.

According to Chapin and Russell-Chapin, "The delicate and intricate symphony of the brain's electro-chemical processes is what determines its current state of healthy brain regulation" (2014, p. 20). We know there are many variables that disrupt this balance and brain regulation and often create many of the psychological and physical problems that you and your clients bring into the counseling arena. You already know many of the factors impeding brain health and a dysregulated brain. To better understand what may cause dysregulation, take your first practical inventory presented in this book. It is called the Neurological Risk Assessment (Chapin & Russell-Chapin, 2014, pp. 9–10) and will explain for you and your clients possible causes of brainwave dysregulation.

Practical Reflection 1: Neurological Dysregulation Risk Assessment

Answer the following screening as honestly as you can. If you don't know the answer, you may want to ask a parent or relative. Tally the number of potential sources of dysregulation for you. What surprises you the most?

_____

_____

_____

_____

Neurological Dysregulation Risk Assessment

Name (or Child's Name):_____ **Age:** __ **Date:** _____

Current Problem, Symptom, or Complaint:_____

Please read each potential source of neurological dysregulation and indicate whether or not it may be a risk factor for you or your child.

1. **Genetic Influences**: Grandparents, parents, or siblings with mental health or learning disorders (including attention deficit hyperactivity disorder), post-traumatic stress disorder, depression, generalized anxiety disorder, substance abuse, personality or other severe psychological disorders (bipolar or schizophrenia).

   Yes   No

   ___   ___

2. **Pre-natal Exposure:** Maternal distress, psychotropic medication use, alcohol or substance abuse, nicotine use, or possible exposure to environmental toxins including genetically modified foods, pesticides, petrochemicals, xenestrogens in plastics, heavy metals (lead/mercury), and fluoride, bromine, and chlorine in water.

   Yes   No

   ___   ___

3. **Birth Complications:** Forceps or vacuum delivery, oxygen loss, head injury, premature birth, difficult or prolonged labor, obstructed umbilical cord, or fetal distress.

Yes   No

—— ——

4. **Disease and High Fever:** Sustained fever above 104 degrees due to bacterial infection, influenza, strep, meningitis, encephalitis, Reyes Syndrome, PANDAS, or other infections or disease processes.

Yes   No

—— ——

5. **Current Diagnosis:** Of mental health, physical health, alcohol abuse, substance abuse, or learning disorder.

Yes   No

—— ——

6. **Poor Diet and Inadequate Exercise:** Diet high in processed food, preservatives, simple carbohydrates (sugar and flour), genetically modified foods, foods treated with herbicides, pesticides, and hormones, low daily water intake, high caffeine intake, and lack of adequate physical exercise (20 minutes, 7 times a week).

Yes   No

—— ——

7. **Emotionally Suppressive Psychosocial Environment:** Being raised or currently living in poverty, domestic violence, physical, emotional, or sexual abuse, alcoholic or mentally unstable family environment, emotional trauma, neglect, institutionalization, and inadequate maternal emotional availability or attachment.

Yes   No

—— ——

8. **Mild to Severe Brain Injury:** Experienced one or more blows to the head from a sports injury, fall, or auto accident (with or without loss of consciousness), or episodes of open head injury, coma, or stroke.

Yes   No

—— ——

9. **Prolonged Life Distress:** Most commonly due to worry about money, work, economy, family responsibilities, relationships, personal safety and/or health causing sustained periods of anxiety, irritability, anger, fatigue, lack of interest, low motivation or energy, nervousness, and/or physical aches and pains.

Yes   No

——   ——

10. **Stress Related Disease:** Includes heart disease, kidney disease, hypertension, obesity, diabetes, stroke, hormonal and/or immunological disorders.

Yes   No

——   ——

11. **Prolonged Medication Use, Substance Use, or Other Addictions:** Including legal or illegal drug use, substance abuse, or addiction (alcohol, drugs, nicotine, caffeine, medication, gambling, sex, spending, etc.) and overuse of screen technologies (cell phones, video games, television, computers, internet, etc.).

Yes   No

——   ——

12. **Seizure Disorders:** Caused by birth complications, stroke, head trauma, infection, high fever, oxygen deprivation, and/or genetic disorders, and includes epilepsy, pseudo-seizures, or epileptiform seizures.

Yes   No

——   ——

13. **Chronic Pain:** Related to accident, injury, or a disease process, including back pain, headache and migraine pain, neck pain, facial pain, and fibromyalgia.

Yes   No

——   ——

14. **Surgical Anesthesia, Chemotherapy, and/or Aging:** Can cause mild cognitive impairment, insomnia, and depression and be related

to emotional trauma, loss and grief, chronic illness, physical decline, reduced mobility, physical, social, and emotional isolation, and decreased financial security.

Yes   No

—   —

Scoring and Interpretation: Total Number of "Yes" Responses _____

In general, the greater the number of "yes" responses, the greater the risk of significant neurological dysregulation. However even one severe "yes" response could cause significant neurological dysregulation and result in serious mental, physical, or cognitive impairment (Chapin & Russell-Chapin, 2014, pp. 8–10).

There are self-regulation skills that can be practiced to assist in re-regulating the brain. There are other interventions such as counseling, neurotherapy, and neurofeedback that we will discuss in Chapter 8.

For now research has demonstrated that human beings can control much of their sympathetic and parasympathetic nervous system (Chapin & Russell-Chapin, 2014). Helping you new counseling students learn about personal self-regulation skills will directly influence how you teach and counsel your clients. You will also be healthier yourselves. Throughout this text and integrated within each chapter, you will have the opportunity to read and practice several of the self-regulation skills. The skills being emphasized will be diaphragmatic breathing, use of imagery, sleep hygiene, gut/brain connection and nutrition, exercise, skin temperature control, heart rate variability, neurotherapy and neurofeedback, harmonics, and mindfulness training.

The first self-regulation skill for Chapter 1 is the practice of diaphragmatic breathing. This may sound a little silly, but most people do not breathe correctly. Runners, singers, and musicians may have been trained to breathe well, but the average person just breathes automatically, and many are shallow breathers or chest breathers.

The diaphragm is a dome-shaped, inspiratory muscle that contracts and flattens when breathing. This muscle is located underneath the superior thoracic cavity (Marieb, 2012, p. 20). The benefit of this type of breathing improves the functioning of the brain through better absorption of glucose and oxygen. In turn, this will improve overall daily performance and often reduce anxiety, as the body begins to relax.

Typically normal breath rates are between 12 and 15 breaths per minute. According to Schwartz and Andrasik (2003) children two to five years old breathe more often, about 25 to 30 breaths per minute, five- to twelve-year-olds, 20 to 25 times per minute, and older than twelve, 15 to 20 times per minute. For clients to learn the relaxation response, the breathing cycle needs to be between four and six breaths per minute (Russell-Chapin, 2016, in press).

> **Diaphragmatic breathing:** Focused breathing through the diaphragm to assist in relaxation and better absorption of glucose and oxygen.

Another way to visualize and practice this rhythmic breathing is counting slowly to five while inhaling through the nose and then exhaling to the count of five through open, pursed lips. That equates to six cycles of a ten count for one minute or six cycles per minute. Imagine "smelling roses" while inhaling, and "blowing out candles" while exhaling. An additional bonus of this skill is that with relaxation also comes increased skin temperature, which brings on greater relaxation. We will discuss more of skin temperature control later in the text.

Practical Reflection 2: Breathing Demonstration

Continue journaling with each practical reflection exercise. Begin to focus on your breathing. How do you naturally breathe? Read again the paragraph above on diaphragmatic breathing. Practice breathing through your diaphragm. One way to visually see this pattern is to lie down on the floor or on your bed. Place a fairly large book over your diaphragm. As you breathe in through your nose to the count of 5, you should be able to push that book and see it rise. When you exhale to the count of 5, you should be able to see the book go down. Practice this for at least eighteen cycles or three minutes. If you don't want to use a book, then just place your hand on your diaphragm, and push it out when exhaling. What did you notice as you practiced diaphragmatic breathing? Write it down here.

_____
_____
_____
_____

Risk-taking

Another very important ability that needs to be examined is taking risks during class and with your clients. There is an old saying: you will get out of this course what you put into it! Practica and internships are some of the most challenging, demanding, and essential courses in your graduate education. Not only must you "turn theory into practice," but each of you must face individual fears and be willing to take risks as a budding counselor and as a valued peer supervisor to your classmates. This takes courage!

Risk-taking: Assessing personal anxiety and fears and courageously changing old ways to facilitate new behaviors.

Carl Jung (1954) once stated that one cannot be courageous unless one has been afraid and fearful! What a great statement. One of your first challenges in field experience then is to face your fears and take calculated professional and personal risks. For example, in this course, each of you may be required to demonstrate your counseling skills through video recordings, case presentations, simulations, and portfolio demonstrations. Showcasing your skills takes courage in itself. Insecurities are heightened, and you want to do well in front of your professor and peers.

Try to remember an important distinction: when others are offering feedback about your work, their comments do not reflect upon you, the person, only on your skills. If this dichotomy is recognized, then you will desire the feedback even more, as it helps you to grow without the insecurities of approval.

Practical Reflection 3: Identifying Fears and Concerns

Right now, continue your reflective journal for this chapter. First jot down your fears and concerns about your field experience. These feelings and thoughts do not have to be shared with anyone. However, the more you are willing to share, the sooner you will begin to experience the concept of universality. Almost everyone in this class will have similar thoughts and feelings.

_____

_____

_____

_____

_____

Goal-setting

Once you begin this course, you must decide "what exactly do you want out of this experience." Some students say they just want to complete the requirements with as little work as possible and jump through the necessary hoops. However, those students who see their field experience as a powerful opportunity for growth will thrive! This kind of structured, organized, small group supervisory opportunity will not be as easily accessible again in your professional life. Seize this time with optimism, and watch yourself change and grow as you never thought possible!

Decide what you want out of this course and set, at least, four tangible and measurable goals for yourself. Begin thinking about your prioritized goals for the field experience. Be sure to share with your classmates. Publicly stating your goals will offer additional motivation and investment to achieve your desired outcomes. As you accomplish these goals, get into the habit of periodically setting new and additional goals.

The importance of goal-setting seems to have the support of all helping professions. Not only does it strengthen the supervisee and supervisor relationship, but it offers specific and objective strategies to guide you through the learning process. You, your instructor, and supervisor will want to set your goals during one of your first supervisory sessions. Be sure to set short-term and long-term goals, reviewing and evaluating the goals through the field experience (Curtis, 2000).

For example, here are four sample goals that can help direct your field experience.

1. Even though I'm here a short time, I'd like to be able to become part of the total community of this service agency or school system. By the end of the first three weeks, I will have read the service directory with agency rules and guidelines, and I will introduce myself to three new co-workers each week.
2. I'd like to learn how to take corrective feedback positively. Too often, I fear hearing what others say. By the end of the first nine weeks, with my supervisor, I will work to learn to use the feedback as a mechanism for change, not personal attacks.
3. To increase my skill confidence, I will practice one new counseling skill every week and discuss with my supervisor its effect and outcome.
4. I will be prepared for my individual supervision session with structured Supervision Questions explaining my supervision needs.

Practical Reflection 4: Establishing Professional Goals

Now begin your list of goals for this field experience. Courageously describe the outcome goals that you know you must learn to be a competent helping professional. These goals may have some similarity to others in this class, but your goals must be individualized to meet your differing needs. List a total of four goals: two short-term and two long-term goals.

_____

_____

_____

_____

Feedback

As you think about your goals, review your strengths and liabilities and "pick the brains" of your university instructor, your on-site supervisors, and your classmates who each bring wisdom and expertise for their input. Use this time constructively. Challenge yourself and your classmates to become the best helping professionals that you can.

The only way this challenge can take place, though, is to promise that constructive feedback will be offered. Constructive or corrective feedback is aimed at assisting you in changing some aspect of a particular skill.

> **Feedback**: A communication skill offering perceptions, observations, and information that the receiver may use to facilitate change.

Please remember, too, that when asked for, feedback is best received! Ask for specific feedback during your individual and class supervisory sessions. It must and should be your responsibility as a supervisee to request what you need and want. Do not leave that up to others. Very little will be gained, if you leave your needs to others.

Also, very little will be gained if you offer only positive and vague feedback to yourself and your peers. We often hear students say comments such as, "You were wonderful with that client. I am so impressed with your skills." Those words are nice to hear, but they will not help anyone grow and improve.

Please offer feedback that is constructive and very specific. In the next section, we will offer an example of one method of assisting you with constructive feedback using a form that can be used with videos or live supervision. For now, though, remember the 80/20 rule of offering feedback. Make sure that 80 percent of the given feedback is positive and stated first, and then the remaining 20 percent of constructive feedback can be heard. Demonstrating your skills is scary, as most of us do want approval from others. With the 80/20 method, you will receive needed support and have the courage to move forward.

Practical Reflection 5: Corrective Feedback

What corrective feedback do you need at this moment in your field experience? Ask for corrective feedback.

_____
_____
_____
_____

Respect

Many of you have been with your professors and classmates for several courses. Some relationships have developed if you have taken risks and built necessary trust. If you are honest with your needs, fears, and concerns, the odds are that your fellow students will follow suit. Basic assertiveness at its best is asserting your thoughts, feelings, and ideas. Showing mutual respect, the underpinnings of assertiveness, will allow your field experience to flourish and produce extremely beneficial results. Practice the guideline that assertion breeds assertion, non-assertion breeds non-assertion, and aggression breeds aggression.

In your beginning theory class, you learned that empathy, unconditional positive regard, and congruent behaviors assist clients in building rapport and trust (Rogers, 1957). These same components are necessary for helping you and your classmates engage in trusting relationships and environments. Use your active listening skills and nonjudgmental actions with clients as well as your teachers, supervisors, and peers.

Power

Another often unspoken ability that is needed is that of personal and professional power. One definition of power is the ability to influence others due to the nature of the situation. There are many different layers of power in the helping professions. There is a power differential between counselor and client, counselor and supervisor, and counselor/student and professor. Each layer has its unique feature. In the varying combinations, one member of the dyad comes to the other party because of expertise and skills that the former does not yet possess. Seeking guidance, wisdom, and knowledge from another places you in a disadvantaged position with power. Knowledge is power, and this power needs to be used cautiously and carefully.

Power: The ability to influence the behaviors of others through direct or indirect maneuvers.

In the counseling relationship, the counselor has the power from the beginning because the client is in a vulnerable state and is seeking help and relief. It is your job as a helping professional to lessen and eradicate that power through listening nonjudgmentally and allowing the client to solve individual concerns and make personal decisions.

There is a parallel process in counseling and supervision. You enter into the supervisory relationship seeking guidance and wisdom. One large difference, though, is the fact that your supervisor and instructor, unlike counselor and client, do have an evaluative aspect to their job responsibilities. Because of evaluation and grading duties, faculty do have some power over your behaviors and attitudes as a student.

> **Supervision**: A structured approach to assist differing developmental and competency levels of helping professionals with a more experienced professional.

We all use power every day, and power can have healthy consequences and negative consequences. There are certain power skills you can utilize as a student to level out the playing field. As a student and counselor-in-training, the most important power skill you must utilize is to ask for what you need and clarify concerns. If you have the courage to do so, the odds are you will get what you desire, particularly if you believe your supervisor is using her/his power unfairly.

All the abilities discussed in this chapter are interwoven together in a collaborative fashion. Developing and using these abilities may be risky, but for the outcome of your field experience it will be riskier not to use these abilities. All of the abilities described in this chapter are so essential if your field experience is to be successful, your supervisory relationship is to prosper and grow, and you are to grow and polish your counseling skills.

Practical Reflection 6: Power Differentials

Describe a time when a helping professional used power inappropriately. What action could you have taken to display the appropriate use of self-respect and clarification of personal needs?

_____

_____

_____

_____

Multicultural Issues

Another essential ability is the understanding of multicultural issues. The term "multiculturalism" has become increasingly inclusive over the years. Whereas once it referred specifically to ethnic/racial differences, multiculturalism encompasses language, race/ethnicity, spiritual orientation, gender, sexual orientation, and many other factors. Cultural issues have become so broad that many now state that all counseling is multicultural and list the following factors as important potential components in the individual or group sessions (Ivey, Pedersen, & Ivey, 2001, pp. 2–3):

- Family context
- Social systems context
- Demographic context
- Status context
- Life experience context.

Culture is made up of all these issues and more. You and each of your clients bring unique cultural experiences to the session. If your client is going through a divorce and you have never had that experience, you are engaged in a cross-cultural encounter even though you and your client may be similar on all other issues. There is a culture of cancer survivors, a culture of Iraq veterans, a culture of those who have immigrated to another country, a culture of survivors from recent natural disasters.

The field experience will test your ability to understand and be empathic with others. There are those who say, "If you haven't been there, you can't understand." There is no question that if you have not been addicted to cocaine, you likely cannot fully understand the issues your client faces. At the same time, your difficult life experiences will be helpful and your empathic understanding, listening, and demeanor will make an important difference in the life of your client.

Understanding the process of change allows you to guide others through the system with your own special and unique orientation to the world, even if you have not gone through that particular problem. As you become more deeply immersed in the field experience, continue to sharpen your understanding and awareness of the infinite multicultural issues underlying all helping.

Practical Reflection 7: Multicultural Concerns

When have you experienced being judgmental of another culture? Discuss the many varying dimensions of that experience.

_____
_____
_____
_____
_____

Positive Resources and Personal Strengths

A final ability that will prove invaluable to you is learned optimism. In your beginning skills course, you began to appreciate the importance of the positive asset search (Ivey, Ivey, & Zalaquett, 2014). Drawing out the client's strengths, especially during painful and discouraging times, allows your client to regain personal power and focus on the concerns with a sense of renewed strength. Your client can remember that life has been better and not so difficult. If your client survived and surpassed other trying times, then this experience can also be surpassed as well.

As with your clients, you, too, are entering a somewhat scary and vulnerable field experience. Use the skill of the positive asset search to reframe your challenges in your internship. We believe it is true that you can find strengths in your weaknesses and weaknesses in your strengths! Your optimistic attitude will allow the entire field experience to blossom.

By now you are beginning to know and understand yourself well. What are your strengths? Remember back to another time in your life, when you were challenged and feeling insecure. Look at those resources to see which ones can generalize to your situation now. Perhaps special friends or family got you through, or you noticed that regular exercise regulated your stressors. Some of you may find that spiritual resources guided you. No one resource is the answer. We believe it is true that you can find strengths in your weaknesses and weaknesses in your strengths. Your optimistic attitude will allow the entire field experience to blossom.

Practical Reflection 8: Emphasizing Your Personal Strengths

Write down some of your personal strengths. Which of these strengths assisted you through a major transition and a difficult challenge during another period in your life? How are you utilizing these same resources currently in your field experience?

_____
_____
_____
_____

Other Key Issues for the Success of Your Field Experience, Practicum, and Internship

Appreciating this time in your professional journey is paramount to your success. Here are a few additional resources that will help your field experience be successful.

Scheduling appointments. To enjoy weekly supervision, first schedule weekly appointments that are set at regular times. This method assures you and your supervisor that your weekly obligations are important to you. Do not assume your supervisor will arrange for these meetings. Supervisors are very busy with other duties; your supervision is just one extra responsibility.

Owning defensiveness. You must not allow your insecurities to get in the way of receiving feedback. Early on in one of your first supervision sessions, as your supervisor is offering suggestions, you may find yourself thinking, "I know what I like, and I like what I know. Stop offering me other ideas to confuse me!" At that moment begin to recognize and own any personal defensiveness. It is critical that you try not to be defensive. Try to turn your resistance into receptiveness to your supervisors' and peers' feedback. When you feel yourself shutting down, getting hurt or angry about someone's comments, and being generally inflexible, try to respond with "Please tell me more so I can better understand the intention and reasoning behind this." It is not easy to do, but remember there is a multitude of methods for counseling others! The more flexibility you learn, the more you will enjoy counseling clients who are different than you are and the more helpful you can be to a diverse population of people.

> **Resistance:** Conscious or unconscious action designed to protect a client or supervisee from uncomfortable material or situations.

Understanding change. This next situation will eventually happen to you, as it has occurred with every person in the counseling profession and every person in the world! Sometimes you will just feel stuck in the counseling session. Theories and techniques do not work, and you feel as if you don't comprehend any of the needed conceptual ideas for your client. Remember that change can be a difficult journey. It is, however, one of the few constants in the world, so it is important that you understand about the change process, for you as well as your clients. Most of us do not like change. It goes against the status quo, and often our bad situation or techniques are just fine, as at least they are familiar. Another Carl Jung paraphrase comes to mind (1954), "If something is not working, don't keep doing the same thing!" If you follow his sage advice, whenever you feel stuck or confused, remember to experiment with another technique or theory. We think the confusion is a healthy place to be. If you are confused, you are not stuck. You are moving to another place, the stagnation has left, and the change process has begun.

An example of the change process is illustrated in a story about a small boy named Sam. He lived with his very strict father whom Sam feared very much. One day Sam and his friends were playing baseball in the front yard, and Sam hit the ball into the neighbor's side window, shattering it into little pieces. The children scattered away in all directions knowing they were all in big trouble. Sam tried to think what to do. He knew his father would be furious, as he had told the children not to play ball in the front yard. Sam could not force himself to tell the truth to his father. His fear of his father's punishment was greater than the pain of telling the truth and facing the future consequences.

Very few of us are willing to change, not our clients or ourselves, until the fear of the unknown is less than the current pain! That can be stated in the opposite way, as well, by stating that you will not change unless the current pain is greater than the fear of the unknown. So anytime you begin to struggle in your field experience, sit down and face your pain and fears. Decide what you can do to move to the next phase. This would be a great topic for your individual supervision sessions!

Needing a personal counselor. The topics of supervision will vary greatly. You have been encouraged to ask for what you want and pick the brains of your supervisors. Sometimes, though, you need to let the supervision process unfold naturally. Sometimes, you won't even know what it is you need or want. That, too, is all right. Sometimes you may need to talk about yourself and not the client. If you let that happen, your client will indirectly benefit, as you have allowed yourself to deal with factors in your life that may be interfering with your role as a counselor. We are not suggesting that you engage in counseling with your supervisor. That is crossing an ethical boundary of dual relationships, but you can deal with immediate concerns. If there is more to the issue, please allow your supervisor to refer you to a helping professional or find a counselor for yourself. Every person can benefit from personal counseling. Your field experience is a very stressful time, so personal counseling would serve you as a useful tool and resource.

Transference and countertransference. There is another way you can tell if you may need counseling during your practicum and internship. If you think your supervisor is "the best thing since cut grass" or "he must be the best supervisor in the entire world" or "she doesn't understand anything about this case," you may be experiencing the phenomena of transference. This also may be occurring if you are thinking about your supervisor frequently.

Transference: Passing personal characteristics of significant others in past relationships onto a therapist, supervisor, or others.

Sometime during your field experience, you may be asked whether you like all your clients all the time. Many students new to the helping professions will hesitate and answer, "Yes!" It is truly healthy to like and even dislike clients. You don't have to like someone to work with them. However, liking a client too much or disliking clients too much may be particularly dangerous transferential issues. When this happens to you, and it will, be sure to discuss it with your supervisors.

Be cautious of extreme emotions during the supervisory process. This intense experience and an often deep supervisory relationship are rich and fertile ground for personal growth and unfinished business with others. Your supervisor may be the one person who can help you to deal with old issues. From several decades of providing counseling services, it seemed as if every time we had unfinished business in our lives, it would walk right into our offices! It is then that we know it is time to enter into personal counseling.

Don't be afraid to seek counseling when you need it the most! The flip side of this coin is, of course, countertransference. You may sometimes find that your supervisor has issues too. That should be of no surprise to you, as everyone does. If you do feel that your supervisor is placing unfair expectations on you or placing emotions onto you that are not yours, please have the courage to address that with him or her. Often it will be the immediacy you need to assist you both in growing. If this doesn't work, contact your university supervisor or vice versa.

Countertransference: A phenomenon where a person in authority transfers personal qualities of significant others from the past onto subordinates.

Practical Reflection 9: Analyzing Past Transference and Countertransference Issues

Discuss with your classmates any times you now realize may have been transference or countertransference issues?

_____

_____

_____

_____

Summary and Personal Integration

This chapter emphasizes the importance of getting started correctly by identifying fears and concerns that may interfere with your progress. Eight needed abilities and skills were addressed to assist you in growing during your field experience:

- neurocounseling, self-regulation, and diaphragmatic breathing
- risk-taking
- goal-setting
- feedback
- respect
- power
- multicultural issues
- optimism and available resources.

Each of you came to your field experience with unique skills and expertise. Try not to compare your strengths with those of others but focus on your current strengths and resources. Take a deep breath—you are just getting started, remember? Seriously, continue to practice your breathing!

Practical Reflection 10: Integration

Identify at least one major ability from Chapter 1 that will have the most impact on your personal growth during your field experience.

_____

_____

_____

_____

_____

Summary List of Resources

Resource A: Glossary of CIRF Skills
Resource B: Microskill Classification: Transcript of Rachel and Lori
Resource C: Counseling Interview Rating Form
Resource D: Counseling Interview Rating Form
Resource E: Counseling Interview Rating Form
Resource F: Supervisory Style Inventory
Resource G: Author's CIRF Quantification of the Case of Stephen
Resource H: Student Practicum/Internship Agreement
Resource I: Practicum/Internship Contract
Resource J: Adult Informed Consent Form
Resource K: Child Informed Consent Form

Resource L: Release of Confidential Information
Resource M: Site Supervisor Evaluation of Student Counselor's Performance
Resource N: Microcounseling Skills Used in Differing Theoretical Approaches
Resource O: Supervisee Perception of Supervision
Resource P: Microskills Hierarchy
Resource Q: Case Presentation Outline Guide
Resource R: Counseling Interview Rating Form
Resource S: Author's Quantification of CIRF—Summarization and Processing Skills of the Case of Darryl
Resource T: The Case of Darryl with Skill Identification
Resource U: Web Addresses for Professional Organizations and Codes of Ethics
Resource V: ACA Code of Ethics and Standards of Practice
Resource W: Indirect Evidence: Methods for Evaluating the Presence of Non-therapy Explanations
Resource X: Rotter's Locus of Control Scale
Resource Y: The Lifestyle Assessment Survey, Form C
Y.1   Therapeutic Lifestyle Changes Inventory
Resource Z: Chi Sigma Iota Advocacy Themes
Z.1   Advocacy Competencies

References

Bailey, A. (1986). Faculty leaders in profile. *Change*, July/August, 18, 24–32, 37–47.

Barks, C. (1995). *The Essential Rumi*. San Francisco: HarperCollins. Reprinted by HarperCollins Publisher, Inc.

Chapin, T. & Russell-Chapin, L. (2014). *Neurotherapy and Neurofeedback: Brain-based Treatments for Psychological and Behavioral Problems*. New York, NY: Routledge.

Curtis, R.C. (2000). Using goal-setting strategies to enrich the practicum and internship experiences of beginning counselors. *Journal of Humanistic Counseling, Education and Development*, 38, 194–205.

Ivey, A., Pedersen, P., & Ivey, M. (2001). *Intentional Group Counseling*. Pacific Grove, CA: Brooks/Cole.

Ivey, A.E., Ivey, M.B., & Zalaquett, C.P. (2014). *Intentional Interviewing and Counseling* (8th edn). Pacific Grove, CA: Brooks/Cole.

Jung, C.G. (1954). *The Practice of Psychotherapy*, vol. 16. London: Routledge and Kegan Paul.

Marieb, E.N. (2012). *Essentials of Human Anatomy and Physiology* (10th edn). San Francisco: CA, Pearson.

Rogers, C. (1957). The necessary and sufficient conditions of therapeutic personality change. *Journal of Consulting Psychology*, 21, 95–103.

Russell-Chapin, L. (2016, in press). The power of neurocounseling and self-regulation. In J. Edwards, S. Young, & H. Nikels (eds.), *The Handbook of Strength-based Practices: Finding Common Factors*. New York: Routledge.

Russell-Chapin, L. & Jones, L. (2014). Neurocounseling: Bridging brain and behavior. September, *Counseling Today*, American Counseling Association.

Russell-Chapin, L. & Jones, L. (2015). Neurocounseling: Bringing the brain into clinical practice. *Fact Based Health*, 2/3/2015, http://factbasedhealth.com/neurocounseling-bringing-brain-clinical-practice/

Schwartz, M.S. and Andrasik, F. (2003). *Biofeedback: A Practitioner's Guide* (3rd edn). New York, NY: Guilford.

Thompson, M. & Thompson, L. (2003). *The Neurofeedback Book*. Wheat Ridge, CO: Association for Applied Psychophysiology & Biofeedback.

2

REVIEWING AND ANALYZING CASES

Microcounseling Supervision

Perhaps most excitingly, we are uncovering the brain basis of our behaviors—normal, abnormal and in-between. We are mapping a neurobiology of what makes us us.

—Robert Sapolsky

If you take what your client gives you, you will rarely be lost in the counseling process. If you do get lost, attend, attend, and attend!

—Lori Russell-Chapin

Overview

Reviewing counseling interviews and analyzing case presentations are essential teaching strategies for every helping profession educational program. This chapter assists you in reviewing those basic microcounseling skills that are used in some fashion in every theoretical orientation and counseling interview. This chapter focuses on a type of supervision called Microcounseling Supervision that provides a vocabulary guide and constant examination of personal counseling style. You will examine and practice using the Counseling Interview Rating Form (CIRF). The CIRF is an instrument that can be utilized for qualitative and quantitative feedback from counseling interviews. Other methods of supervision will be presented later in the text, but Microcounseling Supervision is presented first as a foundation for listening to counseling interviews and reviewing necessary skills.

Also with the advances in neuroscience and neurocounseling, counseling educators and students need to understand the implications of using intentional counseling skills with their clients and their clients' brains. Each counseling skill presented in this chapter has an impact on a particular function in the brain. These will be discussed here.

Goals

1. Correlate neurocounseling and neuroscience brain functions to the counseling interview and skills.
2. Deliver constructive feedback to others and appreciate the importance of individual constructive feedback.
3. Label and identify which counseling skills are being used during one of your recorded counseling interviews using the Counseling Interview Rating Form (CIRF).
4. Use the CIRF to quantify and qualify other students' video recordings.
5. Identify the three basic components of the Microcounseling Supervision Model.
6. Plan and deliver a concise case presentation.

Key Concepts: Microcounseling Supervision

Two of the most important learning strategies in your field experience are reviewing video recordings of counseling sessions and analyzing case presentations.

Obtaining feedback from your classroom supervisor, on-site supervisor, and your peers about your sessions and case presentations are crucial to your personal development and growth as a new counselor and helping professional. This feedback is essential not only for your personal growth but also to the growth of your clients. In this chapter, a method for providing personal feedback is presented using the Microcounseling Supervision Model (MSM) and the corresponding Counseling Interview Rating Form (CIRF). Before we thoroughly investigate the MSM and analyze intentional skills, you also need to imagine how every intentional skill you learn has a correlating intentional location and function in your brain and that of your client.

The Brain and Its Functions

When you strategize what intentional skills will bring about the best response for your clients, we now want you to also enlarge this strategy to include neurocounseling, bridging brain and behavior, that was discussed in Chapter 1.

The authors of this textbook encourage every counseling student to take another anatomy and physiology course or review the one you had as an undergraduate. The reason we want you to take a new course, though, is that so much new information has been discovered about the brain. In Chapter 2 we will briefly discuss several important aspects of the brain and the corresponding functions. These functions will allow you to see where each of your many counseling skills is directly working. This understanding will make you a much more efficient and capable counselor.

You will remember that the brain is divided into three major components: the forebrain, midbrain, and hindbrain (Carter, 2014). Although they communicate with each other, communication can be local, regional, and global. The forebrain handles complex reasoning. The midbrain coordinates our sleep, motor coordination, breathing, and reflexes. The hindbrain acts as a relay station between the forebrain and the hindbrain through our eyes and ears (Chapin & Russell-Chapin, 2014).

Head Map of Functions

Each of these brain components can be separated into more specific brain locations and functions. Neurofeedback, another type of neuromodulation, is an intervention that Lori, one of the authors, uses to assist clients with training the dysregulated aspects of the brain. Neurofeedback (NFB) is a noninvasive method that trains the brain to use needed brainwaves for particular tasks using the principles of operant and classical conditioning (Chapin & Russell-Chapin, 2014). Sensors are placed on the head using a format called the 10–20 System.

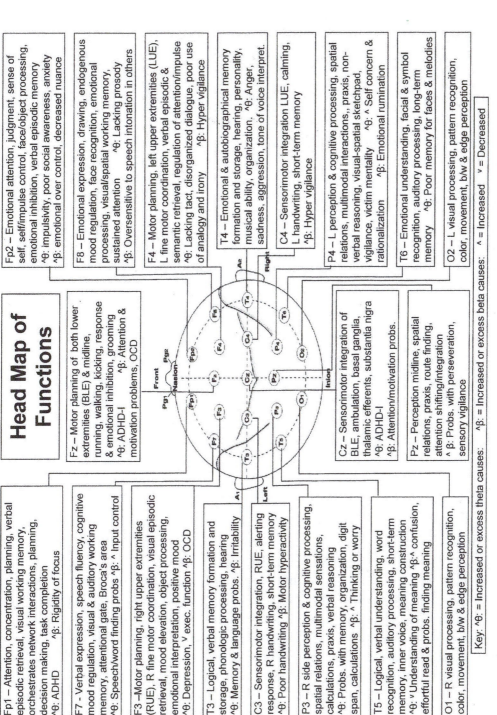

Figure 2.1 **Head Map of Functions** illustrates the 10–20 System of brain site location used in EEGs as well as brain functions (Anderson, 2010). © 2015 John S. Anderson. Permission granted by John S. Anderson

Neurofeedback: A noninvasive neurotherapy technique, biofeedback for the brain, that regulates the dysregulation in the brainwaves through an EEG amplifier and a computerized software program. Neurofeedback (NFB) uses the principles of classical and operant learning to condition and train the brainwaves. NFB is another self-regulating intervention.

Figure 2.1 shows this 10–20 System, and it also labels the specific locations and functions of the brain. Carefully read through the Head Map of Functions as these descriptions and functions will be the same places that many of our counseling skills will activate.

Head Map of Functions: This map labels the locations and functions of the human brain using the 10–20 System of Classification.

Practical Reflection 1: Intentional Skills and Brain Functions

After reading the Head Map of Functions, list three intentional counseling skills you know you use with clients. What location of the brain do you think you are engaging? Explain.

_____

_____

_____

_____

In Chapter 1 you were introduced to the importance of self-regulation skills for you and your clients. The first self-regulation skill to practice was diaphragmatic breathing. Each chapter self-regulatory skill will build upon the next, and by the end of the book, you will have a greater appreciation for neurocounseling and the need for self-regulation. A bonus is that you will feel healthier!

The second self-regulation skill being introduced in Chapter 2 is the use of imagery for yourself and your clients. One of the goals of self-regulation is the concept of brainwave state flexibility (Kershaw & Wade, 2011). Being able to use the right brainwave at the right time for the right task is paramount to healthy living (Chapin & Russell-Chapin, 2014). When it is time to sleep, your slow delta waves (0–4 hertz or cycles per second) assist in falling asleep at nighttime. When it is time to focus to read this material, your busier beta waves (13–18 hertz) transition into alertness when you need to read and comprehend.

Brainwave state flexibility: Achieving brainwave state flexibility allows counselors and clients to rehearse and improve their self-regulation by utilizing needed brain waves for intentional activities. Brainwave state flexibility practices moving up or down brainwaves as tasks are required such as practicing imagery when relaxation is needed to produce theta (5–8 hertz) and alpha (9–12 hertz) waves.

As you know, not every person's brain is healthy enough and regulated enough to be able to have that brainwave state flexibility. One method of teaching brainwave flexibility is the use of imagery where essential brainwave states can be utilized and practiced through relaxation exercises, scripts, and visualizations.

Practical Reflection 2: An Intentional Imagery Exercise

Read through the following scripted imagery exercise. You may prefer to have a friend or fellow practicum/internship student read it for you as you engage in the exercise.

Begin to focus on your diaphragmatic breathing. With the next inhalations, take that rich oxygenated breath to any part of your body that might have tension from the day. With the next breath that you exhale, take that stress and tension and gently push it out through your fingertips and your toes. As you continue, and your body begins to relax, envision sitting across from one of your clients for the first time. You see the details of their clothing. You listen to the tone of their voice. You are hearing her or his story, noting emotions, cognitions, and behaviors that play a central role in present functioning. You are developing the therapeutic relationship by empathizing, mirroring, attuning, and establishing resonance. The difference this time around is that you are also focusing on neurocounseling and how you can bridge the gap between your client's brain, behaviors, and symptoms.

Suddenly this new emphasis opens up an entirely new territory for additional knowledge, skills, treatment, and outcome possibilities. You begin to understand how neurocounseling teaches your clients about their physiology and how the brain impacts behaviors and emotions. You begin to understand how selecting an intentional skill of paraphrasing may resonate with your client feeling safe and listened to for the first time in a long time. This emotional safety engages the mirror neurons in the brain and activates parts of the pre-frontal cortex. You can visualize all of the 100 billion neurons firing in the brain. It is a beautiful sight.

Teaching neurocounseling to your clients helps them better understand how they are more than just thoughts and behaviors. Better understanding the functions of the brain offers you and your clients a deeper understanding of who they are. Your clients seem relieved with this large picture of self. You feel more confident with your intentional selection of skills knowing how and why they work in the brain. You realize you have activated your theta and alpha waves through this imagery exercise. You are relaxed and content. (Adapted from Russell-Chapin, L.A. & Jones, L. (2014).)

Reflect on this imagery exercise. How does your body feel? What brainwave states were flexibly achieved? What did you learn?

_____

_____

_____

_____

The Microcounseling Supervision Model

Now let's get busy and focus on the Microcounseling Supervision Model as a standardized approach assisting you in reviewing, offering feedback, teaching, and evaluating microcounseling skills. The Microcounseling Supervision Model has three major components:

1. Reviewing Skills with Intention,
2. Classifying Skills with Mastery, and
3. Processing Supervisory Needs.

Its tenets are based on microcounseling skills first reported by Ivey et al. (1968), and all the skills correspond to the five stages of the counseling interview.

Microcounseling Supervision: Supervision that allows you to work independently and in peer group supervision to understand the fundamentals of the counseling process and interview. Microcounseling skills are used in almost every model of supervision, and this model of supervision builds a strong foundation for needed basic skills. It has three stages: (1) Reviewing Skills with Intention, (2) Classifying Skills with Mastery, and (3) Understanding the Supervisory Process.

Microcounseling Supervision offers a way for you to learn to give constructive feedback that incorporates your strengths and areas for improvements by following the format of the CIRF. In beginning skills classes, you were encouraged to give others feedback. Usually, the comments were very positive, "You were great" or "I liked the way you paraphrased." During your field experiences, though, more than positive feedback must be given. If constructive feedback is not provided to you as students in field experiences, progress will be stagnant and perhaps nonexistent.

We discussed in Chapter 1 that feedback is not about you, but it is about a particular skill or process! Also, remember that it is your responsibility to ask your peer group, supervisor, and instructor for specific needs and wants during your supervisory time together. Feedback that is requested is best received. Request what you want and need. You know where you struggle, even if you don't know what to ask. When you take ownership of your counseling progress, you will feel less insecure and vulnerable about your counseling style, supervision, and having others view your counseling session recordings!

As you may remember, microcounseling skills are used in some fashion in every theoretical orientation. You practiced these skills in your beginning skills courses and every course after that. Many of you role-played using these same microcounseling skills. Therefore, the beauty of Microcounseling Supervision is it teaches you, the student, and your supervisors a natural method for reviewing your counseling sessions and offering feedback, regardless of theoretical orientation (Russell-Chapin & Chapin, 2012).

Lambert and Ogles (1997) described microcounseling skills as an approach that facilitates the general purposes of psychotherapy no matter what the theoretical orientation. The effectiveness of microcounseling skills training has been researched for decades (Miller, Morril, & Uhlemann, 1970; Scissons, 1993). In 1989, Baker and Daniels analyzed 81 studies on microcounseling skills training. Their finding concluded that microcounseling skills training surpassed both the no training and attention-placebo-control comparison. Daniels (2014, 2002) has followed microcounseling research for many years and now has identified over 450 data-based studies on the model.

Russell-Chapin and Sherman (2000) found, even with the effectiveness of the microcounseling approach, little consistency in the strategies used actually to measure and evaluate counseling students' skills and digital recordings. Russell-Chapin and Sherman (2000, p. 116) stated, "The need for quantifying counselor skills becomes increasingly important as the counseling profession continues to develop and refine standards for counselor competence."

The Counseling Interview Rating Form (CIRF) was designed in response to the need to accurately and effectively quantify skill during supervision sessions (Russell-Chapin & Sherman, 2000). The CIRF has a variety of functions, but it is mostly used as a method of providing positive and corrective feedback for your recorded counseling sessions. This form provides a method for evaluating the five stages of the counseling interview and the micro and macro counseling skills. A quantitative score as well as qualitative comments add to its many supervision benefits. Refer to a blank CIRF (Resource C) in the back of this chapter and follow along to learn how to use this form.

> **Counseling Interview Rating Form (CIRF)**: The Counseling Interview Rating Form is an instrument that provides a method for evaluating the five stages of the counseling interview and microcounseling and influencing skills. A quantitative score can be derived as well as qualitative comments. A copy of the CIRF is included at the end of this chapter.

The Three Components of Microcounseling Supervision

Reviewing Microcounseling Skills with Intention

The first component of the Microcounseling Supervision Model is essential to the efficacy and efficiency of the remaining sections. Once you are comfortable and secure with defining and reviewing the 43 microcounseling skills, then you can rapidly enter into the second phase. However, please initially take your time and ensure that you understand each skill definition along with the underlying intention of that skill. *Intention* is defined as choosing the best potential response from among the many possible options.

You are not looking for the "right" solution and skill, but you are selecting responses to adapt your counseling style to meet the differing needs and culture of clients (Ivey, 2002; Ivey et al. 2014). With intentionality you anticipate specific interviewing results if you use certain skills. For example, if you want your client to continue expressing emotion, a basic reflection of feeling would be a wise skill to choose. Your client laments, "Today was my little boy's first day of kindergarten!" The counselor's reflection of feeling is, "There must be differing emotions going on inside. You could be sad, lonely, scared yet excited."

> **Intentionality**: Selecting a specific counseling skill in anticipation of a particular interviewing client response.

Practical Reflection 3: Reviewing Skills with Intention

A glossary of the 43 microcounseling skills with their intentionality is provided in Resource A at the end of this chapter. Read through the list of skills by yourself and circle the skills you do not understand or the ones that do not seem familiar. List the skills that are unfamiliar to you. Begin to talk to your classmates about the unfamiliar skills and their intentionality. Once your review is complete, you can move to the second stage of Microcounseling Supervision.

_____

_____

_____

_____

Classifying Skills with Mastery

Let's get started in the first step in Microcounseling Supervision by practicing, defining, and reviewing all the microcounseling skills. One of the easiest methods to begin classifying skills with mastery is to have examples of someone else demonstrating the microcounseling skills and their uses. Do you remember the case of Rachel from the Preface? Rachel was introduced in Chapter 1, as the client Lori faced for her first counseling interview. An edited transcript of that session follows. As you read the transcript from the session, classify the microskills that Lori used in the space provided. We will classify the first response with you. Lori is just listening and nodding. You would classify that skill as a "minimal encourager." Was Lori's skill done with intention? In other words, was Lori successful with her choice of skills? In this case, we think Lori's choice did work, as Rachel does continue talking, and her resistance begins to lessen. Continue classifying Lori's counseling responses. Then compare your ideas with our classifications on the following page.

As you read and classify the skills in this session, note that Lori's life experience is indeed different from Rachel's. The two people have varying cultural experiences. Acknowledging that difference early in the interview is important. If you are a White European American and your client is African American, for example, the same frank discussion of differences can be helpful.

Practical Reflection 4: Classifying Skills with Mastery

Example Interview: The Case of Rachel

The following is a transcript of Lori's first counseling session. Rachel, a 71-year-old client, was hesitant to join into the counseling relationship. At that time, Lori was a new counselor and in her late twenties. Rachel immediately took control of the session. She chose not to sit down and wandered around the counseling office.

Notice in this example that the Microskill Classification column is on the left and the transcript is on the right-hand side of the page. Classify each of Lori's counseling responses. Then turn to Resource B to compare your classifications with ours.

Microskill Classification Transcript of Rachel and Lori:

Microskill Classification	Transcript of Rachel and Lori
Minimal Encourager	1. Rachel: Honey, what could you possibly have to offer? You are a child with very little life experience, and you will never be able to help or understand my problems.
	2. Lori: (nods and listens)
	3 Rachel: How could you ever help me?
	4 Lori: Rachel, you are probably correct. I have not lived as long as you, and I don't have as much life experience as you. All I can do is listen to you and see if a counseling relationship develops. How does that sound to you?
	5. Rachel: (finally sits down) It sounds fine, but it won't do any good. You see John and I were happily married for fifty years! He died quite suddenly six months ago, and I just don't know what to do.
	6. Lori: Having your husband be an important part of your life for so long and die unexpectedly must be devastating. I am very sorry.
	7. Rachel: (pausing and looking at me) Do you have any idea what this is like?
	8. Lori: I truly don't know what it is like to lose a husband, but I do know what it is like to lose a loved one; my father died when I was 25. I was scared and very sad.
	9. Rachel: You are right, it is not the same, but at least you know some of what it feels like.
	10. Lori: So we have a few things in common, and one of your concerns we could work on in counseling is about the loss of your husband. Is that right?
	11. Rachel: Yes, I would like to work on that, and I guess, I'd like to talk about what to do with myself now that John is gone. We did so much together; it is like my left arm has been cut off.

12. Lori: Having John gone hits you at many different levels. Not only was he your companion with whom you did everything, it is also like a piece of you is missing as well.

13. Rachel: Yes, yes. There are many different levels. All three of our children are grown, but they so miss their dad AND now they are calling me constantly to see if I am all right. Honestly, they are driving me crazy with their questions and concern! My youngest wants me to leave our home and move away with him.

14. Lori: Rachel, I noticed that when you began talking of your children, your voice became higher and louder; you almost seemed agitated. Tell me more about your children and your relationship.

15. Rachel: I love my children, but we all have our own lives. It feels like now they suddenly think I am incapable of living by myself. I am only 71 years old! I still drive my car; I play duplicate bridge; I tutor first graders in reading . . . . well, I mean I used to do those things.

16. Lori: Let me see If am truly understanding the situation. You miss your husband very much and are lonely, but recently your three children are trying to coddle you and even persuade you to possibly move away and live with them. You believe you are quite capable of living on your own without John, as you USED to do many independent things. Many activities you and John did together, but some of these things sound as if you even did them without John. Am I correctly understanding the gist of it all?

17. Rachel: Yes, yes. (Rachel became silent again; I sat quietly with her for several very long minutes.) I miss the things John and I used to do! I miss my old life.

18. Lori: Rachel, what do you miss about your old life?

19. Rachel: We were both retired, so we had the freedom to travel. We went everywhere. I have so many memories of our travels and years together. We have many friends in this town and throughout the country.

20. Lori: Those memories serve as a reminder of the great times together but they also remind you of your losses. Rachel, how many of those friends have you contacted recently?

21. Rachel: I received hundreds of cards and memorials. I answered each one with a hand-written thank-you note. But, I have not contacted anyone for a get-together since John's death.

22. Lori: Your loneliness goes deeper than John. Am I close?

23. Rachel: (crying) I miss my entire old life.

24. Lori: The sadness and loss seems overwhelming.

25. Rachel: I don't know what to do.

26. Lori: Rachel, you have gone through six very difficult months. Even in this office you have exhibited many varying emotions, from shock to sadness to anger. These are very similar to the stages of grief. Your feelings are very normal and valid. The consequences of John's death seem to have shattered your old life. Let's set up several counseling goals to help you re-structure your life and feelings.

27. Rachel: I wouldn't even know what goals to set.

28. Lori: You have already offered me several ideas, and there are many alternative ways to start. The first goal is to openly share your grief with others. You have done a wonderful job in here just by telling me your varying feelings and thoughts. I would like you to be this specific with your three children as well. Between now and our next session, you need to contact each of your children telling them how you miss John and their dad and also how you feel about their coddling?

29. Rachel: Yes, I will call each child.

30. Lori: The only other goal I would like us to set today is that you will contact one of your duplicate bridge friends to find out the next arranged game time. Are you willing to do that?

31. Rachel: (smiles slowly) I am not sure about that one, but I will try.

32. Lori: We have about 15 minutes left in our session. We have covered a lot of territory in our short time. I think I understand the depth of your loss. John must have been a great partner. You miss him so much, and you are lonely. You would like to have your old life back. Topping it all off are your children who love you very much and are very concerned about you living alone. I have also learned you have given up much of what you used to enjoy such as bridge, tutoring, and traveling.

33. Rachel: We did cover a lot of territory. Until we started talking, I didn't realize how much I have lost.

34. Lori: What part of the counseling session helps you understand why you have been so sad?

35. Rachel: Lots of things help me understand, but I am still somewhat confused.

36. Lori: Rachel, let's clarify even more then. What did we work on today that makes sense to you?

37. Rachel: Well, what I said earlier about not just John's dying, but I am sad about losing so much of my previous life.

38. Lori: You are sad about many of your losses, and today you stated that you are willing to regain control of at least two areas in your life. You will let your children know you love them but are very capable of living alone AND you said you would call a duplicate bridge friend.

39. Rachel: I did say that, didn't I?!

40. Lori: Yes, you did! I took from today's session that your feelings and grief are, indeed, valid and very normal. Rachel, you came here today very hesitant, and when you saw me, you knew I couldn't be of help. (Feedback/Evaluation of Session) How are you feeling about us now?

41. Rachel: I still think you are very young. But you said you would listen and you did. Thank you, my dear child.

42. Lori: Rachel, it was a pleasure to work with you. What would you like to do about setting up another appointment?

Now that you have had a chance to review and classify many of the essential skills, you may recognize that several skills are closely correlated and could be identified in several categories. For example, take a look at Lori's number 20 response. Lori stated, "Those memories serve as a reminder of the great times together, but they also remind you of your losses." We classified that response as a reflection of meaning as the purpose was to expand Rachel's thoughts. It could also be an example of exploration/understanding of the concern.

Talk to your classmates about those similarities, differences, and intentionalities. The more you can verbally articulate those differences and similarities, the sooner you will be able to choose which skills may be more intentionally needed at which times!

Processing Supervisory Needs

Now it is time for you to enter the third components of the Microcounseling Supervision Model and begin summarizing and processing these skills on the Counseling Interview Rating Form (CIRF, Resource C) as well as other important dimensions of the session. Before you begin the actual using of the Counseling Interview Rating Form, you need additional information about the instrument, itself.

The Counseling Interview Rating Form (CIRF)

A major component of Microcounseling Supervision is the Counseling Interview Rating Form (CIRF). The CIRF was originally developed for a counselor education program, but it has been used in both educational and clinical settings. The CIRF is the structured underpinnings of Microcounseling Supervision, as it provides a format for evaluating the five stages of the counseling interview as described by Ivey et al. (2014) and the microcounseling skills used in the counseling interview.

The CIRF was created by including the essential microcounseling and influencing skills taught in many helping professional programs. Two categories of skills are included: (a) microcounseling and influencing skills (Ivey et al., 2014); and (b) counseling interview stages (Ivey et al., 2014). The CIRF is divided into six sections that correspond to the five stages of a counseling interview, plus one additional section on Professionalism. The sections that correspond to Ivey's counseling interview are the (a) Opening, (b) Exploration, (c) Action, (d) Problem-Solving, and (e) Closing sections. Listed within each section are skills or tasks that are seen in that stage of the interview. For example, the Opening section includes the specific criteria of greeting, role definition, administrative tasks, and beginning.

Skill Definitions and Glossary: Forty-three counseling skills are used in the Counseling Interview Rating Form. All skills are defined in Resource A.

Scoring the CIRF

While watching one of your current recorded sessions or participating in a live counseling supervision session, you will complete the CIRF and tally the number of times a certain skill is used with frequency marks. If you saw the skill demonstrated five different times, you would mark a frequency tally each time. Values are assigned after the counseling session to indicate the level of mastery achieved for each skill. Write in the ratings of 1, 2, or 3 for each of the 43 listed skills that were observed. These ratings were developed using Ivey's et al.'s (2014) mastery scores as a model. Although Ivey originally identified four levels of mastery, the CIRF combines levels 1 and 2 to form a single level: identification and basic mastery. Ivey et al. (2014) describe *mastery* as using the skills with intention with an observable, desired effect on the client. You would offer a score of 1 if you only saw a counselor using that skill with little or no effect on the client. A score of 2 says the counselor used the skill with mastery and intention and a score of 3 says the counselor was demonstrating and teaching a new skill or concept to the client. As you can imagine, a score of 3 is used sparingly.

The CIRF includes space for comments next to each skill, so any reviewer can make notes or write the counselor's actual statements while viewing the session. These comments are extremely important to the supervisory session, as these comments can offer the counselor true examples of skills and processes used during the interview. The last page of the CIRF consists of space for providing written feedback on the strengths and areas of improvements. During Microcounseling Supervision, all peer supervisors, and the instructor will use the narrative space to provide constructive feedback.

If using the CIRF for quantifying counseling sessions into grades, the total values are tallied, with an A corresponding to 52 points and higher (i.e., at least 90% of the total points). This cut-off score requires scoring in the mastery range on all the essential skills denoted by an "X" on the CIRF. Essential skills are those deemed necessary for an effective interview as determined by the CIRF authors and the microcounseling approach to training (Russell-Chapin & Sherman, 2000).

Supervisory Process

Practical Reflection 5: Summarizing and Processing Skills

Now turn to the Counseling Interview Rating Form (CIRF) (Resource C). Again use the interview with Lori and the Case of Rachel and begin summarizing skill usage with frequency tallies. Go through the transcript again and use a frequency tally for each of Lori's counseling responses. At the end of the session or during each response, see which of Lori's responses represent basic mastery and active mastery. Remember basic mastery is defined as being able to demonstrate the skill during the interview, and active mastery shows Lori producing specific and intentional results from the chosen counseling skill.

The final step is to compare your ratings with ours (Resource D). In a regular classroom, this final step will be discussing your ratings with your classmates and instructor. Once the CIRF has been tallied by the members of the supervisory team, the narrative process for Microcounseling Supervision can begin. If you are the student counselor presenting the video and case presentation, ahead of time you have been asked to formulate needed supervisory questions and concerns. These issues are addressed by a team in a round-robin fashion going over supervisory concerns, strengths, and areas for improvement. The very last question asked of you will be, "What did you learn in supervision today, which will assist you in more effectively working with this client?"

Many of these comments may come from the Strengths and Area for Improvement area of the CIRF. The comments on these sections will help you immensely to progress forward. Lori's comments were from her supervisor, Dr. Ivey. After reading the section on Case Presentation, you will discover that many of Lori's supervisory questions and concerns were answered.

Uses of the CIRF

The CIRF is useful as an evaluative tool for supervisors and peers and self-evaluation. By using this form as a central foundation to Microcounseling Supervision, you can approach supervision time with less vulnerability as the environment of supervision is not threatening but validating. Also as an evaluation tool, the CIRF is an excellent teaching tool. Use the CIRF to identify areas and skills frequently used and those skills that were not being demonstrated effectively.

Case Presentation

Another essential skill for any helping professional is creating a clear case presentation. Case presentation skill is an important part of Microcounseling Supervision as the structure allows you to present your confidential, written case study to a small group of your counseling peers and instructor orally.

You have already received permission from your client and have placed that Consent Form in the client's file. Then you preview your digital recording and begin writing down major components of the case. Here is one method in written outline and narrative form to assist you in professionally sharing essential information about your client. Your case presentation can be offered first to your supervision group, and then the recording is watched in conjunction with scoring the CIRF, or you may prefer to view the counseling session recording first and then present the case presentation. Either approach is fine, but make an intentional decision about the order. We sometimes prefer to watch the recording first and score the CIRF, as the case presentation may skew some classmates' opinions about certain client characteristics and situations. Either way you will need to share your supervisory questions and concerns.

Decide what order to present the case presentation, and be sure to watch the session recording from beginning to end. It is often better to begin the supervisory processing by having your classmates voice your strengths. Then request the feedback you need. As the trust continues to build, your classmates may offer insights that you have not seen. An easy method for offering feedback is to follow the format of the CIRF. Ask your colleagues to state the comments you demonstrated showing particular strengths and even liabilities.

You may want to provide written copies of the report at the very beginning of the case presentation. It seems helpful to all to have the information in front of each team member or class member. After the supervision session is over, all copies go back to the supervisee to destroy. Even though client names have been shortened, blanked out, or in initial form, it is wise to shred these reports for confidentiality reasons.

You may want to collect all the CIRFs to see all the comments from your peers and supervisor. At this point, you may want to add all your scores and find the average score for a final grade. You will notice on the CIRF that Lori received a score for her interview with Rachel. She received a total of 58 points out of a possible 86 points if each skill were demonstrated with active mastery. How does that compare with your scoring of the Case of Rachel?

**Practical Reflection and Self-assessment 6:
Establishing Your Counseling Skills Baseline**

Now that you are familiar with the Counseling Interview Rating Form, watch one of your previous counseling session recordings that is relatively recent. Your self-assessment task is to classify each of the microcounseling skills you demonstrated. Using another blank (Resource E) CIRF, place a frequency tally in the column marked Frequency every time you demonstrate a skill. Be sure to write down as many of the actual statements in the column labeled Comments. Once your entire session is classified, then go back and offer the ratings in the column marked Skill Mastery Rating. You can add up your scores if you want, but right now a grade is not the most important item. This initial baseline of skills helps you discover those skills you are often using and with intention. Also, look for those counseling skills that you avoid and are not being used. The skills you are not choosing to use are just as telling as your frequently identified skills! Use this baseline information to assist you in goal-setting and future practice.

Self-assessment: Continue to watch your recordings of counseling sessions. View the session recording alone or in peer supervision groups. Use the CIRF to compare your score with others in your group. Continue to look for the skills you are frequently using, as well as those places where a void in skills may be occurring. The skills you are not using often may serve as your goals for the next counseling interview and supervisory session.

Practical Reflection 7: Understanding Microcounseling Supervision

As you practice using the Microcounseling Supervision Model, which of the three components will be most helpful to you now: Reviewing Skills with Intention, Classifying Skills with Mastery, or Understanding the Supervisory Process?

_____
_____
_____
_____

Summary and Personal Integration

Reviewing your counseling sessions and analyzing case presentations are essential to the growth of novice helping professionals. In Chapter 2 the following points were presented to help facilitate skill development:

- Expand your counseling conceptualization by including neurocounseling to comprehend the brain and its functions when selecting counseling skills.
- The Microcounseling Supervision Model can be used to assist you in building a foundation necessary for effective counseling and developmental growth. It provides natural building blocks for better understanding basic attending behaviors and influencing skills.
- The CIRF assists you in developing a system for reciprocal supervision where you, your colleagues and the instructor can offer constructive feedback. A "magic dance" of supervision begins where an easy and natural flow can encourage you to be receptive to new ideas and interventions. The CIRF not only reviews and teaches you how to classify specific skills and behaviors but how to evaluate their intention as well. Finally, the Counseling Interview Rating Form assists you in examining whether the goals of each interview stage are being achieved. Practice using the CIRF and experience the natural flow of Microcounseling Supervision.

Practical Reflection 8: Integration

Based on the information gained in Chapter 2, list at least two skills and/or strategies that will assist you in more effectively reviewing sessions and analyzing cases.

_____

_____

_____

_____

Resource A: Glossary of CIRF Skills

Opening/Developing Rapport Skills

Definition	Intention
Greeting: A simple acknowledgment to the Client	Build rapport
Role Definition/Expectation: Description of the counselor roles and intention of counseling; Confidentiality and its limit.	Provide structure

(*Continued*)

Definition	Intention
Administrative Tasks: Procedures necessary for counseling such as Client Rights; Payment; Scheduling and Intake Forms	Clarify procedures
Beginning: An open-ended question demonstrating to the client the interview is starting such as "What do you want to work on today?"	Offer an expansive method of beginning the interview

Exploration Phase/Defining the Problem Micro Skills

Definition	Intention
Empathy/Rapport: Behaviors and attitudes indicating understanding and active listening	Encourage the client to continue
Respect: Offering genuine acknowledgment of client's concerns	Build rapport
Nonverbal Matching: Using body gestures and positions to mirror the client's	Build rapport and acceptance
Minimal Encourager: An occasional word or "uh, uh" encouraging the client to continue	Encourage the client to continue
Paraphrasing: Actively re-phrasing in the counselor's own words and perceptions what the client has stated such as "Your mother died recently and you miss her."	Create understanding of client's words
Pacing/Leading: Allowing the client to direct the interview flow by counselor matching of words and verbal intonation; Counselor directing when interview flow needs transition	Encourages comfort, discourages resistance
Verbal Tracking: Consistent following of client's verbal direction and themes	Create continuity from client's content
Reflect Feeling: Paraphrase the client's feelings such as "How sad that must be."	Increases understanding of client's feelings
Reflect Meaning: Paraphrasing the client's deeper level of experience such as "Death can be an ending and perhaps a beginning."	Increases wider perspective
Clarifications: Eliminating confusion of terms by seeking clearer understanding of client's words	Eliminates confusion of terms
Open-ended Questions: Asking global questions for the purpose of receiving maximum or infinite amount of information such as "What do you miss the most about your mother?"	Receives maximum or infinite amount of information
Summarization: Paraphrasing a cluster of themes or topics during the interview providing transition and/or closure	Provides for transition and/or closure

(*Continued*)

(Continued)

Definition	Intention
Behavioral Description: Informing the client of what you observe of a behavior or mannerism; "When we began talking about sister and mother's relationship, I noticed your eyes teared up and you moved your chair away from me."	Eliminates assumptions about behaviors and assists in client awareness
Appropriate Closed Questions: An intentional question used to obtain a finite amount of information such as "How old were you when your mother died?"	Gains finite amounts of information
Perception Check: A periodic moment to ask the client if your perceptions or ideas about the concern are accurate; "Is that accurate concerning your sister and mother's relationship?"	Check counselor's perception and accuracy
Silence: Allowing purposeful, quiet reflection during the interview	Allows for purposeful, quiet reflection during the interview
Focusing: Consistent and intentional selection of topic, construct, and/or direction in the session	Aids in direction of the session
Feedback: Offering information to the client concerning attitude and behavior such as "Last week you came here with crumpled clothes, but today you have washed your hair and clothes."	Provides awareness about behaviors, thoughts, and feelings

Problem-solving Skills/Defining Skills

Definition	Intention
Definition of Goals: Statements stipulating directions, outcomes and goals of the client	Stipulates directions for counseling
Exploration/Understanding of Concerns: Using needed micro skills to discover the nature of the concern	Collects essential information about client's concern
Development/Evaluation of Alternatives: Assisting the client in creating a myriad of options for problem solution; Assessing the potential and possibilities surrounding each option	Assesses the potential and possibilities surrounding each option
Implement Alternative: Actively planning and articulating necessary steps for placing option into reality	Assists in putting ideas into action
Special Techniques: Any counseling intervention used to assist the client in deeper understanding of the concern such as imagery or an Empty Chair	Provides for the needs of individual clients
Process Counseling: Helping the client understand special themes and dynamics involved in the problem such as loss and fear	Allows for deeper understanding of client issues

Action Phase/Confronting Incongruities

Definition	Intention
Immediacy: Stopping the interview and immediately seeking clarification about a dynamic or observation in the client or between the counselor and client; "You stopped talking after your Dad was mentioned. What is happening right now?"	Keeps the sessions in the here and now
Self-disclosure: Offering relevant, helpful, and appropriate information about the counselor for the purpose of client assistance; "When my father died, I was 21 years old. My compass was gone, and I was lost."	Assists the client in universality of life
Confrontation: Pointing out client discrepancies between words, behaviors, thoughts	Helps the client to become aware of thoughts and actions
Directives: An influencing statement specifying an action or thought for the client to take; "The next time you visit your Mother's grave, I suggest you write a poem expressing your fears and loneliness."	Offers needed structure for differing developmental client needs; shows acceptance
Logical Consequences: Exploring the results/consequences of the client's actions and solutions; the consequences can be natural or logical	Points out results of client decisions
Interpretation: Presenting a new frame of reference on the client's concern possibly through different theoretical orientations; "It may be that the death of your mother forces you to be alone with yourself and your own fears."	Presents a new frame of reference on the client's concern

Closing/Generalization

Definition	Intention
Summarization of Content/Feeling: Closing the session by tying together themes involving subject matter and emotions	Ties together the counseling themes
Review of Plan: Organizing the desired outcome into a plan and reviewing it with the client	Reminds the client of previously discussed ideas
Rescheduling: Arranging for another session if needed	Provides additional counseling opportunities
Termination of Session: Offering appropriate generalizations from counseling to the client's outside world when goals have been achieved	Brings counseling outcomes to the real world
Evaluation of Session: Asking the client to reflect on the essentials of each interview; "What will you take from today's session that will assist you between now and our next meeting?"	Provides tangible counseling outcomes for the client and counselor
Follow-up: Connecting with the client about previous sessions, topics, and homework assignments	Allows for continuity between counseling sessions

Professionalism

Definition	Intention
Developmental Level Match: Assessing the client's developmental level and selecting counseling interventions accordingly	Creates intentional responses corresponding to client needs
Ethics: Following a set of ethical guidelines provided by a professional organization; Making appropriate ethical decisions	Assists in remaining prudent in decision-making process
Professionalism: Making appropriate professional decisions following unwritten and written organizational mores and guidelines	Adds respect to counselor and client

Resource B

Microskill Classification	Transcript of Rachel and Lori
	1. Rachel: Honey, what could you possibly have to offer? You are a child with very little life experience, and you will never be able to help or understand my problems.
Nonverbal Encourager	2. Lori: (nods and listens)
	3. Rachel: How could you ever help me?
Pacing Paraphrase Open-ended Question	4. Lori: Rachel, you are probably correct. I have not lived as long as you, and I don't have as much life experience as you. All I can do is listen to you and see if a counseling relationship develops. How does that sound to you?
	5. Rachel: (finally sits down) It sounds fine, but it won't do any good. You see John and I were happily married for fifty years! He died quite suddenly six months ago, and I just don't know what to do.
Reflection of Meaning and Empathy/Rapport	6. Lori: Having your husband be an important part of your life for so long and die unexpectedly must be devastating. I am very sorry.
	7. Rachel: (pausing and looking at me) Do you have any idea what this is like?
Self-disclosure	8. Lori: I truly don't know what it is like to lose a husband, but I do know what it is like to lose a loved one; my father died when I was twenty-five. I was scared and very sad.
	9. Rachel: You are right, it is not the same, but at least you know some of what it feels like.
Reflection of Meaning/Goal-setting	10. Lori: So we have a few things in common, and one of your concerns we could work on in counseling is about the loss of your husband. Is that right?

(Continued)

Microskill Classification	Transcript of Rachel and Lori
	11. Rachel: Yes, I would like to work on that, and I guess, I'd like to talk about what to do with myself now that John is gone. We did so much together; it is like my left arm has been cut off.
Paraphrasing/Reflection of Meaning/Pacing	12. Lori: Having John gone hits you at many different levels. Not only was he your companion with whom you did everything, it is also like a piece of you is missing as well.
	13. Rachel: Yes, yes. There are many different levels. All three of our children are grown, but they so miss their dad AND now they are calling me constantly to see if I am all right. Honestly, they are driving me crazy with their questions and concern! My youngest wants me to leave our home and move away with him.
Behavioral Description/Leading	14. Lori: Rachel, I noticed that when you began talking of your children, your voice became higher and louder; you almost seemed agitated. Tell me more about your children and your relationship.
	15. Rachel: I love my children, but we all have our own lives. It feels like now they suddenly think I am incapable of living by myself. I am only 71 years old! I still drive my car; I play duplicate bridge; I tutor first graders in reading . . . . well, I mean I used to do those things.
Summarization	16. Lori: Let me see if I am truly understanding the situation. You miss your husband very much and are lonely, but recently your three children are trying to coddle you and even persuade you to possibly move away and live with them. You believe you are quite capable of living on your own without John, as you USED to do many independent things. Many activities you and John did together, but some of these things sound as if you even did them without John. Am I correctly understanding the gist of it all?
	17. Rachel: Yes, yes. (Rachel became silent again; I sat quietly with her for several very long minutes.) I miss the things John and I used to do! I miss my old life.
Verbal Tracking/Open-ended Question/Exploration/Understanding of Concerns	18. Lori: Rachel, what do you miss about your old life?
	19. Rachel: We were both retired, so we had the freedom to travel. We went everywhere. I have so many memories of our travels and years together. We have many friends in this town and throughout the country.

(Continued)

(Continued)

Microskill Classification	Transcript of Rachel and Lori
Reflection of Meaning/Exploration/Understanding of Concerns	20. Lori: Those memories serve as a reminder of the great times together but they also remind you of your losses. Rachel, how many of those friends have you contacted recently?
Interpretation/Paraphrase	21. Rachel: I received hundreds of cards and memorials. I answered each one with a hand-written thank-you note. But, I have not contacted anyone for a get-together since John's death.
Appropriate Closed Question	22. Lori: Your loneliness goes deeper than John. Am I close?
	23. Rachel: (crying) I miss my entire old life.
Reflection of Feeling	24. Lori: The sadness and loss seems overwhelming.
	25. Rachel: I don't know what to do.
Leading/Teaching Special Technique	26. Lori: Rachel, you have gone through six very difficult months. Even in this office you have exhibited many varying emotions, from shock to sadness to anger. These are very similar to the stages of grief. Your feelings are very normal and valid. The consequence of John's death seem to have shattered your old life. Let's set up several counseling goals to help you re-structure your life and feelings.
	27. Rachel: I wouldn't even know what goals to set.
Goal-setting	28. Lori: You have already offered me several ideas, and there are many alternatives ways to start. The first goal is to openly share your grief with others. You have done a wonderful job in here just by telling me your varying feelings and thoughts. I would like you to be this specific with your three children as well. Between now and our next session, you need to contact each of your children telling them how you miss John and their dad and also how you feel about their coddling?
	29. Rachel: Yes, I will call each child.
Goal-setting/Appropriate Closed Question	30. Lori: The only other goal I would like us to set today is that you will contact one of your duplicate bridge friends to find out the next arranged game time. Are you willing to do that?
	31. Rachel: (smiles slowly) I am not sure about that one, but I will try.
Summarization of Content and Feeling	32. Lori: We have about 15 minutes left in our session. We have covered a lot of territory in our short time. I think I understand the depth of your loss. John must have been a great partner. You miss him so much, and you are lonely. You would like to have your old life back. Topping it all off are your children who love you very much and are very concerned about you living alone. I have also learned you have given up much of what you used to enjoy such as bridge, tutoring, and traveling

Microskill Classification	Transcript of Rachel and Lori
	33. Rachel: We did cover a lot of territory. Until we started talking, I didn't realize how much I have lost.
Open-ended Question/Evaluation of Session	34. Lori: What part of the counseling session helps you understand why you have been so sad?
	35. Rachel: Lots of things help me understand, but I am still somewhat confused.
Clarification/Evaluation of Session	36. Lori: Rachel, let's clarify even more then. What did we work on today that makes sense to you?
	37. Rachel: Well, what I said earlier about not just John's dying, but I am sad about losing so much of my previous life.
Review of Plan	38. Lori: You are sad about many of your losses, and today you stated that you are willing to regain control of at least two areas in your life. You will let your children know you love them but are very capable of living alone AND you said you would call a duplicate bridge friend.
	39. Rachel: I did say that, didn't I?!
	40. Lori: Yes, you did! I took from today's session that your feelings and grief are, indeed, valid and very normal. Rachel, you came here today very hesitant, and when you saw me, you knew I couldn't be of help. (Feedback/Evaluation of Session) How are you feeling about us now?
	41. Rachel: I still think you are very young. But you said you would listen and you did. Thank you, my dear child.
Open-ended Question	42. Lori: Rachel, it was a pleasure to work with you. What would you like to do about setting up another appointment?
	43. Rachel: Could we meet the same time next week?
Pacing/Termination of Session	44. Lori: Let's check. That looks like an open time. Thanks, Rachel.

Resource C

Counseling Interview Rating Form

Counselor: _____   Date: _____

Observer: _____   Recording Number: _____

Observer: _____   Audio or Video; please circle _____

Supervisor: _____   Session Number: _____

For each of the following specific criteria demonstrated, make a frequency marking every time the skill is demonstrated. Then assign points for consistent skill mastery using the ratings scales below. Active mastery of each skill marked by an X receives a score of 2 and should be seen consistently on every recording. List any observations, comments, strengths, and weaknesses in the space provided. Providing actual counselor phrases is helpful when offering feedback.

Ivey Mastery Ratings

3   Teach the skill to clients (teaching mastery only)
2   Use the skill with specific impact on client (active mastery)
1   Use and/or identify the counseling skill (basic mastery)

To receive an A on a recording at least 52–58 points must be earned.
To receive a B on a recording at least 46–51 points must be earned.
To receive a C on a recording at least 41–45 points must be earned.

Specific Criteria	Frequency	Comments	Skill Mastery Rating
A. OPENING/DEVELOPING RAPPORT			
1. Greeting X			
2. Role Definition/ Expectation			
3. Administrative Tasks			
4. Beginning X			
B. EXPLORATION PHASE/DEFINING THE PROBLEM MICRO SKILLS			
1. Empathy/Rapport			
2. Respect			
3. Nonverbal Matching X			
4. Minimal Encourager X			
5. Paraphrasing X			
6. Pacing/Leading X			
7. Verbal Tracking X			
8. Reflect Feeling X			
9. Reflect Meaning X			
10. Clarifications X			
11. Open-ended Questions X			
12. Summarization X			
13. Behavioral Description X			
14. Appropriate Closed Question X			
15. Perception Check X			
16. Silence X			
17. Focusing X			
18. Feedback X			

(Continued)

Specific Criteria	Frequency	Comments	Skill Mastery Rating

C. PROBLEM-SOLVING SKILLS/DEFINING SKILLS

1. Definition of Goals
2. Exploration/Understanding
    of Concerns   X
3. Development/Evaluation of
    Alternatives   X
4. Implement Alternative
5. Special Techniques
6. Process Counseling

D. ACTION PHASE/CONFRONTING INCONGRUITIES

1. Immediacy
2. Self-disclosure
3. Confrontation
4. Directives
5. Logical Consequences
6. Interpretation

E. CLOSING/GENERALIZATION

1. Summarization of
    Content/Feeling   X
2. Review of Plan   X
3. Rescheduling
4. Termination of Session
5. Evaluation of Session   X
6. Follow-up   X

F. PROFESSIONALISM

1. Developmental Level Match
2. Ethics
3. Professional (punctual, attire, etc.)

G. Strengths:

Area(s) for Improvement:

TOTAL: <u>52</u>

Resource D

Counseling Interview Rating Form

Counselor: Lori Russell-Chapin   Date: 5/5/2015
Observer: _____ Recording Number: 1
Observer: _____ Audio or Video; please circle
Supervisor: Allen Ivey _____ Session Number: Initial

For each of the following specific criteria demonstrated, make a frequency marking every time the skill is demonstrated. Then assign points for consistent skill mastery using the ratings scales below. Active mastery of each skill marked by an X receives a score of 2 and should be seen consistently on every recording. List any observations, comments, strengths, and weaknesses in the space provided. Providing actual counselor phrases is helpful when offering feedback.

Ivey Mastery Ratings

3   Teach the skill to clients (teaching mastery only)
2   Use the skill with specific impact on client (active mastery)
1   Use and/or identify the counseling skill (basic mastery)

To receive an A on a recording at least 52–58 points must be earned.
To receive a B on a recording at least 46–51 points must be earned.
To receive a C on a recording at least 41–45 points must be earned.

Specific Criteria	Frequency	Comments	Skill Mastery Rating
A. OPENING/DEVELOPING RAPPORT			
1. Greeting X			
2. Role Definition/Expectation			
3. Administrative Tasks			
4. Beginning X			
B. EXPLORATION PHASE/ DEFINING THE PROBLEM MICRO SKILLS			
1. Empathy/Rapport	I	I am very sorry	2
2. Respect			
3. Nonverbal Matching X			
4. Minimal Encourager X	I	Nods	2
5. Paraphrasing X	I	Having lost John hits you at so many levels	2

(Continued)

Specific Criteria	Frequency	Comments	Skill Mastery Rating
6. Pacing/Leading X	II	Rachel, you are probably correct	2
7. Verbal Tracking X	III	What do you miss about your old life?	2
8. Reflect Feeling X	III	You are lonely	2
9. Reflect Meaning X	III	Having your husband be an independent part of your life for so long and die unexpectedly must be devastating	2
10. Clarifications X			
11. Open-ended Questions X	IIII	How does that sound to you?	2
12. Summarization X	II	Let me see if I truly understand the situation	2
13. Behavioral Description X	I	I noticed when you began talking about your children your voice became higher and louder	2
14. Appropriate Closed Question X	III	Am I close?	2
15. Perception Check X	III	Is that right?	2
16. Silence X	I	Listening	2
17. Focusing X	I	Coddling	
18. Feedback X	I	Rachel, you came here today very hesitant . . .	2
C. PROBLEM-SOLVING SKILLS/ DEFINING SKILLS			
1. Definition of Goals X	II	The first goal is to openly share your grief with others	2
2. Exploration/Understanding of Concerns X	II	How many of those friends have you contacted lately?	2
3. Development/Evaluation of Alternatives X	I	There are many alternative ways to start	2
4. Implement Alternative			
5. Special Techniques			
6. Process Counseling	II	Today you stated that you are willing to re-gain control of at least. . . .	

(*Continued*)

(Continued)

Specific Criteria	Frequency	Comments	Skill Mastery Rating
D. ACTION PHASE/CONFRONTING INCONGRUITIES			
1. Immediacy	II	How are you feeling about us now?	2
2. Self-disclosure	I	My father died when I was 25.	2
3. Confrontation			
4. Directives	I	You will contact one of your duplicate bridge friends.	2
5. Logical Consequences	I	The consequences of John's death seem to have shattered your old life.	2
6. Interpretation	I	Your loneliness goes deeper than John.	2
E. CLOSING/GENERALIZATION			
1 Summarization of Content/Feeling X	I	We have covered a lot of territory. . .	2
2. Review of Plan X	I	Today you stated that you are willing. . .	2
3. Rescheduling	I	What would you like to do about setting up another appointment?	2
4. Termination of Session			
5. Evaluation of Session X	II	What did we work on today that makes sense to you?	2
6. Follow-up X			
F. PROFESSIONALISM			
1. Developmental Level Match	I	(assessing Rachel's developmental level as a 1 or 2)	2
2. Ethics			
3. Professional (punctual, attire, etc.)			

G. Strengths:

1. I liked the way you were able to build rapport with Rachel using the microcounseling skills and going with her resistance.

2. The intentional use of reflections of feeling and meaning seemed to assist Rachel in better understanding her sadness.

Areas for Improvement:
1. Be cautious about asking too many opened and closed questions.
2. Let her brainstorm more ideas for grieving such as creating a memorial for John, etc.
3. Even though Rachel read the Service Agreement describing confidentiality, be sure to discuss it next time.

TOTAL: <u>58</u>

Resource E

Counseling Interview Rating Form

Counselor: _____   Date: _____

Observer: _____   Recording Number: _____

Observer: _____   Audio or Video; please circle

Supervisor: _____   Session Number: _____

For each of the following specific criteria demonstrated, make a frequency marking every time the skill is demonstrated. Then assign points for consistent skill mastery using the ratings scales below. Active mastery of each skill marked by an X receives a score of 2 and should be seen consistently on every recording. List any observations, comments, strengths, and weaknesses in the space provided. Providing actual counselor phrases is helpful when offering feedback.

Ivey Mastery Ratings

3   Teach the skill to clients (teaching mastery only)
2   Use the skill with specific impact on client (active mastery)
1   Use and/or identify the counseling skill (basic mastery)

To receive an A on a recording at least 52–58 points must be earned.
To receive a B on a recording at least 46–51 points must be earned.
To receive a C on a recording at least 41–45 points must be earned.

Specific Criteria	Frequency	Comments	Skill Mastery Rating
A. OPENING/DEVELOPING RAPPORT			
1. Greeting X			
2. Role Definition/Expectation			
3. Administrative Tasks			
4. Beginning X			
B. EXPLORATION PHASE/DEFINING THE PROBLEM MICRO SKILLS			
1. Empathy/Rapport			
2. Respect			
3. Nonverbal Matching X			
4. Minimal Encourager X			
5. Paraphrasing X			
6. Pacing/Leading X			
7. Verbal Tracking X			
8. Reflect Feeling X			
9. Reflect Meaning X			
10. Clarifications X			
11. Open-ended Questions X			
12. Summarization X			
13. Behavioral Description X			
14. Appropriate Closed Question X			
15. Perception Check X			
16. Silence X			
17. Focusing X			
18. Feedback X			
C. PROBLEM-SOLVING SKILLS/DEFINING SKILLS			
1. Definition of Goals			
2. Exploration/Understanding of Concerns X			
3. Development/Evaluation of Alternatives X			
4. Implement Alternative			
5. Special Techniques			
6. Process Counseling			

(*Continued*)

Specific Criteria	Frequency	Comments	Skill Mastery Rating

D. ACTION PHASE/CONFRONTING INCONGRUITIES

1. Immediacy
2. Self-disclosure
3. Confrontation
4. Directives
5. Logical Consequences
6. Interpretation

E. CLOSING/GENERALIZATION

1. Summarization of Content/Feeling   X
2. Review of Plan   X
3. Rescheduling
4. Termination of Session
5. Evaluation of Session   X
6. Follow-up   X

F. PROFESSIONALISM:

1. Developmental Level Match
2. Ethics
3. Professional (punctual, attire, etc.)

G. Strengths:
I liked the way you paced with Stephen. Your play therapy interventions worked well and assisted Stephen in talking.

Area for Improvement:
Next time be sure to explore Stephen's grief and attempts at grieving.

TOTAL: 52

References

Anderson, J. (2010). *Professional EEG Biofeedback Certification Training*. San Rafael, CA:.Stens Corporation.

Baker, S.B. & Daniels, T. (1989). Integrating research on the microcounseling program: A meta-analysis. *Journal of Counseling Psychology*, 36, 213–222.

Carter, R. (2014). *The human brain book* (2nd edn). New York, NY: DK.

Chapin, T. & Russell-Chapin, L. (2014). *Neurotherapy and Neurofeedback: Brain-based Treatment for Psychological and Behavioral problems*. New York, NY: Routledge.

Daniels, T. (2002). Microcounseling research: What over 450 data-based studies reveal. In A. Ivey, M. Ivey, & R. Marx (eds.), *Leader guide to Intentional Interviewing and Counseling*. Pacific Grove, CA: Brooks/Cole.

Daniels, T. (2014). A review of research on microcounseling 1967–present. In A. Ivey, M. Ivey, & T. Daniels (eds.), *Intentional Interviewing and Counseling: CourseMate Interactive Website*. Belmont, CA: Brooks/Cole.

Ivey, A.E. (2002). *Intentional Interviewing and Counseling* (4th edn). Pacific Grove, CA: Brooks/Cole.

Ivey, A.E., Normington, C.J., Miller, C., Morrill, W., & Haase, R. (1968). Microcounseling and attending behavior: An approach to prepracticum counselor training. *Journal of Counseling Psychology*, 15(5), 1–12.

Ivey, A.E., Ivey, M.B., & Zalaquett, C.P. (2014). *Intentional Interviewing and Counseling: Facilitating Client Development in a Multicultural society* (8th edn). Belmont, CA: Brooks/Cole.

Kershaw, C.J. & Wade, J.W. (2011). *Brain Change Therapy*. New York: Norton.

Lambert, M.J. & Ogles, B.M. (1997). The effectiveness of psychotherapy supervision. In C.E. Watkins, Jr. (Ed.), *The Handbook of Psychotherapy Supervision* (pp. 421–446). New York: Wiley.

Miller, C., Morrill, W., & Uhlemann, M. (1970). An experimental study of pre-practicum training in communicating test results. *Counselor Education and Supervision*, 9, 171–177.

Russell-Chapin, L.A. & Chapin, T. (2012). *Clinical supervision*. Pacific Grove, CA: Brooks/Cole/Cengage.

Russell-Chapin, L.A. & Jones, L.K. (2014). Three truths about neurocounseling. *Counseling Today*, American Counseling Association, 57(3), 20–21.

Russell-Chapin, L.A., & Sherman, N.E. (2000). The counseling interview rating form: A teaching and evaluation tool for counselor education, *British Journal of Guidance and Counseling*, 28(1), 115–124.

Sapolsky, R.M. (2004). *Why Zebras don't get Ulcers*. New York, NY: Holt.

Scisson, E.H. (1993). *Counseling for Results: Principles and Practices of Helping Professions*. Pacific Grove, CA: Brooks/Cole.

3

BECOMING EFFECTIVE AS A SUPERVISEE

The Influence of Placement Setting

You can only take your clients as far as you have gone yourself.

Overview

This chapter introduces you to effective supervision and the influences your placement settings may have on the structure, amount, and type of supervision available. You need to be knowledgeable enough about the supervisory process to assist the supervisor in the efficacy of the supervision process. You will learn about which supervision style matches your personal preferences and the special counseling considerations and implications that certain placement settings bring. The Case of Stephen is introduced, illustrating the unique needs in a school setting. We stress the importance of evaluating supervision and its impact on you. The third self-regulation skill of sleep hygiene is introduced.

Goals

1. Understand the self-regulation skill of sleep hygiene and how it relates to overall health.
2. Assess personal preferences for the differing dimensions of supervision.
3. Take responsibility for individual supervision needs.
4. Understand the unique supervision needs and skills of the settings of community agencies, schools, private practice, and hospital-based treatment programs.
5. Share forms and contracts establishing clear expectations for you, the agency, and the client.
6. Understand the need for evaluation and its benefits.

Key Concepts: You and Supervision

There are many differing dimensions of effective supervision. It is an area that has been the focus of much research from theoretical perspectives to outcome results. We discuss more theoretical models of supervision and further inform on counseling outcome research later in the text, but for the purpose of getting you started, five different aspects of becoming an effective supervisee are addressed.

Supervision: A distinct manner of approach and response from an experienced supervisor to a supervisee's questions and needs

As you read this chapter, work at assessing honestly what you desire out of supervision and what your needs and expectations are from your supervisor.

These ideas should correlate with the goals, expectations, and counseling base-line from Chapters 1 and 2. Read each section and write down your preferences and self-acknowledgments.

If you are willing to address these issues, you will have a very successful and powerful supervision experience. The five areas for this chapter are determining which supervisory style works for you, discerning the unique influences of your placement setting, collecting and sharing needed information from your placement setting, understanding the supervision evaluation, and adjusting attitudinal perspectives. Once again before we get started in discussing effective supervision and settings, another essential self-regulation skill must be added to diaphragmatic breathing and imagery.

Self-regulation Skill of Sleep Hygiene

The third self-regulation skill emphasized is understanding the need for proper sleep hygiene. Many of us seem to be sleep deprived and expect to still function in a healthy manner. How can you perform well in school and with your clients if you don't have enough sleep? You can begin modeling for your clients by practicing the first three self-regulation skills of breathing, imagery, and sleep hygiene.

Becoming aware of your sleep habits and patterns is the first step in establishing proper sleep hygiene. Often people don't understand the necessity of quality sleep to mental health. As a graduate intern, enough sleep often goes by the wayside. Begin to observe your routine for going to bed and getting up. Have you scheduled them realistically for the same time every day? There are several additional healthy sleep hygiene rules to implement. For example if possible, no eating a heavy meal right before bedtime; exercise during the day but not at night; no or little daytime napping; no discussing of "heavy" or emotional issues right before going to bed; no drinking alcohol or too much caffeine during the day and none at night (Saxon, Etten, & Perkins, 2015).

Adults need approximately seven to eight hours of sleep per night. Teen-agers need even more. Neuroscientists have recently discovered why sleep is so important. The glial cells that often don't conduct electrical activity during the day are thriving at night acting as "garbagemen" for our brains, clearing unnecessary brain debris and toxins (Parker, 2014). When not enough sleep is obtained, too many toxins accumulate, and the brain and body don't function efficiently.

Educating you and your clients about the pineal gland, a small cone-shaped gland that is found next to the optic nerve and in the third ventricle of the brain, is important to understanding sleep hygiene (Marieb, 2012). The pineal gland produces and secretes significant amounts of the hormone melatonin. Teaching clients about screen time at night helps in comprehending why bright lights such as cell phones, televisions and laptops tell the pineal gland to stop making melatonin. Melatonin is necessary for proper sleep (Russell-Chapin, 2016). Melatonin is produced in smaller amounts especially for the aging population, reinforcing the importance of exercise and getting outside when possible. Research is suggesting that melatonin acts as an antioxidant and a regulator of our mitochondrial cellular functioning (Srinivasan et al., 2011). Taking nightly melatonin may help with the aging of the mitochondrial cell body.

Melatonin: A hormone secreted from the pineal gland that regulates sleep.

Practical Reflection and Self-regulation Skill 1: Sleep Hygiene

Keep a journal of your nightly sleep hygiene habits. What is one change you could begin that will assist you in self-regulation of your sleep?

_____

_____

_____

_____

Determining Which Supervision Style Works Best for You

Supervision style is often very individual and very different. A basic definition of supervision style suggests that it is a distinctive manner of approach and response to supervisees' needs for a helping professional who has more expertise and experience than the supervisee (Friedlander & Ward, 1984; Russell-Chapin & Chapin, 2012). There is some outcome research on what makes effective supervision, and yet it still is a somewhat uncharted territory. It appears that there is not one distinct style of supervision that is best for everyone. You must understand the varied dimensions of the supervisory process to assist in building the best situation for your supervisory experience. As we present each aspect of supervision, you need to be looking for the best match of supervision dimensions for you.

At the end of this chapter Resource F is a Supervisory Style Inventory (SSI) (Friedlander & Ward, 1984). You may want to take the inventory now, or read through this chapter and then take the SSI. Regardless of when you take the SSI, your results will help you understand better what will make supervision more effective for you based on your preferences.

Developmental Styles of Supervision

There is much research about the developmental nature of supervision. The two major assumptions in developmental supervision are that you, the counselor in training, go through different developmental stages depending on your supervision needs. Secondly, just as you would assess the developmental level of your client in counseling, your supervision developmental level is assessed and requires different types of supervisory responses (Russell-Chapin & Chapin, 2012; Stoltenberg, McNeill, & Delworth, 1998). One way to think about your developmental level is to focus on your experience and knowledge.

Developmental supervision: Supervisees progress through a series of predictable levels or stages as they learn the skills of the counseling process.

Hersey, Blanchard, and Johnson (2000) expanded that concept by dividing developmental or maturity level into four different styles: structured, encouraging, coaching, and mentoring. Again for each level of supervisee developmental maturity or each different situation you present, your supervisor will respond accordingly. In the Maturity Stage 1 (M1), you might tell your supervisor that you don't know how to proceed with a particular client. An M1 structured supervisory response would be to explain in detail what to do, "Try utilizing those basic interviewing skills. During the next interview, please use at least three reflections of feeling and meaning." In the M2 stage, you may tell your supervisor that you are working with a client, and you were able to conceptualize the case and necessary treatment interventions. An M2 encouraging supervisory response is, "You have worked hard on this case and thought it out thoroughly; I like how you stated treatment goals." In the M3 stage, you are excited to share the details of the case and request additional ideas. An M3 coaching supervisory response may sound like, "Using the intentional skill of self-disclosure seemed to work, but how did it change the focus of the session?" In the final stage, M4, you tell your supervisor in a confident manner how the case is developing.

You have very few questions. An M4 mentoring supervisory response is, "It is fun to share cases and hear how others intervene."

Practical Reflection 2: Preferred Maturity Dimensions

Of the situational/maturity dimensions mentioned, list supervision aspects that you prefer now such as structure, encouragement, coaching, or mentoring.

_____

_____

_____

_____

Other supervision theorists believe there are varying approaches to supervision such as either expressive or instrumental (Russo, 1993). Supervisors who use expressive approaches tend to be extraverts, enjoy people and relationships, and easily build rapport. Expressive supervisors focus on how you are interacting with your clients and supervisors. An expressive response may sound like, "You seem very comfortable with your clients, and your warm and friendly demeanor puts people at ease." Supervisors who prefer instrumental approaches tend to be introverts, encourage outcomes and goal-setting, and are comfortable handling conflict in general. An instrumental supervisory response may be, "I noticed that you used open-ended questions when exploring your client's concerns. When your client began to cry openly, however, you quickly asked a closed question and did not focus on his emotions. Next time you need to be willing to let your client sob."

Another supervision variable, according to Ladany, Marotta, and Muse-Burke (2001), is as trainees gain general experience, they become more adept at conceptualizing clients. In their research, the Supervisory Style Inventory (SSI) was administered to measure student supervisees' perceptions of their supervisors. One of the outcomes of the research was that trainees preferred supervisors who were moderately high on all three styles: attractive, interpersonally sensitive, and task-oriented.

Trainees rated Attractive supervisors as warm, supportive, and often friendly. Interpersonally sensitive supervisors were seen as invested in the therapeutic process and what was happening to you the student. The task-oriented supervisor provides structure to the supervision session and focuses on goals and task (Friedlander & Ward, 1984).

Practical Reflection 3: The Best Fit Supervisory Styles

Based on what you know about yourself, what style of supervision best fits your current supervision needs in the areas of attractiveness, interpersonal sensitivity, and task orientation? What were the results of your SSI?

_____

_____

_____

_____

You and Your Supervision Setting

Now that you have a better understanding of some of the styles involved in supervision, you must be able to comprehend how your placement site influences the type of supervision you receive. As each supervisor is different and unique, so is the actual placement site. Notice these differences, but look for some similar features that will illustrate consistency across professions. You and your fellow students will have practicum and internship experiences in a variety of settings, including schools, community agencies, hospitals, and private practice. Each setting, as well as individuals and groups served, has unique needs and special opportunities for your counseling growth.

School Settings

Primary, Middle, and High Schools. In both public and private schools, as a school intern you will provide a variety of typically short-term, developmental academic, career, and social/personal counseling to students. Group counseling, parent and teacher consultation, and crisis intervention are among the more common services performed.

University and Community College. In college and university settings, you will gain experience in individual and group counseling, as well as outreach programming, crisis intervention, and academic counseling and development. Many counseling centers have several helping professionals on staff who work closely with student services such as residence life and health services, to provide for the mental health needs of both traditional and nontraditional age students.

Primary, Middle, and High Schools

School counselors' roles continue to change. You may become more focused on developmental education and the mental health needs of the school community as well as administrative opportunities. At some schools, the counselor intern may be the only mental health professional on site, while at others, the intern is part of a system that includes school counselors, school social workers, school psychologists, and student assistance program (SAP) professionals. SAP professionals are often outside, contracted providers. Private schools may provide an even broader opportunity for developing a school counseling program. At each school level, the intern must become familiar with the developmental needs of the age group concerned and appropriate programs and interventions both academically and socially.

Supervision. For school counselor interns, a credentialed school counselor must conduct the supervision. Be sure to check with your state board of education to understand the credentialing procedures in your state.

Sometimes locating a supervisor is a challenge when there is only one school counselor per school district who works with a number of different schools. Many school counseling interns do not have a site supervisor located in the same building so they are not as readily accessible as at other sites. Although the intern may have an administrative supervisor on the site such as the school principal, it is vital to be assertive about asking for and getting the support necessary on site. In cases where site supervision is not as effective as desired, the university supervisor and group supervision with fellow students become more important. Interns should attempt to improve the situation with their on-site supervisor and involve the university supervisor as necessary. Some schools will not have an office readily available for the counselor intern's use. Basic needs for the counselor intern are a space that provides for privacy and the ability to keep the client's visit confidential. Without this, school-age clients will not feel comfortable voluntarily seeking out the school counselor.

For all settings where the site supervisor is not directly on site, and in all school settings, interns should make themselves aware of emergency procedures. Schools should have crisis plans and perhaps even crisis teams to act when necessary. Many schools team with community agencies providing additional support to the school when necessary.

School or Agency procedures for mandatory reporting are also necessary. Understand your state's laws and regulations for mandated reporting of sexual, child, and elder abuse.

Colleagues. Many school counselors find themselves as "one of a kind" in their work setting. To avoid isolation, networking with school counselors in the district and beyond, as well as through professional organizations, is a necessity. The lack of understanding of what school counselors do and issues of confidentiality can lead to feelings of isolation as well. One of our group of three school counseling interns maintains monthly meetings five years after graduation, finding the resulting support and peer supervision invaluable in their role as school counselor. Another networking system is the use of the Internet and e-mail. You can use the International Counselor Network at LISTSERVE@ UTKVM1.UTK.EDU to find colleagues online who can support your efforts and discuss related concerns. Obviously you would need to be discreet when discussing problems by avoiding names and other identifying references due to the nonconfidential nature of the Internet.

Clients. In school settings, the clients might be students, parents, teachers, or groups of students. Counselor interns will get referrals from teachers who become aware of student concerns or behavior, from parents or guardians, the administration (particularly involving students with disciplinary problems), and from self-referrals. An intern in a school that did not previously have a school counselor must develop referral relationships and educate school staff about all that school counselors can do, and in some cases, what they can't do! Basic forms and permissions need to be developed, as well as policies and procedures for handling confidential material such as progress notes and intake information.

The counseling emphasis is short-term counseling aimed at assisting the student in learning ways to apply problem-solving skills to issues of concern. Opportunities for group counseling are many. School counselor interns have successfully facilitated grief groups, social skills groups, academic improvement groups, play therapy groups, and even groups for parents.

Consultation with teachers and parents is another major focus for the school counseling intern.

Confidentiality. When working as a counselor with school-age children and in school settings, special legal and ethical considerations arise concerning confidentiality. School counselor interns should understand and implement the types of permission required by the school for their involvement in individual and group counseling. Questions such as "Under what circumstances can a child work with the school counselor without parent or guardian prior permission?" and "What counseling records does the parent or guardian have legal access to?" should be answered.

Additionally, the intern and his or her site supervisor should address questions regarding what information can be released to referral sources such as teachers and administrators. Lawsuits have raised issues about counselor liability in circumstances such as suicide, drug abuse, abortion, and even success in college. School counselor interns need to be familiar with reporting procedures, the duty to warn, and when to refer a student to community resources, among other responsibilities. It is essential that you obtain your personal liability insurance. Many organizations offer student malpractice/liability insurance, including the American Counseling Association (ACA), American Mental Health Counseling Association (AMHCA), and National Association of Social Workers (NASW). Check to see if your educational institution covers you and what its requirements for insurance are as well.

Practical Reflection 4: Current Supervisory Expectations

What are your current expectations about supervision? Settings: List them here and be sure to share with your supervisors.

_____

_____

_____

_____

The Case of Stephen

As you read the Case of Stephen, begin to focus on the special needs that a school placement site may bring. Think about the supervision needs of Lori as she begins to understand the complexities of Stephen's counseling needs.

Stephen was referred to Lori during her days as a school counselor/school psychologist. She spent twenty hours a week as a school counselor in a rural Western town and the remaining twenty hours a week as a school psychologist for the same district administering tests and facilitating multidisciplinary case study teams.

Stephen's mother was very upset as Stephen was falling behind in his studies and continuing to lose interest in his friends and his love for soccer.

Stephen's father committed suicide six months prior to Lori interviewing this eleven-year-old boy. His dad had been in a high-pressured administrative position, and the company had filed for bankruptcy. Stephen was the person to find his dad's body hanging in the family basement. This rural community had few mental health resources, but the family was seen by their church pastor immediately following the funeral.

You may want to follow along using a blank Counseling Interview Rating Form (CIRF), introduced in Chapter 2. Below is the second counseling interview between Stephen and Lori. To compare your scores with ours, see the completed CIRF in Resource G.

LORI: Stephen, it is good to see you again. What do you want to work on today?

STEPHEN: (Silence.)

LORI: (Silence.)

STEPHEN: I don't want to work on anything. It is so boring in here.

LORI: It is boring in here. Let's go to the play therapy room.

STEPHEN: That must be for babies, but it has to be better than here!

LORI: (The play therapy room was two doors down.) Play with anything you want.

STEPHEN: (He wandered around for several minutes and became intrigued with the small sand play area. Stephen picked up a large plastic dinosaur and began chasing the smaller dinosaurs.)

LORI: Those smaller dinosaurs must be scared. The big one may feel pretty powerful and in control.

STEPHEN: Yah.

LORI: Stephen, when was the last time you felt powerful and in control?

STEPHEN: I guess it was before my dad died. (A tear trickled slowly down his cheek.)

LORI: Stephen, that must have been so scary and sad when your dad died. I am so sorry that your dad killed himself and felt he had no other options. I am sorry that you found your dad dead in the basement.

STEPHEN: (Our eyes meet for the first time and both of us are crying.) It was awful! Why did he have to leave us?

LORI: (Silence.) I don't know, Stephen. It is important, though, that you begin talking about your thoughts and feelings surrounding your dad's suicide.

STEPHEN: I don't want to talk about it. It hurts too much.

LORI: (Silence.) Do you like to read?

STEPHEN: Sometimes.

LORI: Let's not talk then but read instead. I have a wonderful book called The Hurt. It is quite easy to read and probably too simple for you. Perhaps we could read it together and then you may want to tell the story to your younger brother, Abe.

STEPHEN: Whatever.

LORI: (We read the book together, alternating reading pages out loud.) This is one of my favorite stories. What does it mean to you?

STEPHEN: It is a pretty good book. Abe would like it. He doesn't talk much either. It is a story about a little boy who stops talking about his hurt feelings. The hurt moves into his room. The little boy becomes more sad and lonely, and the hurt gets as big as his room.

LORI: That must be how Abe feels. I guess that may be how you feel too, Stephen!

STEPHEN: I guess it is.

LORI: Tell me what things you have tried to make your hurt go away.

STEPHEN: I have worked hard around our house helping my mom.

LORI: That must be a huge responsibility for the oldest man in your house.

STEPHEN: It is, but mom needs my help. She doesn't have anyone else.

LORI: So in order to be the man and maybe even take the place of your dad, you can't focus on your studies and fun things like soccer because you have so much to do around the house.

STEPHEN: I have lots to do and besides soccer is for kids.

LORI: The man of the house can't have fun anymore?

STEPHEN: Sure, I guess.

LORI: (I picked up an inflatable beach ball and threw it at Stephen. He caught it with a surprised look on his face.) Let's play ball for a while. Look where you caught the ball using your left thumb. What word is written on that section of the ball?

STEPHEN: Hopeless.

LORI: Talk to me about your hopeless feelings.

STEPHEN: Everything is hopeless. Nothing seems to get better. Everyone says time will make it better, but it hasn't.

LORI: Time alone is not healing your hurt. In fact, it gets bigger by doing nothing.

STEPHEN: Maybe.

LORI: Let's keep throwing the ball. (I dropped it this time, so I picked it up strategically. My thumb happened to land on the word devastated.) One of the last times I was devastated was when my dad died. I was 25 years old, so older than you. I do remember, though, thinking my world had crumbled and feeling abandoned.

STEPHEN: Well, I bet you didn't have to see your dad hanging from a rope!

LORI: No, Stephen, I did not. I can't imagine how difficult that must have been.

STEPHEN: I tried to save him, you know.

LORI: I didn't know that.

STEPHEN: I got on a chair and cut him down with a knife we had. He fell to the floor. I thought maybe I killed him by the fall. I then tried helping him breathe like I had seen on TV.

LORI: You were very brave, Stephen.

STEPHEN: It didn't do much good, did it?

LORI: You couldn't save his life, but maybe you helped him in his death. What do you think your dad wants for you in his death?

STEPHEN: (Long pause.) He wants me to be happy.

LORI: What do you need to do to be happy and alive?

STEPHEN: I don't know.

LORI: Guess with me then.

STEPHEN: Have some fun. Study hard. Take care of Mom and Abe. Stuff.

LORI: Let's have some more fun here. I have one more game to play, and then we will close up. Do you know the game of Tic, Tac, Toe?

STEPHEN: Sure.

LORI: You can draw the needed squares on this paper. Our goal is to work on your having more fun and studying harder. So every time you place an X, you must come up with one idea how to have fun and study harder. When I place my O, I will offer some ideas too. Go. (We played the game until the "cat" won, and all the squares had an X or O.)

LORI: Stephen, you have played and worked a lot in our time together. What will you take with you from our session today that you can use in the week to come?

STEPHEN: Well, this hasn't been as boring as I thought! I guess I learned that my hurt had gotten really big! I have to remember to tell Abe the story.

LORI: Your hurt is really big. You were able today to make it much smaller by talking about your thoughts and feelings. Would you like to borrow the book to read to Abe?

STEPHEN: Sure. I will bring it back next week.

LORI: Stephen, thanks for working and playing with me. During the next week, I need you to work and play again. What is one thing that you will work on and one thing that you will play?

STEPHEN: (He smiled at me.) I will turn in my science homework, and I will play with Abe.

LORI: Those two tasks sound important and even fun. When shall we make the next appointment?

STEPHEN: I could make it after my soccer practice next Wednesday.

LORI: See you then, Stephen. I hope Abe will like the book too.

Practical Reflection 5: School Counseling Supervisory Needs

What unique supervisory needs are presented in the Case of Stephen? Think about Stephen's age, school life, homework, family, and so on.

_____

_____

_____

_____

Colleges and Universities

Practicum and internship experience in the counseling center at a community college, college, or university offers a variety of opportunities ranging from crisis intervention to career development and counseling. Professional counselors and other mental health professionals deal with the range of presenting concerns of college students, faculty, and administration staff at the college or university counseling center. As a part of student affairs and student services, counseling center staff typically work closely with administrators and even faculty in dealing with the mental health needs on campus.

Supervision. The counseling center director or his or her designee serves as site supervisor. If there are specialists in the center, such as a substance abuse counselor or eating disorders expert, the intern may seek their supervision concerning certain clients. Weekly staff meetings are usually held to discuss cases, plan programming efforts, deal with administrative matters, and share information regarding the types of clients and presenting concerns being encountered. As a community within the larger community, it is necessary to learn and communicate trends and issues with which students deal. Learning the intake process, limits of treatment provided, and referral sources are matters dealt with early on in supervision.

The intake process entails learning to conduct a complete assessment in order to recommend treatment options. For some counseling centers, the intake process is separate from treatment, with the intake counselor recommending the most appropriate treatment provider within or outside of the counseling center. Many centers offer in-service education programs, as well as the opportunity to sit in on counseling sessions for observation.

Colleagues. Professionals working in college counseling centers come from a variety of backgrounds, including social work, psychology, and counseling.

Counseling centers may also use paraprofessionals and interns from various academic departments to provide services. Paraprofessionals can be students who are trained as peer counselors, providing information and support to students on a variety of issues and concerns. Counseling interns may be involved in training of paraprofessionals in helping skills. Colleagues may have developed certain areas of expertise that will be useful for consultation as you work with clients with a variety of presenting concerns.

Clients. Clients in college and university counseling centers may range from the traditional age college freshmen experiencing being away from home for the first time, to the older international student seeking a degree far from home. Many adjustment problems come to the attention of counseling centers. Students may have difficulty adjusting to college life, residence hall life, new relationships, old relationships, family relationships, choosing a major or program of study, and career direction, among other issues. Other concerns typically dealt with in counseling centers include depression, eating disorders, substance abuse, and anxiety disorders. Occasionally, serious mental illness such as schizophrenia emerges in late adolescence. Older adults are returning to college or starting later than the traditional age and may experience concerns needing attention through the counseling center.

An important part of working in a counseling center is outreach programming. Interns develop teaching and presentation skills by providing information to groups of students about topics of interest and concern such as substance abuse, eating disorders, sexual and relationship abuse, and stress management. Presentations on academically-oriented topics such as time management, test anxiety, and study skills present opportunities to develop skills while providing important preventive services. Additionally, many students benefit from participation in group counseling, where topics can range from body image to career exploration. Counseling interns have found success in establishing such groups even in centers where group participation has not previously been offered or established.

Confidentiality. Although the limits of confidentiality are the same in the counseling center, it can be difficult for students to seek services, fearing that others will consider them "crazy" if they have visited the counseling center. Normalizing the process of seeking mental health services is a challenge to all professional counselors, and college and university counseling centers have worked toward this end. Outreach programming is one way that counseling centers provide students with information about services offered. Informally learning about the intake process and meeting a person who works as a counselor can alleviate some of the fear of using counseling services.

Those who refer students to the counseling center include faculty, residence hall personnel, family members, and others. Interns need to learn what is appropriate to share with referral sources, depending on the releases of consent signed, as well as university policy and legal status of the client. Educating referral sources about the importance of confidentiality and its limits also assists in the process.

Community Agencies

Community agencies provide diverse opportunities for counseling with special clients, ranging from agencies providing services for the elderly, victims of sexual assault and domestic violence, foster care and child welfare, to those with persistent mental illnesses and substance abuse problems.

In many agencies, counselor interns work as part of a treatment team, along with psychiatrists, social workers, case managers and caseworkers, as well as with professionals from other agencies involved with a client. Additionally, in many cases, counselor interns may be working with the judicial system when their clients have court-mandated treatment obligations or are involved in legal matters. Individual, family, and group counseling, including in-home treatment, as well as psychoeducational programming, assessment, and case management activities, may all be part of the counselor intern's work at an agency.

Supervision. In community agencies, counselor interns may have a variety of opportunities for supervision in addition to the designated site supervisor. Many agencies have teams of service providers, and at team meetings, specific cases are presented for consultation, supervision, and information sharing. Valuable input can be gained from others working directly with the client's case as well as other team members. The case presentation format is useful for sharing necessary information about a client so other team members can assist and respond. At many agencies, a variety of professionals and paraprofessionals provide services, expertise, and experiences to share with a counselor intern. Informal supervision may often occur during the day as the counselor intern seeks input from available colleagues.

One of the challenges of working at a community agency is the paperwork necessary for documentation of services. Supervision will include getting feedback on the appropriate documentation of services according to funding and accrediting sources. It is important to build in time during working hours to complete documentation, whether written or dictated.

As at any site, counselor interns should learn what emergency procedures are on site. Examples of emergencies include a suicidal client, a client threatening violence, and potential danger at a home visit. Interns should be trained in procedures and emergency agency contacts when the site supervisor is not available.

Colleagues. After training and a certain amount of time spent at the agency, interns find themselves feeling and being treated as a full staff member. Colleagues will be from a variety of professional training backgrounds including psychology, social work, and human services, as well as counseling. Learning from each can add greatly to the internship experience.

At agencies with residential settings, a variety of service providers work with clients around the clock. Communication among shifts is vital for continuity in treatment. Opportunities for continuing and in-service education are provided by many agencies; it is important to find out what is available and participate. Many agencies use volunteers in different capacities as well. As an intern, recognizing the value of and participating in the training and education of volunteers is an additional opportunity for professional development. Although you may find yourself being treated as a full member of the staff and find many opportunities for learning, remember to set limits on what you take on as an intern.

Clients. At community agencies, counselor interns work with clients in outpatient, residential, home-based, and community-based settings. You might work with an agency that serves victims of violence, the elderly, children and families, substance abuse, involuntary clients, clients involved with protective services, and any number of presenting concerns.

Many agencies serve a specified clientele based on funding sources. For example, an agency serving elderly clients might only provide services to those over 65, or a children's agency may only serve those 18 years or younger. Other agencies affiliate with a religious organization and may have restrictions on the types of services provided.

Many agencies provide counseling and mental health services to clients who are mandated or directed to seek treatment. A parent attempting to regain custody of a child might be court ordered to complete substance abuse treatment and parenting classes. A child or adult adjudicated in the legal system may be mandated for counseling as part of successfully completing probation. In these cases and others, clients may have a variety of feelings and responses to the counselor assigned. In addition, most clients in this situation will have signed a release of information for the counselor to report progress to the referring agent.

Establishing a therapeutic relationship can be difficult under these circumstances. In the initial session, it is important to ask the client their feelings about the referral and reflect and acknowledge those feelings as legitimate.

Clients usually direct negative feelings at the referring source and, once acknowledged and legitimized, the counselor can move toward establishing some beginning trust in the relationship. When working with mandated clients, it is also necessary to discuss the limits of confidentiality with the referring source as well as the consequences for choosing not to follow through with counselor recommendations. For example, when working with clients on parole mandated for outpatient substance abuse treatment, clients should be asked what the consequences would be for choosing not to comply with treatment. When presenting treatment as a choice, and, even though to choose not to comply meant violating parole, clients may feel more empowered about their choice for treatment.

Confidentiality. The ethical obligation of protecting your client's right to confidentiality has certain limits within the context of working in community agencies, particularly in circumstances where the counselor intern is a mandated reporter. As a mandated reporter, counselor interns must report incidences of suspected physical or sexual abuse or neglect of children and the elderly to appropriate authorities. Counselors can become aware of abuse or neglect from primary sources and secondary sources.

The limits of confidentiality should be stated so that all clients and their guardians understand under what circumstances the counselor must break confidentiality without client consent. The agency should have a standard form of informed consent that includes information regarding the confidentiality of client information. When working with children, interns must know who is the legal guardian of the child because this is the person with a legal right to the child's information. Client information may be shared with counselor intern and supervisor, and with other members of a treatment team within the agency without violating confidentiality. Clients should, however, be made aware of who will have access to their information.

An example is gaining client permission to record sessions for supervision or class assignments. Clients should be given explicit information about who will be viewing the session, under what circumstances and for what purpose, and how the recording will be disposed of.

Private Practice

In private practice, one or more licensed professionals organize their company to provide counseling services. These services may include individual, family, and group counseling as well as organizational consulting and Employee Assistance Programs. Although many private practices have set fees and clients may use insurance coverage to help pay for services, some use a sliding fee scale, particularly for services provided by a counselor intern.

Private practice settings may specialize in certain areas such as Christian Counseling, Neuro feedback, or Court Evaluations; however, most offer comprehensive, generalist practice. Counselor interns in private practice settings typically are exposed to a diverse clientele with a variety of presenting concerns.

Supervision. In a private practice setting, there are several opportunities for supervision. Your supervisor might be a licensed psychologist, a licensed clinical social worker, a licensed professional clinical counselor, or even a psychiatrist. In each case, it is vital to understand the training and approach to counseling and psychotherapy that your supervisor has.

In addition to the one-on-one supervision of your site supervisor, you will typically be involved in staff meetings and group supervision meetings as well. You may find that you bring a different, perhaps more developmental perspective to the understanding of client concerns. Staff meetings will also include marketing, client service, and other aspects of maintaining and growing the practice. Training by individuals within the practice and opportunities to attend other training sessions may be available. If your supervisor is also the owner of the practice, you may have opportunities to be involved in development of the organization and its client base. Due to the nature of most private practices, your supervisor will typically be heavily involved in client services and may be limited to the one hour of weekly scheduled supervision time. Interns can make the most of supervision by being prepared with questions, reviewed recorded sessions, and administrative concerns.

Colleagues. Practitioners working in private practice come from many fields of the helping professions, including counselors, social workers, and psychologists, as well as pastoral counselors and others who have met licensing standards.

Your colleagues will typically be working for a percentage of the fees they bring to the practice; for example, the practitioner receives 50 percent of the fees generated and 50 percent goes to the practice for overhead expenses such as administrative support, office rent, and equipment. In other cases, practitioners might work for the practice for an hourly wage, and, as an employee, have withholding taxes, liability insurance, and other expenses taken care of by the employer. Some private practices now are choosing to only take fee for service rather than being on provider lists for insurance.

With the working structure of a private practice, staff meetings or supervision usually structures time with colleagues. Occasionally, when clients cancel or do not show for an appointment, there is the opportunity for collegial visits.

Clients. For most practitioners and clients in private practice, the greatest challenge for providing service can be managed care. Managed care began as an effort to control skyrocketing costs of medical and mental health care and provide some standardization of medical and mental health treatment protocols. Although managed care has met these goals in some ways, in many cases client treatment has changed dramatically and not always for the good. In the past, insurance companies may have covered unlimited numbers of sessions for mental health treatment.

Presently, most companies require the approval of services and documentation of treatment goals, progress, and success for services to be covered. Private practitioners apply to managed care companies to become network service providers. This process can take months, and the practitioner generally accepts a lower fee than usually charged to become a participating provider. Additionally, some companies limit the type of mental health provider who can provide treatment. Clients make choices for treatment and providers based on what managed care companies will approve. Many times the managed care company allows an assessment to determine what treatment is indicated. The managed care company might conduct the assessment, or an employee assistance program or other company contracted by the managed care company might be utilized. Recommendations are then made for the client's treatment, and a suitable network provider is sought. Depending on the requirements of the managed care company, interns might not be deemed suitable for providing treatment, even under the supervision of the established provider.

One of the challenges for interns in a private practice is getting enough direct client counseling hours. Although there may be ample opportunity for psycho-educational presentations, pro bono work, and other supportive work such as administering and scoring tests, interns rarely have established referral sources for clients. Developing a referral base is essential for success; churches, physicians, other interns, and schools might be places to contact. A sliding fee scale for interns' services can also assist in establishing a client base. When potential clients are referred to the practice and cannot afford regular fees, intern services at reduced fees can be a viable option for many.

Confidentiality. As in community agencies, clients need to be informed what the limits of confidentiality are in a private practice. Additionally, clients must be informed as to who will see or hear recordings of the intern's counseling sessions. Many interns have difficulty asking clients to agree to sessions being recorded for supervision and course expectations.

Informing the client as to the purpose of the recording, who specifically will see it, and how it will be disposed of can assist the client in agreeing to the request. It may also help to remind the client that, as a counselor in training, your supervisors and classmates provide valuable feedback for learning. Many an intern who has difficulty with clients agreeing to have sessions recorded, when asked about their approach, will have put the process in a negative light, thereby making it easier for the client to reject the request.

Some clients will give consent if their back is to the camera and only the counselor intern's face can be seen. Although not ideal, it assists in learning to be able to gauge client reactions and nonverbal communication. This setup can work for most supervisees and supervisors. Children usually readily agree to recording and as long as the parent and legal guardian approves, it is helpful to get permission from the child as well. Letting the child see the camera, view a few minutes of recording, and generally become comfortable with the process can assist in lessening the impact of recording when the session starts. A general discussion of how students have successfully obtained agreement from clients will facilitate the process for those who are more hesitant.

Hospital-based Treatment Programs

Hospitals provide mental health treatment programs on an inpatient, partial hospitalization, and outpatient basis. Programs range from eating disorders to attention deficit hyperactivity disorder (ADHD) clinics to substance abuse, and may serve all age groups. Most hospital-based programs utilize group therapy as a primary treatment, particularly at the inpatient and partial hospitalization levels of treatment. Counselor interns will work with a variety of treatment providers including nurses, psychiatrists, psychologists, and social workers.

Supervision. Greater numbers of professional counselors are being hired to work in hospital-based settings and different capacities than ever before. Depending on the program selected the supervisor's training can range from psychiatry to social work to mental health nursing. A professional counselor's identity and niche are important in mental health treatment in hospital-based settings as treatment focus moves away from a strict medical model to a more holistic, even developmental model.

Supervision may entail learning the supervisor's theoretical approach and foundation and sharing of the intern's emergent theoretical beliefs. If the program is inpatient or partial hospitalization, opportunities for supervision may occur at several times throughout the day or week. Frequently, a team approach is used in treatment. During team meetings, client cases are discussed with each member of the team contributing ideas, impressions, information, and recommendations.

Colleagues. As stated previously, colleagues and treatment team members come from a variety of training backgrounds. Interns may find themselves co-leading a treatment group or other therapeutic interventions and disagreeing with the approach used by their colleague. Counseling interns may find themselves at odds with the approaches used by other professionals who may not have counseling training yet are providing counseling services. Learning from each other is vital in improving services offered to clients. Interns should be open to learning from the experiences of others and willing to share what they have learned as well.

Clients. Clients in hospital-based settings, particularly those in inpatient and partial hospitalization, are suffering more acute phases of mental disorders. Inpatient programs attempt to stabilize the client through medication and treatment and then release the client to follow-up services in an outpatient or partial hospitalization program. The client will receive a diagnosis of their condition, possibly be involved with psychological testing, and receive group and individual counseling as part of their treatment. Additional services may include medical treatment, occupational therapy, and discharge planning. For some hospital-based treatment programs, a specific diagnosis or cluster of diagnoses are treated in a specialized program. Examples include substance dependence, eating disorders, and gambling addiction. Inpatient, mental health treatment programs exist for children, adolescents, and adults.

Confidentiality. Confidentiality can be challenging in inpatient and partial hospitalization programs as clients and staff members interact. Clients and even staff members who are always on duty when on the unit can also challenge boundaries. All treatment professionals who interact with clients chart or record the interaction, so there is a record of all treatment the client receives. In this way, those who work other shifts and other treatment team members have information about what happened with the client while they were not present. Many interns have found electronic hospital charting of progress notes to be different than what is required in an agency. An important part of training is learning what belongs in a client's chart or record, because it is the master record of the client's treatment while hospitalized.

Practical Reflection 6: Influences of Field Experience Settings

How is your practicum and internship setting influencing your field experience and your supervision? Analyze this from the standpoints of supervision opportunities and structure, colleagues, clients, and confidentiality.

_____

_____

_____

_____

Collecting and Sharing Needed Information

As you can see, the type of placement site does influence your counseling and supervisory experience. Another essential component of your overall experience is sharing information about yourself once you have selected a placement setting. As soon as you have taken the opportunity to let your supervisor get to know who you are, we hope you will ask your supervisor to share his or her collective wisdom. Learning about theoretical orientations and others' training experiences can be fun and interesting. Reciprocity is a treasured relationship builder.

We all fear that which we don't understand and is unknown, so you can alleviate some of that anxiety by letting your supervisor know as much relevant information about you as possible. If you have an updated resume, please make copies for your supervisor and instructor. Your field experience instructor may have special forms to assist you with sharing this information and other course requirements. If not, Resources H through L are provided for you to use or adapt. Several of the forms were adapted from classic materials developed by Dimick and Krause (1980).

These forms and needed information may also assist your counseling program in following the necessary accreditation guidelines for field experience and supervision. Remember to use the forms your educational institution and agencies have first. The forms presented here are only examples for you to use if needed.

Two forms that protect you, your institution, and your placement site are the Student Practicum/Internship Agreement and the Practicum/Internship Contract.

The Student Practicum/Internship Agreement and an extra copy will assure all that you have read your professional code of ethics, you understand the policies of the professional organization, you have proof of student liability and malpractice insurance, and you agree with and understand the field experience expectations laid out before you (see Resource H for a sample form). Resource I is an example of a contract between the University and the actual field placement site clarifying the expectations and roles of each party. Keep an extra copy of everything just in case some information gets lost!

Your field experience forms may include a log sheet to help you in accurately and consistently collecting your weekly field experience hours. Your instructor will let you know when to turn in your hours, but you need to find a method of habitually writing down your hours of direct and indirect service hours. Direct service hours are any counseling activity where you are actively and directly working with clients, such as individual and group counseling, educational workshops, and consultations where you are presenting materials. Indirect service hours are those where you are not directly working with clients, but are an essential part of your counseling responsibilities, such as case notes, client files, pertinent reading, supervision sessions, staff meetings, and class time. In CACREP accredited counseling programs, you must acquire a minimum of 700 clock hours for the entire field experience with at least 240 indirect hours. The specific breakdown is 100 hours for practicum and 600 hours for the internship.

Practical Reflection 7: Student Practicum/Internship Agreement

After looking at the Student Practicum/Internship Agreement, what other valuable information would you want to include? What might your instructor want you to include?

_____

_____

_____

_____

_____

Three other important forms for you to become familiar with are an Informed Consent Form for Adults and Children. These forms are essential to you, the intern counselor, and to the client; they clarify the counseling relationship and expectations. Clients should receive copies of these forms and copies should be kept in the client's file. The Adult Client Informed Consent Form ensures that the client understands who you are and the extent of your counseling training. In addition, it offers approval for recording the session. The Child Client Informed Consent Form offers approval for you to counsel a child or minor, and it could also provide a place for you to share needed information with others. It is important to have the effective dates the contract begins and ends.

The third needed form is the Release of Confidential Information form. This information protects confidentiality and stipulates exactly what information can be shared with whom, and specific dates. Resource L is an example, but be sure to use the customized form from your counseling setting if requested. Official institutional letterhead is essential for identification. Resources J, K, and L are offered as examples, but your individual universities and settings may have similar forms developed for their unique population and settings.

Evaluation of Your Work in the Placement Setting

Earlier in the chapter, you learned that true supervision will always include an evaluation component. It seems you are in a constant state of evaluation when receiving feedback on your weekly counseling sessions. This formative assessment helps you develop your skills, and there will be a formal or summative evaluation, usually at a midpoint in the semester and at the end of the semester. Be sure to ask these important questions about the evaluations. How much are they worth point-wise in proportion to your entire grade? Who will get to see them? Where do they go? When do you get to review the evaluation? (Sweitzer & King, 1999).

There are different types of evaluations, such as narratives and open-ended questions or Likert-type scales numbering from 1 to 6. Resource M is a sample Site Supervisor's Evaluation of Student Counselor's Performance that uses a Likert-type scale (Hackney & Nye, 1973). Notice the different categories used to examine your counseling competencies: supervision comments, the counseling process, the conceptualization process, and additional suggestions. Be sure to set up a special supervision session for your midterm evaluation or use a regularly scheduled appointment to review your evaluation. There is also a place for your signature and that of your supervisor. Review your supervisor's evaluation carefully and work on areas that need improvement in the next time period. In many programs, students have the opportunity to evaluate the supervisor as well. This mechanism provides the supervisor with important information to improve his or her skills. If any problems arise that cannot be resolved between the supervisor and supervisee, the university instructor can act as a third-party mediator.

Practical Reflection 8: Evaluation Concerns

What are your biggest concerns about the evaluation process? Talk among your classmates about their concerns.

_____

_____

_____

_____

Summary and Personal Integration

This chapter outlined unique variables influencing your supervisory experiences:

- The third self-regulation skill of proper sleep hygiene was emphasized.
- In the section on Determining Which Supervisory Style Works for You, information was shared so you could select the best supervision match for your cognitive and emotional style of interviewing and counseling.
- In You and Your Supervision Setting, each placement setting was presented listing special considerations, learning opportunities, and skill development.
- Sample forms and evaluation procedures were offered to assist you and your school and agency in gathering and sharing needed counseling information.
- The final section comprised attitudinal perspectives that may be strengths, but if not addressed could cause potential supervisory problems.

Practical Reflection 9: Integration

Which of the supervisory dimensions will assist you most in becoming a productive and effective interviewer, counselor, and supervisee?

_____

_____

_____

_____

Resource F

Supervisory Style Inventory*

For trainees' form: Please indicate your perception of the style of your current or most recent supervisor of psychotherapy/counseling on each of the following descriptors. Circle the number on the scale, from 1 to 7, which best reflects your view of him or her.

For supervisors' form: Please indicate your perceptions of your style as a supervisor of psychotherapy/counseling on each of the following descriptors.

Circle the number on the scale, from 1 to 7, which best reflects your view of yourself.

NOT VERY   VERY

1. Goal-oriented   1 2 3 4 5 6 7
2. Perceptive   1 2 3 4 5 6 7
3. Concrete   1 2 3 4 5 6 7
4. Explicit   1 2 3 4 5 6 7
5. Committed   1 2 3 4 5 6 7
6. Affirming   1 2 3 4 5 6 7
7. Practical   1 2 3 4 5 6 7
8. Sensitive   1 2 3 4 5 6 7
9. Collaborative   1 2 3 4 5 6 7
10. Intuitive   1 2 3 4 5 6 7
11. Reflective   1 2 3 4 5 6 7
12. Responsive   1 2 3 4 5 6 7
13. Structured   1 2 3 4 5 6 7
14. Evaluative   1 2 3 4 5 6 7
15. Friendly   1 2 3 4 5 6 7
16. Flexible   1 2 3 4 5 6 7
17. Prescriptive   1 2 3 4 5 6 7
18. Didactic   1 2 3 4 5 6 7
19. Thorough   1 2 3 4 5 6 7
20. Focused   1 2 3 4 5 6 7
21. Creative   1 2 3 4 5 6 7
22. Supportive   1 2 3 4 5 6 7
23. Open   1 2 3 4 5 6 7
24. Realistic   1 2 3 4 5 6 7
25. Resourceful   1 2 3 4 5 6 7
26. Invested   1 2 3 4 5 6 7
27. Facilitative   1 2 3 4 5 6 7
28. Therapeutic   1 2 3 4 5 6 7
29. Positive   1 2 3 4 5 6 7
30. Trusting   1 2 3 4 5 6 7
31. Informative   1 2 3 4 5 6 7
32. Humorous   1 2 3 4 5 6 7
33. Warm   1 2 3 4 5 6 7

*Developed by M.L. Friedlander and L.G. Ward (1984).

Scoring Key for SSI

Attractive: Sum items 15, 16, 22, 23, 29, 30, 33; divide by 7.
Interpersonally sensitive: Sum items 2, 5, 10, 11, 21, 25, 26, 28; divide by 8.
Task-oriented: Sum items 1, 3, 4, 7, 13, 14, 17, 18, 19, 20; divide by 10
Filler items: 6, 8, 9, 12, 24, 27, 31, 32

Resource G

Author's CIRF Quantification of the Case of Stephen

Counselor:	Lori Russell-Chapin	Date:	6/2/15
Observer:	_____	Recording Number:	1
Observer:	_____	Audio or Video; please circle	
Supervisor:	A. Ivey	Session Number:	2

For each of the following specific criteria demonstrated, make a frequency marking every time the skill is demonstrated. Then assign points for consistent skill mastery using the ratings scales below. Active mastery of each skill marked by an X receives a score of 2 and should be seen consistently on every recording. List any observations, comments, strengths, and weaknesses in the space provided. Providing actual counselor phrases is helpful when offering feedback.

Ivey Mastery Ratings

3   Teach the skill to clients (teaching mastery only)
2   Use the skill with specific impact on client (active mastery)
1   Use and/or identify the counseling skill (basic mastery)

To receive an A on a recording at least 52–58 points must be earned.
To receive a B on a recording at least 46–51 points must be earned.
To receive a C on a recording at least 41–45 points must be earned.

Specific Criteria	Frequency	Comments	Skill Mastery Rating
A. OPENING/DEVELOPING RAPPORT			
1. Greeting X	I	Stephen, it is good to see you again.	2
2. Role Definition/Expectation			
3. Administrative Tasks			
4. Beginning X		What do you want to work on today?	2

(Continued)

Specific Criteria	Frequency	Comments	Skill Mastery Rating
B. EXPLORATION PHASE/DEFINING THE PROBLEM MICRO SKILLS			
1. Empathy/Rapport	I		2
2. Respect			2
3. Nonverbal Matching X			
4. Minimal Encourager X			
5. Paraphrasing X	I	So in order to be the man and maybe even take the place of your dad, you can't focus on your studies and fun things like soccer because you have so much to do around the house.	2
6. Pacing/Leading X	II	It is kind of boring in here.	2
7. Verbal Tracking X	I	Let's not talk then but read.	2
8. Reflect Feeling X	III	Stephen, that must have been so scary and sad when your dad died.	2
9. Reflect Meaning X	III	That must be a huge responsibility for the oldest man in your house.	2
10. Clarifications X			
11. Open-ended Questions X	III	Stephen, when was the last time you felt powerful and in control?	2
12. Summarization X			
13. Behavioral Description X	I		
14. Appropriate Closed Question X	IIII	Do you like to read?	2
15. Perception Check X			
16. Silence X	IIII		2
17. Focusing X	I		2
18. Feedback X	I	You were very brave, Stephen.	2
C. PROBLEM-SOLVING SKILLS/DEFINING SKILLS			
1. Definition of Goals	I	Our goal is to work on your having more fun and studying harder.	2
2. Exploration/ Understanding of Concerns X	II	What do you need to do to be happy and alive?	
3. Development/Evaluation of Alternatives X	II		2

(*Continued*)

(Continued)

Specific Criteria	Frequency	Comments	Skill Mastery Rating
C. PROBLEM-SOLVING SKILLS/DEFINING SKILLS			
4. Implement Alternative	I	So every time you place an X, you must come up with one idea how to have fun and study harder.	2
5. Special Techniques	III	Let's play ball for a while.	2
6. Process Counseling			
D. ACTION PHASE/CONFRONTING INCONGRUITIES			
1. Immediacy	I	One of the last times I was devastated was when my dad died.	2
2. Self-disclosure			
3. Confrontation			
4. Directives	IIIII	Tell me what things you have tried to make your hurt go away.	2
5. Logical Consequences			
6. Interpretation			
E. CLOSING/GENERALIZATION			
1. Summarization of Content/Feeling X	I	Your hurt was really big. You were able today to make it much smaller by talking about your thoughts and feelings. Would you like to borrow the book to read to Abe?	2
2. Review of Plan X	I	What is one thing that you will work on and one thing that you will play?	2
3. Rescheduling	I	When shall we make the next appointment?	2
4. Termination of Session			
5. Evaluation of Session X	II	What will you take with you from our session today that you can use in the week to come?	2
6. Follow-up X			

Specific Criteria	Frequency	Comments	Skill Mastery Rating
F. PROFESSIONALISM			
1. Developmental Level Match	I		2
2. Ethics			
3. Professional (punctual, attire, etc.)			

G. Strengths:

I liked the way you paced with Stephen. Your play therapy interventions worked well and assisted Stephen in talking.

Area for Improvement:
Next time be sure to explore Stephen's grief and attempts at grieving.

TOTAL: 52

Resource H

Student Practicum/Internship Agreement

Name of Institution Name of Program

Directions

Please complete this form in duplicate, submit one copy to the university supervisor and retain one copy for your own personal student file.

- I have read and understand the (professional organization) ethical standards and will practice counseling in accordance with these standards. Any breach of these ethics or any unethical behaviors on my part will result in my removal from practicum/internship and a failing grade. Documentation of such behavior will become part of my permanent record.

- I agree to adhere to the administrative policies, rules, standards, and practices of the practicum/internship site, including the HIPAA regulations.
- I understand that my responsibilities include keeping my practicum/internship supervisors and my university supervisor informed regarding my field experiences.
- I understand that I will not earn a passing grade in practicum/internship unless I demonstrate the specified minimal level of counseling skill, knowledge, and competence, and complete course requirements as mandated by my course instructor.
- I understand that I must show proof of liability insurance in the amount of at least $1,000,000/$3,000,000 to my university supervisor within 1 week of the semester or session start and before working with any clients. The University reserves the right to determine what insurance carrier the student will use.

Signature: _____ Date: _____

Resource I

Practicum/Internship Contract

_____

Student

This agreement is made on _____ (month/day/year) by and between _____ (Field Site)

and the *Name of Counseling Program and University Name.* The agreement is effective

for a period from _____ (month/day/year) to _____ (month/day/year) for a minimum of 750 clock hours.

Hours worked during University holidays and breaks will be determined by the student and site based on the needs of the school or agency.

The _____ Counseling Program agrees:

1. To assign a University faculty liaison to facilitate communication between the University and the site.
2. To provide an orientation for Site Supervisors and a course syllabus for Practicum/Internship.

3. To notify the students that they must adhere to the administrative policies, rules, standards, schedules, and practices of the site.
4. That the faculty liaison shall be available for consultation with both site supervisors and students.
5. That the University supervisor is responsible for the assignment of a course grade.
6. That the student carries liability insurance in the amount of $1,000,000/$3,000,000 during the entire time this agreement is in effect.
7. That the student will comply with district or organization requirements for a criminal background check.

The Practicum/Internship site agrees:

1. To assign a site supervisor who has the appropriate credentials, time, and interest for training the student and provide a *recent resume* for the site supervisor to the University Program.
2. To provide opportunities for the student to counsel clients who represent the ethnic and demographic diversity of their community (including adequate opportunity to video record counseling sessions) and for evaluating the student's performance.
3. To provide the opportunity for the student to become familiar with a variety of professional activities and resources in addition to direct service (e.g., record keeping, assessment instruments, supervision, information and referral, in-service and staff meetings).
4. To provide the student with adequate workspace, telephone, office supplies, and staff to conduct professional activities.
5. To provide at least one hour of weekly, individual, face-to-face on-site supervision including supervisory contact which involves some examination of student work using audio/video recordings and/or observation.
6. To provide written evaluation of student's work based on criteria established by the University program.
7. To comply with the University's policy that **students may not under any circumstance transport clients** when they are serving in the capacity of an intern at any practicum or internship site or setting.

Site Supervisor Information:

Printed Name	Address (home/work)	Phone	SS# OR Site FEIN TAX ID#

University Supervisor Information:

Printed Name   Phone

The student's Faculty Advisor approves this site and the student has complied with school district and/or agency requirements for a criminal background check.

Faculty Advisor Signature   Date

University Supervisor Signature   Date

Site Supervisor Signature   Date

Resource J

Adult Informed Consent Form

I _____ agree to be counseled by a practicum/intern student in the (*Program*) at (*Institution*).

    I further understand that I may participate in counseling interviews that will be audio and/or video recorded and/or viewed by practicum/intern students through the use of one-way observation windows. I understand that I will be counseled by a graduate student who has completed advanced course work in counseling. I understand that the student will be supervised by a faculty member of the (*Institution*) (*Program*) and an agency site supervisor.

Client's Signature: _____ Date of Birth: _____

Today's Date: _____ Counselor's Signature: _____

Effective Date: _____ Expiration Date: _____

Resource K

Child Informed Consent Form

I agree for my child, _____, to be counseled during the (*date*) school year by _____, Counselor Intern in the (*Program*) at (*Institution*). I understand that my child may participate in counseling interviews that may be audio or video recorded and/or viewed by practicum/internship students through the use of one-way observation windows. I further understand that _____ _____ has completed advanced coursework in counseling/therapy and will counsel my child. I further understand that a (*Institution*) Professor and an on-site (*Institution*) supervisor will oversee the Counselor Intern.

_____ I agree for my child to be counseled by the Counselor Intern for the (*date*) school year and for those sessions to be video or audio recorded.

_____ I agree for my child to be counseled by the Counselor Intern for the (*date*) school year; however, I do not wish for those sessions to be video or audio recorded.

_____ I agree to have counseling information shared with: _____   Person(s)

Parent/Guardian Signature_____

Date_____ _____ Counselor Intern

Signature _____

Date _____ Date Effective _____ Date Contract Expires_____

Resource L

Release of Confidential Information

I, _____ (your name), give

_____(name of counselor) permission to release and share

_____ (specify exactly what information you want released) to _____ (person wanting the file or information). This release is valid from _____ (today's date) through

_____ (the date this release is no longer valid from your desired date).

_____(Signature of Client).

_____(Signature of a Witness).

Resource M

Site Supervisor's Evaluation of Student Counselor's Performance
(Clinical Mental Health Counseling)

INSTRUCTIONS:

1. The Site supervisor should rate the student counselor on a three-point scale as indicated below.
2. The Site supervisor is encouraged to add pertinent comments at the end of each major function.
3. The Site supervisor and the student counselor must discuss the results of this evaluation and any corrective steps that should be taken.
4. Both the University supervisor and the counseling student must sign this evaluation in the designated area.

Site Name: _____

Date Evaluation Discussed: _____

Student Counselor's Name (printed): _____ ID#_____

Student Counselor's Signature: _____

Site Supervisor's Name (printed): _____

Site Supervisor's Signature: _____

University Supervisor's Signature: _____ Date: _____

Signatures indicate that the written evaluation has been seen and discussed.

Please indicate student proficiency by marking the corresponding value for each area identified in the following tables.

1 Exceeds Expectations—demonstrates consistency and independence
2 Meets Expectations—sporadically competent; requires some guidance and assistance
3 Fails to Meet Expectations—unsuccessful, demonstrates little or no competence

Preparation and Openness to Supervision

Preparation and Openness to Supervision	*1-exceeds*	*2-meets*	*3-fails*
1. Arrives prepared for supervision.			
2. Accepts and uses constructive criticism to enhance self-development and counseling skills			
3. Engages in open, comfortable, and clear written and verbal communication with clients, peers, and supervisors.			
4. Appropriately seeks out additional supervision/consultation when needed.			
5. Identifies questions, concerns, and issues relevant to current cases.			

Comments: _____

Knowledge, Skills, and Practices

Foundations

CACREP Standard	Description	1-exceeds	2-meets	3-fails
B.1.	Demonstrates the ability to apply and adhere to ethical and legal standards in clinical mental health counseling			
B.2.	Applies knowledge of public mental health policy, financing, and regulatory processes to improve service delivery opportunities in clinical mental health counseling.			

Comments _____

Counseling, Prevention, and Intervention

CACREP Standard	Description	1-exceeds	2-meets	3-fails
D.1.	Uses the principles and practices of diagnosis, treatment, referral, and prevention of mental and emotional disorders to initiate, maintain, and terminate counseling.			
D.2.	Applies multicultural competencies to clinical mental health counseling involving case conceptualization, diagnosis, treatment, referral, and prevention of mental and emotional disorders.			
D.3.	Promotes optimal human development, wellness, and mental health through prevention, education, and advocacy activities.			
D.4.	Applies effective strategies to promote client understanding of and access to a variety of community resources.			
D.5.	Demonstrates appropriate use of culturally responsive individual, couple, family, group, and system's modalities for initiating, maintaining, and terminating counseling.			
D.6.	Demonstrates the ability to use procedures for assessing and managing suicide risk.			
D.7.	Applies current record-keeping standards related to clinical mental health counseling.			
D.8.	Provides appropriate counseling strategies when working with clients with addiction and co-occurring disorders.			
D.9.	Demonstrates the ability to recognize his or her own limitations as a clinical mental health counselor and to seek supervision or refer clients when appropriate.			

Comments: _____

Diversity and Advocacy

CACREP Standard	Description	1-exceeds	2-meets	3-fails
F.1.	Maintains information regarding community resources to make appropriate referrals.			
F.2.	Advocates for policies, programs, and services that are equitable and responsive to the unique needs of clients.			
F.3.	Demonstrates the ability to modify counseling systems, theories, techniques, and interventions to make them culturally appropriate for diverse populations.			

Comments: _____

ASSESSMENT

CACREP Standard	Description	1-exceeds	2-meets	3-fails
H.1.	Selects appropriate comprehensive assessment interventions to assist in diagnosis and treatment with an awareness of cultural bias in the implementation and interpretation of assessment protocols.			
H.2.	Demonstrates skill in conducting an intake interview, a mental status evaluation, a biopsychosocial history, a mental health history, and psychological assessment for treatment planning and caseload management.			
H.3.	Screens for addiction, aggression, and danger to self and/or others, as well as co-occurring mental disorders.			
H.4.	Applies the assessment of a client's stage of dependence, change, or recovery to determine the appropriate treatment modality and placement criteria within the continuum of care.			

Comments:_____

RESEARCH AND EVALUATION

CACREP Standard	Description	1-exceeds	2-meets	3-fails
J.1.	Applies relevant research findings to inform the practice of clinical mental health counseling.			
J.2.	Develops measurable outcomes for clinical mental health counseling programs, interventions, and treatments.			
J.3	Analyzes and uses data to increase the effectiveness of clinical mental health counseling interventions and programs.			

Comments:_____

DIAGNOSIS

CACREP Standard	Description	1-exceeds 2-meets 3-fails
L.1	Demonstrates appropriate use of diagnostic tools, including the current edition of the DSM, to describe the symptoms and clinical presentation of clients with mental and emotional impairments.	
L.2	Is able to conceptualize an accurate multi-axial diagnosis of disorders presented by a client and discuss the differential diagnosis and collaborating professionals.	
L.3	Differentiates between diagnosis and developmentally appropriate reactions during crises, disasters, and other trauma-causing events.	

Comments:_____

OVERALL COMMENTS
Evaluator's Summary Comments: _____

_____

_____

Student's Reactions to Evaluation: _____

_____

_____

References

Dimick, K.M., & Krause, F.H. (1980). *Practicum Manual for Counseling and Psychotherapy* (4th edn). Muncie, IN: Accelerated Development Inc.

Friedlander, M.L., & Ward, L.G. (1984). Development and validation of the Supervisory Styles Inventory. *Journal of Counseling Psychology,* 31, 541–557.

Hackney, H. & Nye, S. (1973). *Counseling Strategies and Objectives.* Upper Saddle River, NJ: Prentice Hall.

Hersey, P., Blanchard, K., & Johnson, D. (2000). *Management of Organizational Behavior: Leading Human Resources* (8th edn). Upper Saddle River, NJ: Prentice Hall.

Ladany, N., Marotta, S., & Muse-Burke, J. (2001). Counselor experience related to complexity of case conceptualization and supervision preference. *Counselor Education and Supervision,* 40, 203–219.

Marieb, E.N. (2012). *Essentials of Human Anatomy and Physiology* (10th edn). San Francisco, CA: Pearson.

Parker, S. (2014). The power of sleep. September 22. *Time.*

Russell-Chapin, L. A. (2016, in press). The power of neurocounseling and self-regulation. In J. Edwards, S. Young, & H. Nikels (eds.), *Handbook of Strengths-based Clinical Practices: Finding Common Factors.* New York, NY: Routledge.

Russell-Chapin, L. & Chapin, T. (2012). *Clinical Supervision.* Belmont, CA: Cengage.

Russo, J. R. (1993). *Serving and Surviving as a Human Service Worker* (2nd edn). Prospect Heights, IL: Waveland Press.

Saxon, S. V., Etten, M. J., & Perkins, E. A. (2015). *Physical Change & Aging: A Guide for the Helping Professions.* New York, NY: Springer Publishing Company.

Srinivasan, V., Spence, D. W., Pandi-Perumal, S. R., Brown, G. M., & Cardinalis, D. P. (2011). Melatonin in mitochondrial dysfunction and related disorders. *International Journal of Alzheimer's Disease,* 3263201.

Stoltenberg, C. D., McNeill, B., & Delworth, U. (1998). *IDM Supervision: An Integrated Developmental Model for Supervising Counselors and Therapists.* San Francisco: Jossey-Bass.

Sweitzer, H. F., & King, M. (1999). *The Successful Internship: Transformation and Empowerment.* Pacific Grove, CA: Brooks/Cole.

4

CONTINUING SELF-IMPROVEMENT

Major Supervision Model Categories

Supervision is a privilege and a must, especially when it is created with a trusted mentor.

Overview

Four conceptual models of supervision will be presented as well as one supervision approach. In each model, the general skill of feedback is central, but the feedback process comes from an assumption underlying the basic tenets of the supervision models. Additionally there are several features that are central to all supervision models and approaches. The common supervision factors are: necessary relationships between a supervisee and supervisor; supervisee goals designed for attitude, skill, and knowledge acquisition and competency; and relevant supervision domains such as clinical skills, theories, client dynamics, professional and ethical behaviors, supervisee personal growth, supervisee autonomy, and supervisee monitoring and evaluation (Morgan & Sprenkle, 2007).

Another common aspect of supervision is a structured and perhaps even a foundational and linear template for conducting supervision:

1. Clarify supervision expectations and build supervisory relationships.
2. Explore multicultural backgrounds: similarities and differences.
3. Listen to the supervisee's Supervision Question for each session.
4. Select an appropriate supervision approach and/or model.
5. Discuss diagnosis/conceptualization.
6. Analyze supervision outcomes for each session.

(Russell-Chapin & Chapin, 2012, p. 4)

Experiment with the order of these components and see whether they, too, are a good fit for you. As you continue through your supervision journey during your practicum and internship and hopefully through supervision throughout the life of your counseling career, you will remember the common factors associated with supervision and continue to search for the best supervision fit as you continue to grow and change (Russell-Chapin & Chapin, 2012).

This chapter begins by presenting another self-regulation skill of brain/gut connection and nutrition and stressing the importance of relationship qualities between you, the student supervisee, and your supervisor. Throughout the chapter, you will have reflective opportunities to discover the supervision model that might best match your supervision needs, along with a supervisory method of viewing videotapes. Finally you will assess your supervision needs with a supervisee questionnaire.

Goals

1. Discover how the brain/gut connection impacts you, your counseling, and your supervision.
2. Understand the role that nutrition plays in our lives.
3. Understand the four different models and one approach to supervision.
4. Examine how the Microcounseling Supervision Model relates to the different categories of supervision models.

5. Recognize how the Interpersonal Process Recall (IPR) method can be utilized with most supervision models.
6. Apply the differing supervision models to the Case of Rachel.
7. Identify the supervision model(s) that best fit you and your counseling style and needs.

Key Concepts: Finding the Supervision Match for You

As mentioned in Chapter 2, the Microcounseling Supervision Model (MSM) was introduced to you first as your foundation for learning the needed basic interviewing skills. There are many other supervision models that have emerged throughout the history of the helping professions. We offer additional models to help you as a student have a general understanding of the major categories of supervision: (1) developmental models, (2) theoretical orientation-specific models, (3) social role models, (4) integrated models, and (5) interpersonal process recall.

> **Supervision:** A distinctive manner of approach and response to a supervisee's questions and needs.

Much like studying your counseling theories, these supervision models have many similarities and differences. You will begin to notice that most supervision models emphasize the importance of a healthy supervisee and supervisor relationship, stress the importance of feedback and communication, and have a variety of supervisor tasks and functions. Experienced supervision experts suggest that it is the supervision tasks and roles plus their functions of those tasks that equal the supervision process (Holloway & Carrol, 1999; Kadushin, 1992).

> **Function:** Major responsibilities in supervision of administration, education, and support.

In other words, if you combine the roles and responsibilities of the supervisor with your needs, the counselor in training, then you have a supervision process. After those similarities, each model focuses on its essential and unique

supervision tenets. As you read the following models, try to determine which
model offers you what you need during your field experience. You might find
that your attraction to different models depends on your differing supervision concerns with a variety of clients. The personal changes you experience
as you learn and grow throughout your practicum and internship will also
make a difference in your supervision needs! You may find that each model has
something to offer you! (For additional information about these models see
Russell-Chapin & Chapin, 2012.)

> **Role:** The supervisor role such as teacher, consultant, evaluator and so on
> depends on the needs of the supervisee/student.

Before we go into depth with each supervision model, let's add the next
essential self-regulation skills of the gut/brain axis and the role that nutrition
plays in healthy and engaged living. Most of us were raised understanding the
importance of proper nutrition towards overall health. That may have not mat-
tered much, but now new research is convincing us with science and changing
how we eat and what we need to eat. The latest research is on our gut, its influence on brain dysregulation, and the gut/brain communication connection.
There is evidence that each person's microbiome, an ecosystem of microbes
in the body, impacts many brain disorders (Russell-Chapin, 2016, in press).
Research into the gut-microbiome-brain connection is rapidly gaining approval
among mainstream neurocounselors and neurobiologists and has implications
for the treatment for anxiety and depression (Rook, Raison, & Lowry, 2012).
    According to Mayer (2011), the idea that the gut and the brain are intimately
connected, and that this interaction plays an important part not only in gastrointestinal function but also in certain feeling states and in intuitive decision making, is an integral part of our language, from the phrase "I have a gut
feeling" to "I made an intuitive decision." Research into this neurobiological
gut-brain crosstalk demonstrates a complicated, bidirectional communication
system. Mayer stated, "proper maintenance of gastrointestinal homeostasis and
digestion is likely to have multiple effects on affect, motivation and higher cognitive functions, including intuitive decision making. Moreover, disturbances
of this system have been implicated in a wide range of disorders, including
functional and inflammatory gastrointestinal disorders, obesity and eating disorders" (Mayer, 2011, p. 453).
    This gut-brain-microbe axis has also been labeled the sixth sense or even the
second brain. This connection is focusing on neuroinflammation, illustrating

that affect and physical stress can cause harmful inflammation throughout the body. Most people associate the neurotransmitter serotonin with the brain, but research has found that 95% of serotonin is produced in the gut. According to Ivey and Ivey (2015), "Our total body reacts to external stressors and, at the same time, internal cognitions and 'gut feelings' produce our own internal stress" (Ivey & Ivey, 2015, p. 14).

Here are a few more fascinating facts that we know about the gut/brain connection. Seventy to eighty percent of the body's immune cells are housed in the gut-associated lymphoid tissues. Unconscious interoceptive stimuli from the gut caused by intestinal microbes may affect memory formation, emotional arousal, and affective behaviors (Mayer, 2011).

According to Ivey and Ivey (2015), almost every chemical that controls the brain is also located in the stomach region, including hormones and neurotransmitters such as serotonin, dopamine, glutamate, GABA (gamma-aminobutyric acid), and norepinephrine.

With each passing piece of new research, we know that the typical American diet plays havoc with brain regulation. Many of our diets consist of simple carbohydrates, processed foods such as white bread, potatoes, pasta, and rice. Amen, a brain researcher and clinician, writes that this type of diet often makes a person feel tired, inattentive, and sluggish because blood sugars are lower than needed (Amen, 2001; Chapin & Russell-Chapin, 2014). Chronic changes of homeostasis cause the gut-to-brain signaling to seek and often increase fat-rich diets. High fat diets tend to lead to gut inflammation (Mayer, 2011).

According to Amen (2001) the healthiest diet needs to consist of eight ounces of water for cell functioning and blood flow; protein at every meal for immune functioning; complex carbohydrates such as vegetables and fruits for fiber; and some saturated and monounsaturated fats for brain and neuron health (Chapin & Russell-Chapin, 2014). Ratey and Manning (2014) theorize that our bodies have not evolved at the same pace as our industrialized sciences. Therefore more diseases and allergies occur because the body cannot metabolize these processed foods as well as natural foods. Because of these and other factors, many of our clients are encouraged to work with their physician and a nutritionist and/or dietician to learn more about healthier eating that feeds the body, mind, and soul (Russell-Chapin, 2016, in press).

Practical Reflection 1: Self-regulating What You Eat and Why

For five days in a row, write down everything you eat and drink. Also jot down how you feel physically and emotionally. Begin to observe the impact of healthy foods in daily living. What causations and correlations can you draw from your nutrition and your gut? How might this connection impact your counseling and supervision?

_____

_____

_____

_____

Developmental Models of Supervision

The basic tenets formulating developmental models of supervision are that, as a student, you continue to grow at your own pace with differing needs and differing styles of learning. If this is true, then the major objective during developmental supervision is to discover your personal needs and focus on whatever it takes to maximize your strengths and minimize your liabilities.

Developmental stages: Supervisees progress through a series of predictable levels or stages as they learn the skills of the counseling process.

To manage this developmental nature of learning, the manner in which you and your supervisor interact must also change. As you mature and grow, your needs and wants from your supervisors will also change. In individual counseling, we assess the developmental level of the client and choose a corresponding intervention. A parallel process occurs within developmental supervision.

For example, Stoltenberg (1981) and Stoltenberg and Delworth (1987) formulated a developmental supervision model describing distinct levels of supervisees: beginning, intermediate, advanced, and master counselor. During each level or stage, the job of the supervisor is to structure your supervision, moving from imitative and demonstrative functions at the beginning level to more competent and self-reliant functions at the advanced levels (McNeill, Stoltenberg, & Romans, 1992).

In this model, a strong emphasis is on better understanding you and others around you, your motivational levels, and your ability to become autonomous. Each level includes those three processes (awareness, motivation, and autonomy), and within each level are nine growth areas for you to focus on. See Table 4.1 to better understand each level.

Table 4.1

	Supervisee	Supervisor
Beginning—Level 1	Little experience; dependent on the supervisor	Models needed skills and behaviors; teacher role
Intermediate—Level 2	Less imitative; strives for independence	Provides some structure but encourages exploration
Advanced—Level 3	More insightful and motivated; more autonomous	Listens and offers suggestions, sharing when asked
Master Counselor—Level 4	Skilled interpersonally and cognitively	Provides collegial and professionally consultative functions

The nine growth areas are intervention, skill competence, assessment techniques, interpersonal assessment, client conceptualization, individual differences, theoretical orientation, treatment goals and plans, and professional ethics (Stoltenberg, McNeill, & Delworth, 1998). In developmental supervision, your job and your supervisor's job will be to help you to discover your strengths and locate your areas for improvement. Once you realize this strategy can be a life-long learning pattern, then you, as a helping professional, can be responsible for your own growth throughout your career.

Personal style: Awareness of the natural preference and match assisting each counselor in discovering an approach to counseling and supervision.

Practical Reflection 2: Developmental Model Growth Areas

As you read about Stoltenberg and Delworth's Developmental Model, identify at which level and growth area you currently reside. In which areas might you need and want to grow and learn more?

_____

_____

_____

_____

Theory-specific Supervision Models

Helping professionals who adhere to a specific school of thought and therapy (cognitive-behavioral, psychodynamic, Rogerian, and so on) may believe that naturally it is wise to supervise from that same theoretical orientation.

The major advantage to you is that if you and your supervisor share the same theoretical orientation, it maximizes the modeling that can occur in supervision (Bernard & Goodyear, 1998). Your supervisor could demonstrate discipline-specific skills as well as integrate necessary theoretical constructs.

For example, if your supervisor follows a Rational Emotive Behavioral Therapy (REBT) theoretical orientation, then two main skills would be required during supervision. First you would need to identify the problem and irrational thinking of both you and your client. Then you and your supervisor would select ways to dispute and challenge those same irrational thoughts as a method for changing and learning new, productive thoughts and behaviors (Ellis, 1989; Woods & Ellis, 1996). Behavioral and cognitive-behavioral supervisors will emphasize and expect you to demonstrate more technical mastery than most supervisors (Bernard & Goodyear, 1998). If your supervisor uses a person-centered approach, then the focus may be one of self-discovery and awareness (Rogers, 1961).

Practical Reflection 3: Theoretical Orientation

Think of a supervision moment when your supervisor was demonstrating a specific theoretical orientation skill. For you, what would be the advantages of focusing on one theoretical orientation?

_____

_____

_____

_____

Social Role Models of Supervision

The Discrimination Model of Supervision is an example of a social role supervision model. It has been widely researched and its supporters believe it is an inclusive approach to supervision; its roots are in technical eclecticism (Bernard & Goodyear, 1998). One of the main goals of the Discrimination Model of Supervision is to focus on your needs as a supervisee by being able to respond flexibly with any needed strategy, technique, and/or guidance.

This model is situation-specific, and your supervisor would emphasize two primary functions during each of your sessions: the supervisor's role and focus. There are three roles that your supervisor would take, based on your supervision needs: teacher, counselor, and consultant. You might require your supervisor

Table 4.2

Role	Focus Definition
Process	Examines how you communicate with your client
Conceptualization	Explores your intentions behind the chosen skill interventions
Personalization	Identifies mannerisms used to interact with clients, such as body language and voice intonation

to put on the teacher's hat and role and directly instruct and demonstrate constructs and skills. You might need your supervisor to be in the counselor's role to assist you in locating your "blind spots" or becoming aware of, perhaps, some personal countertransference issues. Finally, there may be times during supervision when you just need your supervisor to bounce back and forth intervention ideas surrounding your client. Your supervisor becomes your colleague and consultant. Each of these roles emphasizes three areas of focus for skill-building purposes: process, conceptualization, and personalization. Study and review Table 4.2 for the definition of each focus area.

Practical Reflection 4: Role and Focus Needs

What role and specific focus would you like your supervisor to display with each of your clients? Select a current case study and request what you need.

_____

_____

_____

_____

Integrated Models of Supervision

Often when helping professionals are asked about their theoretical orientation, many clinicians will state they are eclectic in their views. That does not mean those clinicians don't believe in anything, but instead adhere to theoretical tenets from several theories. To assist helping professionals who favor eclecticism, integrated models of supervision were designed for those who work from multiple theoretical orientations. We have already presented our Microcounseling

Supervision Model (MSM), which falls into the category of integrated supervision. It is our belief that MSM successfully combines and uses many of the skills from a variety of theories and supervision models.

> **Focus:** Specific growth areas for the student in training to concentrate on, from skill competence to personal awareness to interventions.

A Supervision Digital Recording Method:
Interpersonal Process Recall

We have presented four main supervisory models. Many models require that you record digitally your counseling interviews or conduct your sessions in an actual live observation setting. One of the most widely used methods that your instructor may use in class is Kagan's Interpersonal Process Recall (IPR) (Haynes, Corey, & Moulton, 2003). Borders and Leddick (1988) conducted a national survey of counselor educators and found IPR to be one of two distinct methods used during supervision courses.

The main essence of IPR is to create a supervision environment where supervisees can safely analyze their communication styles and strategies.

Kagan believes that most people act diplomatically and often do not say what they actually mean or feel. In supervision, then, your supervisor will encourage you to reflect and interpret your experience in the counseling session (Kagan, 1980). The best way to do that is to view a video of a counseling session and simply stop the recording at any time to discuss essential personal and/or counseling issues.

It was the work of Norm Kagan and Allen Ivey that inspired the development of the Microcounseling Supervision Model that you practiced in Chapter 2. Using the Counselor Interview Rating Form (CIRF) while videotaping is an extension of Kagan's work. Study the following list to see the questions that could be asked while using the Interpersonal Process Recall method (Bernard & Goodyear, 1998, p. 102).

- What were your thoughts, feelings, and reactions? Did you want to express them at any time?
- What would you like to have said at this point?
- What was it like for you in your role as counselor?
- What thoughts were you having about the other person at that time?
- Had you any ideas about what you wanted to do with that?

- Were there any pictures, images, or memories flashing through your mind then?
- How do you imagine the client was reacting to you?
- How do you think the client was seeing you at this point?
- Did you sense that the client had any expectations of you at that point?
- What did you want to hear from the client?
- What message did you want to give the client? What prevented you from doing so?

Practical Reflection 5: Needed IPR Questions

If you could use the IPR supervision method of viewing digitally recorded sessions, which of the above questions would assist you the most during your supervision?

_____

_____

_____

_____

Supervision and the Case of Rachel

You have been studying the Case of Rachel throughout the first section of this book, integrating unique features of Rachel's case study. As we described different models of supervision, it may be helpful to imagine working with Rachel using the supervision models offered. You read how we supervised Rachel using the initial Microcounseling Supervision Model. The main emphasis was on identifying and classifying essential interviewing counseling skills. Microcounseling Supervision fits into the category of Integrated Supervision, as any theoretical orientation could use this approach to supervision. Resource N, Microcounseling Skills Used in Different Theoretical Approaches (Ivey et al., 2014), provides a list of the theories using Microcounseling Supervision. As we offer examples using the four supervisory models and one supervision approach described in this chapter, begin to formulate the supervision approach that best fits with you and your present needs.

Developmental Supervision and the Case of Rachel

You may need to review Rachel's case from previous chapters. She is an older woman whose husband recently died. Rachel's children were trying to help her cope but were interfering with her independence. In Chapter 2, the importance of case presentations is discussed. The actual narrative case presentation for the Case of Rachel is presented in Chapter 5. In that narrative report, Lori had several supervision questions requesting assistance on issues of effectiveness with self-disclosure, diagnosis, Rachel's resistance, personal issues of death, focus of resources, and general strengths and liabilities.

If Dr. Ivey were supervising Lori, and he selected Stoltenberg's (1981) and Stoltenberg and Delworth's model of Developmental Supervision (1987), he would first assess Lori's level of functioning from Level 1 through 4. Dr. Ivey would need to look at Lori's awareness of self and others; her motivation toward the developmental process; and her independent thinking. From her supervision questions and general skills, Dr. Ivey may see Lori's functioning between Level 2 and 3 because she seems aware of her impact on Rachel. The focus of supervision may need to highlight client conceptualization and treatment goals and plans. Dr. Ivey would gently encourage Lori to gain confidence in her own skill development.

Theoretically Oriented Supervision and the Case of Rachel

If Dr. Ivey decided to supervise Lori using a psychotherapy theory-based supervision model, he would choose one theory adhering to its tenets throughout the supervisory process. Using cognitive-behavioral supervision, Dr. Ivey would focus on skills and strategies that Lori may want to use with Rachel. He may also challenge any irrational thoughts Lori may have about personal death issues and need for approval.

In Psychodynamic Supervision, additional emphasis may be on parallel process (Doehrman, 1976). *Parallel process* is the dynamic that occurs in the client/therapist relationship that is played out in the supervisee/supervisor relationship. Dr. Ivey may focus on the resistance that Rachel had during the session and investigate what resistance Lori may have toward him.

Using supervision from Person-Centered Theory, Dr. Ivey would ensure that the basic facilitative conditions were in process throughout the supervision session. Dr. Ivey would emphasize unconditional positive regard, building trust, and creating a genuine environment for Lori to express self-doubts and fears about confidence in her counseling skills (Hackney & Goodyear, 1984).

You have now had the opportunity to read about several different supervision models. Take the time to discover more about you as a supervisee by taking the Supervisee Perception of Supervision questionnaire (Olk & Friedlander, 1992). Answer the statements honestly as you take the inventory (located in Resource O at the back of this chapter). Let your scores from the questionnaire assist you in further defining what you need from supervision.

Social Role Supervision and the Case of Rachel

If Dr. Ivey were supervising Lori using the Discrimination Model of Supervision, what would he need to consider? First, he would have to decide which foci to select and which role to use to accomplish the needed supervision goal. Since this is the first session with Rachel and one of Lori's first clients, Dr. Ivey may choose to focus on Lori's basic intervention skills by being in the role of teacher and counselor. He may actually teach new skills and work on Lori's effect on the client.

The elegance of Discrimination Supervision is that as Dr. Ivey continues to supervise Lori, his foci and roles change across and within sessions (Bernard & Goodyear, 1998). The cardinal rule of any integrative supervision is to customize supervision to meet the needs of the individual supervisee.

In other words, "the 'how' of supervision should parallel the 'what' of supervision" (Norcross & Halgin, 1997, p. 210).

Integrated Supervision and the Case of Rachel

You have already read Dr. Ivey's supervisory responses to Lori using the integrated Microcounseling Supervision Model. Refer back to Chapter 2, if you need to review MSM.

Interpersonal Process Recall and the Case of Rachel

Based upon Lori's Supervision Question, Dr. Ivey may have chosen to use IPR as the needed supervision approach. One of Lori's supervision needs focused on appropriate self-disclosure. One of the many IPR questions is "What message did you want to give the client? What prevented you from doing so?"

By providing a safe environment to explore those two questions, Lori may gain essential information to better understand when her self-disclosure is relevant and effective.

Practical Reflection 6: Your Favorite Supervision Model

Review the models presented. Which one(s) best matches your counseling and supervision style and needs today? What is your best "fit" model for today?

_____

_____

_____

_____

We have discussed the differing models of supervision. Now take the Supervisee Perception of Supervision and learn even more about you and the supervisory process.

Practical Reflection 7: You and Your Supervision Perceptions

Discuss what you learned from taking the Supervisee Perception of Supervision instrument. Which roles are in conflict and which seem unclear? Share your concerns with your colleagues and supervisor.

_____

_____

_____

_____

_____

Summary and Personal Integration

This chapter offered additional models of supervision for you to include in your supervisory knowledge base. Four categories of supervision models were presented: Developmental; Theoretically Oriented; Integrated; Social Role. Examples were offered for each category and your task was to determine which, if any, model was the best fit for your counseling style and supervision needs. A Supervisee Perception of Supervision was offered to assist you in determining your supervisory needs and expectations.

Practical Reflection 8: Integration

As your supervision knowledge base increases, which Chapter 4 constructs will assist you the most in becoming a skilled helping professional? Explain.

_____

_____

_____

_____

_____

Resource N

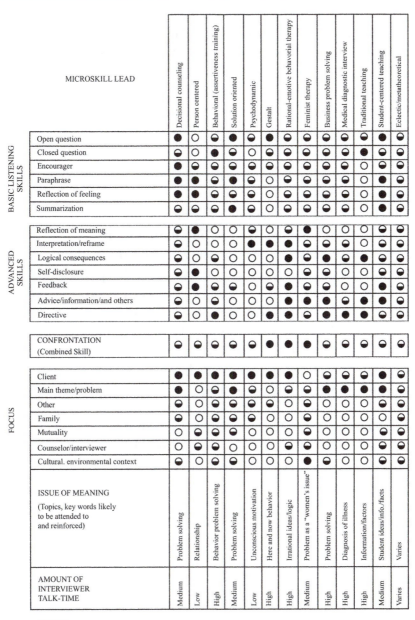

LEGEND
- ● Frequent use of skill
- ⊖ Common use of skill
- ○ Occasional use of skill

Figure 4.1 Resource N shows frequency use of microcounseling skills with other counseling theories. © 2015 Allen E. Ivey.

Resource O

Supervisee Perception of Supervision*

The following statements describe some problems that therapists in training may experience during the course of clinical supervision. Please read each statement and then rate the extent to which you have experienced difficulty in supervision in your most recent clinical training, from 1 (not at all) to 5 (very much so).

I have experienced difficulty in my current or most recent supervision because:

1. I was not certain about what material to present
   to my supervisor.   1 2 ③ 4 5
2. I have felt that my supervisor was incompetent or
   less competent than I.
   I often felt as though I was supervising him or her.   ① 2 3 4 5
3. I have wanted to challenge the appropriateness of my
   supervisor's recommendations for using a technique with
   one of my clients, but I have thought it better to keep my
   opinions to myself.   1 ② 3 4 5
4. I wasn't sure how best to use supervision as I became more
   experienced, although I was aware that I was undecided
   about whether to confront my supervisor.   1 ② 3 4 5
5. I have believed that my supervisor's behavior in one or
   more situations was unethical or illegal and I was
   undecided about whether to confront him or her.   ① 2 3 4 5
6. My orientation to therapy was different from that of my
   supervisor. She or he wanted me to work with clients using
   her or his framework, and I felt that I should be allowed to
   use my own approach.   ① 2 3 4 5
7. I have wanted to intervene with one of my clients in a
   particular way and my supervisor has wanted me to
   approach the client in a very different way. I am expected
   both to judge what is appropriate for myself and also to
   do what I am told.   ① 2 3 4 5
8. My supervisor expected me to come prepared for
   supervision, but I had no idea what or how to prepare.   ① 2 3 4 5
9. I wasn't sure how autonomous I should be in my
   work with clients.   1 2 ③ 4 5
10. My supervisor told me to do something I perceived to be
    illegal or unethical and I was expected to comply.   ① 2 3 4 5
11. My supervisor's criteria for evaluating my work
    were not specific.   ① 2 3 4 5

12. I was not sure that I had done what the supervisor expected me to do in a session with a client. ①2 3 4 5

13. The criteria for evaluating my performance in supervision were not clear. ①2 3 4 5

14. I got mixed signals from my supervisor and I was unsure of which signals to attend to. ①2 3 4 5

15. When using a new technique, I was unclear about the specific steps involved. As a result I wasn't sure how my supervisor would evaluate my work. ①2 3 4 5

16. I disagreed with my supervisor about how to introduce a specific issue to a client, but I also wanted to do what the supervisor recommended. ①2 3 4 5

17. Part of me wanted to rely on my own instincts with clients, but I always knew that my supervisor would have the last word. ①2 3 4 5

18. The feedback I got from my supervisor did not help me to know what was expected of me in my day-to-day work with clients. ①2 3 4 5

19. I was not comfortable using a technique recommended by my supervisor; however, I felt that I should do what my supervisor recommended. ①2 3 4 5

20. Everything was new and I wasn't sure what would be expected of me. 1 2 ③4 5

21. I was not sure if I should discuss my professional weaknesses in supervision because I was not sure how I would be evaluated. 1 ②3 4 5

22. I disagreed with my supervisor about implementing a specific technique, but I also wanted to do what the supervisor thought best. ①2 3 4 5

23. My supervisor gave me no feedback and I felt lost. 1 ②3 4 5

24. My supervisor told me what to do with a client, but didn't give me very specific ideas about how to do it. ①2 3 4 5

25. My supervisor wanted me to pursue an assessment technique that I considered inappropriate for a particular client. ①2 3 4 5

26. There were no clear guidelines for my behavior in supervision. ①2 3 4 5

27. The supervisor gave no constructive or negative feedback and as a result I did not know how to address my weaknesses. 1 2 3④5

28. I didn't know how I was doing as a therapist and as a result I didn't know how my supervisor would evaluate me. ①2 3 4 5

29. I was unsure of what to expect from my supervisor. ①2 3 4 5

SCORING KEY

Role ambiguity items: 1, 4, 8, 9, 11, 12, 13, 18, 20, 21, 23, 24, 26, 27, 28, 29
Role conflict items: 2, 3, 5, 6, 7, 10, 14, 15, 16, 17, 19, 22, 25

MEANING

Look at the responses for each statement. High scores of 4s and 5s validate your feelings and beliefs concerning role ambiguity and role conflict. These concerns need to be shared in supervision.

*Olk, M. & Friedlander, M.L. (1992). Trainee's experiences of role conflict and role ambiguity in supervisory relationships. *Journal of Psychology*, 39, 389–397. Copyright © 1992 by the American Psychological Association. (Reprinted with permission.)

References

Amen, D.G. (2001). *Healing of ADD*. New York: Putnam.

Bernard, J.M. & Goodyear, R.K. (1998). *Fundamentals of Clinical Supervision*. Needham Heights, MA: Allyn and Bacon.

Borders, L.D. & Leddick, G.R. (1988). A nationwide survey of supervisory training. *Counseling Education and Supervision*, 27(3), 271–283.

Chapin, T. & Russell-Chapin, L. (2014). *Neurotherapy and Neurofeedback: Brain-based Treatments for Psychological and Behavioral Problems*. New York, NY: Routledge.

Doehrman, M. (1976). Parallel processes in supervision and psychotherapy. *Bulletin of the Menninger Clinic*, 40, 3–104.

Ellis, A. (1989). Thoughts on supervising counselors and therapists. *Psychology: A Journal of Human Behavior*, 26, 3–5.

Hackney, H.L. & Goodyear, R.K. (1984). Carl Rogers' client-centered supervision. In R.F. Levant & J.M. Schlep (eds.). *Client-centered Therapy and the Person-centered Approach*. New York: Praeger.

Haynes, R., Corey, G., & Moulton, P. (2003). *Clinical Supervision in the Helping Professions: A Practical Guide*. Pacific Grove, CA: Brooks/Cole.

Holloway, E. & Carrol, M. (eds.). (1999). *Training Counselling Supervisors: Strategies, Methods and Techniques*. London: Sage.

Ivey, A.E. & Ivey, M.B. (2015). Allostasis, stress and the microbiota-gut-brain axis. *Counseling Today*. American Counseling Association, 57(12): 14–20.

Ivey, A.E., Ivey, M.B., & Zalaquett, C. (2014). *Intentional Interviewing and Counseling: Facilitating Client Development in a Multicultural Society* (8th edn). Pacific Grove, CA: Brooks/Cole.

Kadushin, A. (1992). *Supervision in Social Work* (3rd edn). New York: Columbia University Press.

Kagan, N. (1980). Influencing human interaction—eighteen years with IPR. In A.K. Hess (ed.). *Psychotherapy Supervision: Theory, Research and Practice* (pp. 262–286). New York: Wiley.

McNeil, B.W., Stoltenberg, C.D., & Romans, J.S. (1992). The integrated developmental model of supervision: Scale development and validation procedures. *Professional Psychology: Research & Practice*, 23, 504–508.

Mayer, E.A. (2011). Gut feelings: The emerging biology of gut-brain communication. *Nature Reviews Neuroscience*, 12, 453–466.

Morgan, M.M. & Sprenkle, D.H. (2007). Toward a common-factor approach to supervision, *Journal of Marital and Family Therapy*, 33(1), 1–17.

Norcross, J.C. & Halgin, R.P. (1997). Integrative approaches to psychotherapy supervision. In J.C.E. Watkins (ed.). *Handbook of Psychotherapy Supervision* (pp. 203–222). New York: Wiley.

Olk, M. & Friedlander, M.L. (1992). Trainee's experiences of role conflict and role ambiguity in supervisory relationships. *Journal of Counseling Psychology, 39*, 389–397.

Ratey, J.J. & Manning, R. (2014). *Go Wild: Free your Body and Mind from the Afflictions of Civilization.* New York: Little Brown.

Rogers, C.R. (1961). *On Becoming a Person.* Boston: Houghton Mifflin.

Rook, G., Raison, C., & Lowry, C. (2012). Can we vaccinate against depression? *Drug Discovery Today, 17*(9–10), 451–458.

Russell-Chapin, L.A. (2016, In press). The power of neurocounseling and self-regulation. In J. Edwards, S. Young, & H. Nikels (eds.). *Handbook of Strengths-based Clinical Practices: Finding Common Factors.* New York: Routledge.

Russell-Chapin, L.A. & Chapin, T. (2012). *Clinical supervision: Theory and Practice.* Belmont, CA: Brooks/Cole.

Stoltenberg, C.D. (1981). Approaching supervision from a developmental perspective: The counselor-complexity model. *Journal of Counseling Psychology, 28*, 59–65.

Stoltenberg, C.D. & Delworth, U. (1987). *Supervising Counselors and Therapists.* San Francisco: Jossey-Bass.

Stoltenberg, C.D., McNeill, B.W., & Delworth, U. (1998). *IDM Supervision: An Integrated Developmental Model for Supervising Counselors and Therapists.* San Francisco: Jossey-Bass.

Woods, P.J. & Ellis, A. (1996). Supervision in rational emotive behavior therapy. *Journal of Rational-Emotive & Cognitive Behavior Therapy, 14*, 135–152.

5

CONCEPTUALIZING THE CLIENT

DIAGNOSIS AND RELATED ISSUES

Overview

The purpose of this chapter is to introduce you to the world of case conceptualization and how it relates to formal client diagnostic systems such as the American Psychiatric Association's *Diagnostic and Statistical Manual of Mental Disorders*, 5th edition (DSM-5) (APA, 2013b).

Information about the fifth self-regulation skill, exercise, will be added to assist you in continuing your personal wellness journey. This is a time when you graduate students become even more focused on clients, comprehensive examinations, and readings. Often your health goes by the wayside. Let's see if we can avoid a major physical crisis by including and practicing the five self-regulation skills presented thus far.

There are many variables involved in the conceptualization and understanding of your client's world. In this chapter, you will be introduced to three case conceptualization strategies: Stages of the Counseling Interview, DSM-5, and Developmental Assessment. These strategies can be used independently and stand alone as methods of conceptualizing your cases.

However, these approaches also work well together to provide you with an in-depth and comprehensive view of your client's world. You will utilize the stages of the counseling interview to provide structure to your conceptualization, dissect the DSM-5 used for diagnosing mental disorders, and view diagnosis from a developmental perspective. At the end of this chapter, you will delve into conceptualization using the Case of Rachel.

Goals

1. Integrate 20 minutes of exercise into every day for graduate school survival.
2. Identify some key issues involved in client case conceptualization.
3. Work with three case conceptualization strategies.
4. Understand how the stages of the counseling interview provide a framework for conceptualizing your cases.
5. Focus on the Diagnoses of the *Diagnostic and Statistical Manual of Mental Disorders*–5th edition (DSM-5) and how they relate to conceptualization regardless of placement setting.
6. Understand how developmental assessment assists in treatment interventions.
7. Use case conceptualization and diagnosis as a tool for enhancing effective counseling and treatment with the Case of Rachel.

Key Concepts: Client Case Conceptualization and the Investigative Nature of Counseling

The world of case conceptualization and its relationship to formal client diagnostic systems such as the DSM-5 (APA, 2013b) is a fascinating and essential aspect of counseling. Client case conceptualization is like being a detective in a mystery case. Each new piece of information tells a different and unique aspect of this major problem that your client has allowed you to hear, see, and investigate. Often once you have put the puzzle pieces together, you may finally see the gestalt of the problem. Ginter (2014) describes case formulation (conceptualization) with DSM-5 as one part of a three-part process. Case formulation is the link between assessment and treatment planning answering the question, "Why is this person, having this type of problem, now?" (Ginter, 2014, slide 2).

> **Diagnostic and Statistical Manual of Mental Disorders, Fifth Edition (DSM-5):** The fifth edition of a classification of mental disorders manual published by the American Psychiatric Association, coding over 400 different disorders.

Whether you choose to include DSM-5 diagnosis of your clients as a part of client case conceptualization is a decision you must make with your on-site supervisor and university instructor. Regardless of your position on diagnosing, it is essential that you be familiar with the diagnostic process to understand the diagnoses of other professionals in the helping professions. Diagnosis can serve as a common and universal communication tool, bringing together clinicians working with people's social, emotional, and physiological concerns.

Your major task is, of course, to work on understanding the client and helping that client achieve counseling goals and resolve issues. DSM-5 diagnoses may offer additional information about the client and case conceptualization. You may use the diagnostic process as yet another piece of information to address the puzzle of effective treatment.

> **Diagnosis:** The use of an assessment tool or strategy to analyze a person's functioning and symptomatology.

Conceptualizing a client's case can be a stimulating and interesting journey. It is a journey that you must not take alone because it is your client's world and perspective and also includes your supervisor's perspective. If you allow your client and supervisor to be active players in the case conceptualization and treatment team, the three of you can learn together. With this team approach, counseling gains and outcomes are more realistic, practical, and efficient.

As you join with your client in asking the needed questions and working together as team players, three cautionary statements must be mentioned.

Confidentiality

The world of counseling builds therapeutic relationships like none other. People often enter your life when they are most vulnerable, afraid, and fragile. One of the reasons the process of counseling works is that you, as the counselor, demonstrate to the client that this place of sharing and working is a haven. Your client must know that all material shared is confidential unless you believe the client may be harmful to self or others or is being abused (children and older adults). As you know, it is this confidentiality that many times is the reason people enter into the frightening journey of self-awareness and growth. Be sure you demonstrate confidentiality by your words, attitudes, and consistent behaviors.

Humble Guest

Another variable that helps in case conceptualization, diagnosing, and treatment is the attitude of respect that emanates from you to your client. You are invited into your client's life as a humble guest. It is a place of honor at the head table. If you have never been in personal counseling as a client, consider your field experience as an opportunity to get into counseling.

There are two reasons for seeking counseling yourself. Remember that you can only take your clients as far as you have gone yourself! You need to be as healthy as possible to serve your clients. Even more importantly, though, you must know what it is like to have the courage to ask a stranger for assistance! Both Lori and Nancy have sought counseling three times throughout their life history. Lori's first time was in her doctoral program, when everyone was gently encouraged to enter counseling. She went begrudgingly, feeling invaded and resentful! Lori also felt scared, embarrassed, and finally relieved, and the list goes on. Nancy first went to counseling while struggling through a divorce. Allen did years of psychoanalytically oriented therapy and found it extremely beneficial in terms of self-learning and growth. We all believe that it assisted us in terms of a broader understanding of what is going on with our clients! Nancy always tells her students that they will never be the best counselor they can be without understanding the experience of being counseled.

From those first counseling experiences, you will learn to surrender to your fears and ask for help. From your position as a client, you will learn how to gain needed strength and new coping skills. Everyone has problems, no one is exempt, and everyone can benefit from a respectful, counseling relationship if you, as the counselor, understand your position of humble guest. There is no greater honor than being asked to be a part of someone's life when they are struggling and scared. Since trust is not established when that client walks into your office, your first counseling task is to honor that client, no matter where they are in life, and begin the delicate task of creating a trusting counseling relationship! You can accomplish that by meeting the client wherever they are and conscientiously beginning to gather all the needed information for case conceptualization, diagnosis, and treatment.

Cautiousness

There are many levels of case conceptualization developed throughout the chapter; however, case conceptualization and diagnosing using the DSM-5 is a serious matter. Once you have gathered all the necessary information, formally checked the criteria in the DSM-5, and discussed the aspects of the case with your supervisor you are finally ready to apply a diagnosis. Please remember that your work and diagnosis may travel with the client wherever he or she goes in life.

If you choose to use DSM-5 diagnosis as part of your case conceptualization, remember that other involved helping professionals, insurance companies, and possibly your client may view your diagnosis. Your client does have the right to view their personal file, and many clients find it helpful if they are part of the naming process that is diagnosing. Consider encouraging your client to be an active participant.

A DSM diagnosis is a serious label and is accomplished through diligent work and knowledge. As with all aspects of your counseling job, take this part of your job very seriously and be cautious about quickly or nonchalantly writing down symptoms, diagnoses, and treatment goals. Before examining further case conceptualization methods, let's add your fifth self-regulation skill, the importance of consistent exercise.

Exercise, the Brain, and Decision Making

We have heard for years that exercise is good for us. Advances in research are beginning to translate into actual practical information helping people better understand the exact science behind the benefits of exercise, especially as it relates to neurobiology and neurocounseling. Dr. John Ratey (2008; Ratey & Manning, 2014) has written about exercise and nutrition and explains how exercise releases brain-derived neurotrophic factors (BDNF). These cascading hormones assist the body in better learning, energy metabolism, and synaptic plasticity. BDNF are activated by glutamate that produces antioxidants and grows new brain cells. Ratey (2008) coined BDNF as the "Miracle Gro" for the brain. Ratey described how the stress from exercise sparked brain growth. Exercise can be too harsh though, but when done correctly it strengthens the infrastructure of nerve cells against damage and disease. Ratey emphasized how healthy stress is a must for survival and growth.

> **Brain-derived neurotropic factors (BDNF):** Cascading hormones that are activated through exercise.

Through Ratey's research, he suggested that a comprehensive exercise routine include six hours a week or 45 minutes to an hour a day of interval training, where the heart rate is very high for short periods and then returns to a lower rate for longer periods.

The most important aspect of exercise, though, is to find a sport or program that meets individual lifestyles and needs whether that be walking, Tae Kwon Do, pickleball, or biking (Russell-Chapin, 2016, in press). During this period in your life, just 20 minutes per day will impact your health and your studies. Perhaps purchasing some wearable technology to assist in recording and maintaining a physically fit body and mind would be worthwhile. There are also free applications on your phone to help you track your workouts. The Apple Watch is another example of wearable technology to keep you more physically aware and fit.

Once you begin to understand how exercise impacts your brain and the decision-making processes, exercise will more easily become a number one priority in your life. It will also help you get better grades! Exercise releases the cascading brain-derived neurotrophic factors (BDNF) or hormones that the body relies on to wake-up and revitalize. Blood flows more freely, releasing positive neurotransmitters such as serotonin, dopamine, or norepinephrine. Exercise also impacts the insulin-like growth factor (IGF-1), vascular endothelial growth factor (VEGF), and fibroblast growth factor (FGF-2) necessary for building new connections and neurons (Ratey, 2008; Ratey & Manning, 2014).

By adding self-regulations skills to your practicum/internship book, we are strongly encouraging you to use the neurocounseling techniques and strategies to help your clients. You need to understand that the brain has two interrelated brain axes. The basic limbic hypothalamic-pituitary-adrenal axis (HPA) releases epinephrine and norepinephrine to control emotional regulation and reactions to stress and other bodily processes such as sexuality, energy storage, and the immune system.

HPA The hypothalamic-pituitary-adrenal brain axis is responsible for emotional regulation.

We want you to see the connection that the HPA has with the second brain axis: the thyroid, anterior cingulate cortex, and the prefrontal cortex (TAP). This axis acts as your control relay station and the brain's main boss. The TAP functions as the major decision maker in managing the sometimes impulsive HPA. You are beginning to see how exercise assists the brain with these two axes to work more productively and effectively for healthier decision making. You are also getting the connection that counseling, as well as exercise, strengthens the TAP by expressing client feelings and thought that can then have a powerful influence on the negative stressors that we experience (Ivey et al., 2014).

TAP The thalamus-anterior cingulate cortex-prefrontal cortex brain axis is responsible for decision making.

Practical Reflection 1: Physical Exercise Plan

What will it take for you to integrate only 20 minutes of physical activity a day into your busy schedule? List one measureable change and one benefit to you from regular exercise.

_____

_____

_____

_____

Case Conceptualization Methods

There are many methods available for viewing the client's worldview and strategically assessing and intervening in the problem. One client conceptualization method that has already been presented to you utilizes the same interview stages presented in the Microcounseling Supervision Model: rapport/structuring, defining the problem, defining the goal, exploration of alternatives, and generalization to daily life (Ivey & Ivey, 2003). You can review those stages in Resource C and by using the Counseling Interview Rating Form (CIRF).

Using the Interview Stages to Conceptualize Cases

It is essential that you can understand the basics of case conceptualization; how you view your client's world and concerns certainly influences your treatment of that client. Using the stages of the interview to assist you in building your case is a natural approach to case conceptualization.

Please take a look at the CIRF or view the Microskills Hierarchy in Resource P. Follow along as we describe each stage.

Notice that the first two stages—rapport building/structuring and exploration/defining the problem—use many of the essential interviewing skills. The intention behind all of these basic skills is to encourage your client to share the concerns that are a focus of the counseling interview. It is at this point that you encourage your client to "tell the story." Hearing the story is the very first phase of the client's case conceptualization.

The most fundamental issue in conceptualization is, what is going on with the client? What are her or his concerns? What might have brought about the problem? What are some critical systems that might impact the client (family, work, and so on)? It is during these two stages that you may begin to use the diagnostic approach to case conceptualization.

During the third stage of the interview, defining goals and problem solving, your task is to analyze the information gleaned and set appropriate goals. What are the counseling goals? The fourth stage, action, and confronting incongruities, is very dynamic and fluid. As client progress is achieved and new awareness gained, you can continue to set new goals and action strategies.

The final stage of closing and generalization assists in case conceptualization by tying up loose ends, summarizing outcomes, and evaluating present and future needs. The stages work together providing you with seamless clues that create a final but ever-growing case agenda. You can use these five stages as a way to organize your interviewing notes, and you can use this model to summarize and conceptualize the interview. You can use it for notes and long-term treatment planning.

Practical Reflection 2: Stages of the Interview

How will the stages of the counseling interview assist you in conceptualizing your cases? Use the stages of the counseling interview to conceptualize a current client's case.

_____

_____

_____

_____

Adding the DSM-5 to the Case Conceptualization

As you develop and conceptualize each case, remember whether you decide to follow the DSM-5 approach or not is a decision you must make. You must follow your agency guidelines as well, but each decision on using the approach can be determined on a client-to-client basis. For Practicum/Internship class, we typically ask that each case presentation includes a DSM diagnosis for practice.

In the past, many counselor educators and social workers believed that there was no place for diagnosing in counseling. Interviewers, more often than not, assist people in effectively dealing with everyday problems and life issues. Although the 2020 Definition of Counseling emphasizes prevention and wellness, many counselors are placed in the position of making a clinical diagnosis (Kaplan et al., 2014). As the counseling and social work fields become more receptive to the idea of clinical diagnosis, the definition of diagnosis expands to include different aspects and layers. Although counselors still work with everyday life problems, the prevalent thinking is that all clinicians working in the helping professions must understand the dynamics of the major diagnostic system to work more effectively with each other.

Diagnosing Using the DSM-5

The DSM-5 provides guidelines allowing you to investigate your client's concerns in order to make an accurate diagnosis. It represents a common language for all mental health clinicians allowing better communication between and among professionals. The DSM-5 helps us choose the most effective treatment plan for our clients and provides information about the prognosis of our client's treatment. The DSM-5 was also designed to assist clinicians in distinguishing whether the client does indeed have a mental disorder (Buckley, 2014).

One of the most important aspects of DSM-5 is the focus on the client's cultural experience. The Cultural Foundations Index (CFI) is an assessment designed to collect cultural information that is important in understanding a client's beliefs that may have an impact on diagnosis and treatment. "The CFI follows a person-centered approach to cultural assessment . . . designed to avoid stereotyping, in that each individual's cultural knowledge affects how he or she interprets illness experience and guides how he or she seeks help" (APA, 2013b, p. 751). Use of the CFI provides you with the opportunity to view your client's world in a much broader manner.

DSM-5 authors did away with the multiaxial system and combined the former Axes I–III from DSM-IV-TR (Mental Disorders, Personality Disorders, and Medical Disorders) as well as the V Codes (Other conditions that may be the focus of clinical attention). Axis IV psychosocial factors have been replaced by severity indices in some cases, and disability/functioning may be assessed using the World Health Organization Disability Assessment Schedule (WHODAS) 2.0 (APA, 2013b). Diagnoses are now recorded with the code and name of the disorder. In cases where more than one diagnosis is present, the focus of treatment or primary diagnosis is listed first. This format follows the way International Classification of Diseases-10 (ICD-10) diagnoses are presented (WHO, 2015). ICD-10 codes replaced the current ICD-9 codes in October, 2015. So, for example, Rachel's DSM-5 diagnoses would appear as follows:

309.0 Adjustment Disorder with Depressed Mood, Persistent (chronic) F43.21
I10 Essential (Primary) Hypertension (This is the ICD-10 code)

The process of accurate diagnosing starts with the presenting problem(s) or major focus of clinical attention the client brings to you. You gather this information from the Client Intake Form, the client's words, and your initial observations during the first intake interview. A thorough biopsychosocial assessment is necessary for accurate diagnosing. You can certainly create your intake form, but please remember first to use the forms from your university and field experience agencies and schools, if available. Important additions to DSM-5 are assessment measures that can be used in the initial interview and then periodically to measure client progress. Cross-cutting Symptom Measures, Severity Indices, the WHODAS, and the CFI are all available for free from APA at http://www.psychiatry.org/practice/dsm/dsm5/online-assessment-measures#Level1.

Nussbaum (2013) describes a step-by-step process for obtaining a differential diagnosis with DSM-5. The first step is to determine if the client is intentionally causing their symptoms for any reason. Next, the clinician determines if the client's symptoms are related to a substance use disorder. The clinician then checks to what extent the client's signs and symptoms are related to a medical disorder. The fourth step involves determining the extent to which the symptoms are related to a developmental conflict or stage. The clinician then determines if the signs and symptoms are related to a mental disorder or if no mental disorder is present. Using this process can rule out factors related to misdiagnosis as well as help the clinician make an accurate diagnosis leading to an informed treatment plan.

Students often ask what they should do if their opinions and observations are different from what the client says is the presenting problem. If the client says the presenting problem is a marriage concern, but during your interview you obtained material that may suggest your client also has an addictive disorder, there seems to be a conflict about what the focus should be.

Your client is telling you the reason she came into counseling is her failing marriage, but you suspect a deeper and separate issue that may be influencing the marital relationship.

There are two different strategies you can follow. First, in a purely ethical sense, it seems logical to write down the presenting problem that your client states and is currently willing to discuss. As the counselor, you can now consider the two diagnoses providing both situations fit. You can also provide a "rule out" as an option, demonstrating that your client may fit this diagnosis but you are not certain and must perform more assessments and obtain more quantitative evidence to rule out this possibility. It is very difficult to focus on a troubled marriage if your client is dealing with addiction concerns as in this example. Clients are not willing to tell you exactly what the counseling problem is because it is too scary, too embarrassing, and too unknown.

Once trust has been established, you can ask an essential exploratory question, "What do you need to tell me that you have been keeping to yourself?" This level of trust allows you to get finally to the depth of the issues. Bergman (1985) refers to this as "fishing for the barracuda!" This part of your investigation is critical to your diagnosis and is the underlying essence of effective diagnosis and treatment.

Until clients feel comfortable enough to trust you with the secrets that they have been hiding for many years, you may not discover that flesh-eating barracuda. Once you find it, you can always add to or change your initial diagnosis and your focus of clinical attention.

Here are the three basic questions you need to be able to answer when diagnosing:

1. What are the major psychiatric symptoms and disorders?
2. What developmental issues are arrested or are currently presenting difficulty?
3. What is their duration and how does their intensity vary (Ginter, 2002)?

These questions integrate well with the questions you asked in Stages I and II of the interview. Hopefully, you are beginning to see how using the interview stages and the DSM-5 can work together.

Personality Disorders

Many clinicians use the DSM-5 and its criteria to indicate severe pathologies such as personality disorders. This is a useful method for corroborating your appraisal results, but please never use the criteria alone. Defer personality disorder labels until you can test your client for personality disorders using one of the many valid and reliable instruments assessing these conditions.

Two of the best personality instruments designed to measure psychopathology are the Millon Clinical Multiaxial Inventory-IV (MCMI-IV) (Millon, 1994, Millon, Grossman & Millon, 2015) and the Minnesota Multiphasic Personality Instrument-2 (MMPI-2) (Hathaway & McKinley, 1989). Both tests can be scored by hand or computer; however, the hand-scored tests offer a more individualized profile because the results refer only to your client. When using a computerized form, the profile is individualized but the treatment suggestions are generic and compared to others having a similar profile. The results are immediate, however. Be cautious and experienced using these tests. When sharing information with clients regarding the results, we do not recommend that you or your supervisor share actual test scores. Remember that your client's life does depend on accurate diagnosis.

If a score must be reported, try sharing the standard error of measurement as the central concept. Determining and objectively analyzing personality disorders are critical steps in the treatment of your client. If your client does score in the personality disorder range, you understand the intensity of your client's concern. A personality disorder influences and affects your client's decision making on a daily basis. The sooner the client understands the impact of the disorder, the more quickly you can assist him or her in becoming more aware of those needs.

Here are the essential questions you need to ask for determining the diagnosis of a personality disorder: (1) Are there any lifelong maladaptive patterns or traits? (2) Do these patterns tend to cause trouble in intimate, social, or work relationships (Ginter, 2002)?

Practical Reflection 3: DSM-5 Strategy and Conceptualization

List your major concerns about diagnosing using the DSM-5.

_____

_____

_____

_____

_____

_____

_____

Developmental Assessment

The third and final strategy adding to your case conceptualization is developmental assessment. As you have learned, stages of the interview and clinical diagnosis offer information about the client's problems, but development diagnosis offers information about your client's style and orientation to the world. Proponents of assessing the developmental levels (Ivey & Ivey, 2003) emphasize that clients enter into the counseling system from an individual and familiar cognitive and emotional frame of reference.

> **Developmental assessment**: Matching the counseling language style with the client's organizational reference to the world.

In Developmental Counseling and Therapy (DCT), Ivey and Ivey (2003; Ivey et al., 2014) suggest that clients offer you clues about how they arrange and organize their world. By matching your words and phrases with the client's worldview, you build rapport and let the client know you do understand the presented views. There are four developmental styles/levels discussed and four recommended appropriate intervention types to match these levels.

Your counseling task is to listen and observe very carefully and match the client's beginning developmental orientation with similar skills and theories. After establishing the client's style, you can intentionally mismatch to assist the client in developmental stretching. Ivey and Ragazio-Digilio (2009) provide key questions that facilitate your client's expression within developmental styles. They state "when clients are able to talk about, think through, and experience multiple ways of expressing emotion, this frees them for more intentional and effective resolutions of their issues" (Ivey & Ragazio-Digilio, 2009, p. 6).

Developmental style 1 (D-1) is a sensorimotor and a "here and now" experience orientation. A client in this style feels and shows emotion deeply and can describe those emotions. Clients may feel overwhelmed and be in a state of crisis. An appropriate development response may be to listen and then respond using a structured directive, assisting the client to move into a more grounded and positive experience.

We will use a hypothetical Susie as an example. Assume that Susie is seeking counseling to talk about mild, but possibly clinical depression. Susie's example statement: Susie begins to weep, "I can't believe my husband is so mean to me and the kids. I am crushed." Her presentation of her problems is somewhat random, and it is hard to follow her logic. She is deeply embedded in her emotions.

Clients in the developmental style D-2 are in the concrete orientation style. These clients are often linear and detailed. Their account of the situation is specific, and the stories are long and involved. In this style, Susie's example statement is: "This morning I woke up at 5:30. I cleaned the house and fed the dog. I got the kids up and dressed at 7:00, had breakfast, and we made the beds. As we were leaving the house, my husband became very critical about the mail piling up and how lazy we all were. We all left the house in tears."

You will find that many clients present their issues in this fashion, and it is important to listen carefully and not become bored or push the client to reflection and analysis too soon. Paraphrasing and Summarization can be especially helpful in showing the client that they have been heard, resulting in fewer repetitions of their story.

A developmental style of formal-operational orientation (D-3) is demonstrated with little detail and feelings, but your client may talk in abstract terms about the problem. Themes, patterns, and self-analysis seem to come easily to people in this style. Susie's example statement: "It always tends to be the same. I try so hard to please him and be a good wife and mother. Perhaps that is the problem; I am trying too hard, but whenever I try hard, my husband becomes critical and harsh." Here you see a more verbal client, one who is often good at examining the self and patterns of thought, action, and feeling.

The final developmental style is dialectical/systemic orientation (D-4). A client in this style tends to have a need to analyze patterns with self-reflection but also the contextual situation. Susie's example statement: "Probably there are many ways to look at this problem. I am sure that when I am overwhelmed and trying hard to keep everything and everybody together and happy that there must be that stress spillover to everyone around me."

This brief discussion of developmental assessment can be valuable to you in several ways. First, it reminds you that clients present their issues in varying styles and that it is essential to meet the client where he or she is at in the moment. As clients progress and change, you will find that their verbal style changes, and you will want to change your mode of working with them. This strategy of developmental assessment has specific implications for treatment as well.

Ashen (1977) offers a different classic developmental assessment method. He believes all people carry mental pictures in their minds of certain situations. It is not until these symbols or images become conscious that the client will be able to make direct and rational choices about these events. A triadic model is presented, demonstrating that clients enter the counseling system using created images (I), somatic responses (S), and related meaning (M). Whichever component a client chooses is the one you want to use first. Once the client knows you understand him or her, it is the counselor's job to gently stretch the client for further understanding of the problem.

For example, a client enters counseling stating he is sad, depressed, and does not feel productive at work. Your client has offered the meaning (M) component of the triad. It is your job to developmentally hook into that meaning component by understanding all of its dimensions. Then gently begin to stretch to the other components looking for additional clues to fill in the treatment story. What are the somatic and physiological symptoms? If he has headaches, when and where does your client most often develop these headaches? What are these headaches telling him from a symbolic point of view? This last question may lead you into the image component of the triad by listening to your client's wordings and phrasings. His headaches might be stating that he feels as if he is between a rock and a hard place. You need to carefully examine his images of "a rock and a hard place."

Developmental assessment offers another strategy in the diagnosis and treatment aspects of counseling. When you imagine the advantages of developmental assessment and combine those clues offered with the counseling stages and clinical diagnosis, your counseling puzzle is almost complete. You receive additional and valuable information with which to work more effectively with your client. In addition, this information assists you to determine the client's goals and treatment plan accurately.

Practical Reflection 4: Your Preferred Developmental Orientation Style

Think back to a time in your life when you were describing one of your problems to a friend or helping professional. Did you offer feelings, thoughts, details, and images? What developmental styles/orientations did you present (D-1 through D-4)? Sensorimotor? Concrete-Operational? Formal operational? Dialectic/systemic?

_____

_____

_____

_____

_____

_____

_____

Goals and Treatment Plans

Every helping professional must be able to design an effective treatment plan with appropriate goals. There are several components for developing accurate treatment plans, but the one cardinal rule seems quite simple: Devise your treatment plan and measurable goals around any or all of the above three strategies—stages of the interview, DSM-5 diagnosis, or developmental assessment. If you follow this formula, your counseling goals will assist you in the implementation of that plan.

In designing your treatment plan and goals, first assess your problem list from the DSM-5 diagnosis(es) and the five stages of the interview as a way to organize a treatment plan. Look at your client's available resources and positive skills, and then identify the lack of meaningful activities, medical limitations, social isolation, and any suicidal ideations. Once your problem list develops, you can begin to prioritize which needs must be addressed immediately, which needs could be addressed in the short term, and which issues will require long-term attention and goals (Ginter, 2002).

Remember, set goals in behavioral terms that are measurable. For example, with Susie, you could give her an assertiveness instrument to determine her basic communication skills. Administering the instrument could be a short-term goal. A long-term goal could be that in six months, you administer the same instrument to Susie. She will have increased her assertiveness rating by at least 10 points. Your goals are critical to the efficacy of the treatment. If you don't have goals, you cannot have direction for change.

Case Presentation Guidelines

Another important aspect of case conceptualization is the skill of presenting your client's case to other professionals. At the end of the chapter, Resource Q provides a sample outline that can assist you in putting all the information down concerning your client and the case study. Follow along using this outline as the Case of Rachel is used to demonstrate a narrative case presentation.

Narrative Case Presentation about Rachel

This is a concise example of a written case presentation about Rachel. Your instructor may want you to add more information, but you can use this format as a skeletal outline or guide. As you are reading this example narrative, think of other pertinent information that may need to go into this presentation. Remember that the purpose of a case presentation is to advise others who may need to work with Rachel or to assist you in your treatment plan and supervisory needs sufficiently.

I. **Introduction**: NAME AND PERSONAL INFORMATION: Rachel S. is a 71-year-old Caucasian woman whose presenting problem is sadness and anger about the death of her husband. She stated, "I just want my old life back." She displayed tangible signs of agitation, tearfulness, and depression. She appears to be stressed over issues of growing older and possibly losing her independence.

II. **History**: PRESENT PROBLEMS: Rachel stated the onset of her problems began when her husband, John, unexpectedly died six months ago of a heart attack. Since that time Rachel reported, "I don't know what to do with myself." She does not eat or sleep regularly. There was no relevant information gained from the Cultural Formulation Interview (CFI).

III. **History of Psychiatric Illness**: There is no reported history of psychological illness.

IV. **Contributing Medical Illness**: From Rachel's Intake Form, the results of a recent physical showed high blood pressure. Rachel stated she was taking her blood pressure medicine on a daily basis.

V. **Brief Family History**: Her husband, John, died six months ago.
They have three grown children who all live outside the state of Wyoming.

VI. **Social History**: Rachel and John were married for 50 years. She is now a widow living on a fixed income, but John left her in a stable financial state. Rachel was a teacher and librarian for 30 years; both she and John had retired to travel and relax. She presently lives alone, but recently her children, especially the youngest child, are encouraging her to move away and live with one of them. Rachel believes she is very capable of living alone.

VII. **DSM-5 Diagnosis/ICD 10**: 309.0 Adjustment Disorder with Depressed Mood, Persistent (chronic), F43.21, I10 Essential (Primary) Hypertension

VIII. **Wellness Focus**:

(A) PHYSICAL: Rachel used to walk through the mall with her spouse three times a week. She is not exercising at all now. She maintains that her previous healthy eating habits are now sporadic. John loved to cook, and now Rachel hates cooking for one. Her sleep patterns are irregular.

(B) SPIRITUAL: According to Rachel's Intake Form, she belongs to a local First Methodist Church. She has been a member there for the past thirty years. She has not attended church since John's funeral.

(C) OCCUPATIONAL: Rachel is a retired teacher and librarian. Before John's death, she was active in several local charity events, bridge, tutoring, and traveling.

(D) SOCIAL: Rachel reported that she and John had many friends and outlets for social activities. She has not contacted any friends since John's death.

(E) EMOTIONAL: Rachel labeled herself a happy person who enjoyed life. Her mother and father are both dead, and she remembers being sad but not devastated when they passed away. She remembered entering counseling one time when she lost her first baby, who was stillborn. Rachel said she only went a few times.

(F) INTELLECTUAL: Rachel stated she enjoyed reading books and articles, both fiction and nonfiction. She discussed that lately she cannot focus long enough to read.

IX. **Prognosis:** Based on the Intake Form information and initial counseling interview, Rachel's counseling outcome and prognosis is good. If she continues to grieve the losses in her life openly and begins to create a new life without her husband, Rachel will develop the needed coping skills.

X. **Treatment Goals in Specific and Measurable Terms:** Four main counseling goals have been set with Rachel. Additional goals may be created as counseling continues.

1. Rachel will openly share her thoughts and feelings about her husband's death with her three children between now and the next two weeks.
2. Rachel will call at least one previous friend every week to arrange a social event.
3. Rachel will take a pre- and post-test Beck Depression Inventory to assess the degree of potential depression.
4. A Lifestyle Assessment Survey will be administered assessing wellness needs.

XI. **Supervision Question(s), Needs, and Wants:** During my individual and group supervision I would like for each of you in my supervisory group to watch for the following skills and problems:

1. Rachel seemed resistant in the very beginning of the counseling session. What could I have done differently to increase her level of comfort?
2. There were so many areas on which to focus. I chose to focus on support resources. Was that the most effective and efficient area of focus?

3. The topic of death is not an easy issue for me. Did I handle my self-disclosure appropriately?
4. Please give me feedback on my diagnosis.
5. What were my strengths? What could I improve upon?

Practical Reflection 5: Case Presentation Additions

As you read the case presentation, what would you add to the overall case study? What did you see as strengths in the presentation? What would you recommend for areas of development and improvement in the case presentation style?

_____

_____

_____

_____

_____

_____

_____

The Case of Rachel: Case Conceptualization with the Stages of the Interview, Clinical Diagnosis, and Developmental Assessment

Stages of the Interview

Using the Stages of the Counseling Interview was helpful in comprehending the content and major concerns of Rachel. In the rapport/structuring stage, Rachel seemed resistant and stuck in her grief. Active listening skills were required. The exploration of concerns/data gathering stage revealed her additional concerns with her children and losing her independence. Stage three, mutual goal-setting, assisted in developing the needed outcomes of counseling. The exploring alternatives stage assisted the case because available resources were discovered. Finally, the generalization and termination stage offered the necessary transitions for overcoming Rachel's grief and moving on to a new life.

DSM-5 Diagnosis

A diagnosis was offered in the narrative case presentation. An explanation of the diagnosis is offered, so you can dissect and compare the codes presented.

DSM-5 Diagnoses:

309.00 Adjustment Disorder with Depressed Mood/F43.21
I10 Hypertension (ICD-10 code)

Rachel came to counseling displaying symptoms of agitation, sadness, loneliness, and confusion. During her interview, Rachel stated these symptoms had continued for a period of six months. For adjustment disorder to be considered, the client must exhibit marked distress in excess of what is expected and display significant social or occupational functioning. When the distress lasts for more than six months, the adjustment disorder is considered to be chronic. Bereavement was considered, as Rachel had valid and legitimate reasons for her grief, but her signs and symptoms seemed more intense than bereavement.

From the intake form and interview, Rachel disclosed that her high blood pressure or hypertension seems to be less manageable since her husband's death. Rachel must keep her blood pressure checked and under control to ensure that her medical condition does not interfere or contribute to the adjustment disorder. There were several psychosocial factors contributing to Rachel's primary counseling concern.

In the counseling interview, Rachel discussed how lonely and sad she continues to be about John's death. She continues by disclosing that her children want her to move away and live with her youngest. These issues must be addressed during counseling as additional goals.

Developmental Assessment

Assessing Rachel's developmental needs seemed obvious as well. She spoke in analogies, such as "It is like my left arm has been cut off." Rachel preferred the Formal-Operational style of patterns and analysis. Lori's comments matched Rachel's words; when summarizing, she commented, "a piece of you is missing." Lori continued to search for meaning, feelings, and themes for the remainder of the counseling session. Rachel was fairly independent, so Lori gave her intentional support, latitude, and a small amount of direct structure as they began goal-setting.

Goals and Treatment for Rachel

The goals and treatment plan for Rachel may follow the diagnosis and developmental assessment. As the treatment priority list is established, It is clear that Rachel is struggling with all the new transitions in her life. Learning about grief and openly sharing with her children was a priority in the short term.

Goal 1.   By the end of next week, Rachel will telephone each of her three children to talk about her grief and loneliness for their father.

Goal 2.   By the end of next week, Rachel will tell her children about her feelings that they are coddling her.

Goal 3.   By the end of next week, Rachel will call one friend to arrange a social outing.

Goal 4.   By the end of the second counseling session, Rachel will have completed a Millon Clinical Multiaxial Inventory-IV and a Beck Depression Inventory-II (BD-II) (Beck et al., 1996).

Goal 1.   By the end of one month, Rachel will have an appointment for a complete physical to check her high blood pressure and to develop a baseline for physiologic needs.

Goal 2.   By the fourth counseling session, Rachel and Lori will evaluate the previous goals for counseling outcomes and if necessary, create new goals.

Goal 3.   By the eighth counseling session, Rachel will retake the BDI to determine if there is a decrease in depression score.

Goal 4.   As counseling progresses, Rachel will work on decision-making strategies for living arrangements, social activities, and projects.

These goals assist Lori in treating Rachel through this difficult period of adjustment to her husband's death. Because of Rachel's development levels, Lori will intentionally use encouragement and positive asset searches to guide Rachel. Gentle confrontations will challenge Rachel to stretch into an inclusive model of wellness.

Summary and Personal Integration

The main emphasis of Chapter 5 was to create a better understanding of the steps involved in case conceptualization and treatment. The self-regulation skill of daily exercise was integrated with the earlier presented skills of diaphragmatic breathing, imagery, sleep hygiene, and the gut/brain connection and nutrition.

- Three strategies to assist in the case conceptualization process were presented: stages of the interview, clinical diagnosis, and developmental assessment.
- Descriptions of the DSM-5 diagnoses were provided with examples of each.
- The Case of Rachel illustrated case conceptualization using the three strategies and emphasizing case presentation, goal-setting, and treatment plans.

Practical Reflection 6: Integration

As you read the material and reflections in Chapter 5, what aspects of case conceptualization will help you the most in effectively understanding your client's case and interventions?

_____

_____

_____

_____

_____

_____

Resource P

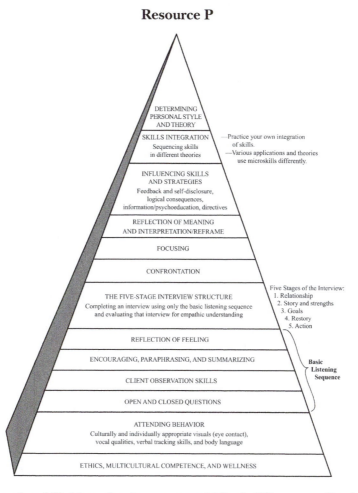

Figure 5.1 **The microskills hierarchy shows a pyramid for building counseling intentionality. (Copyright @1982, 2007, 2015 Allen E. Ivey. Reprinted by permission.)**

Resource Q

Case Presentation Outline Guide

I. Introduction: (a) Abbreviated Name of Client, (b) Age, (c) Gender, (d) Presenting Problem(s) in Client's Words, (e) Present Signs and Symptoms, (f) Relevant Information from Cultural Formulation Inventory (CFI)

II. History: (a) Present Problem(s): (1) Onset, (2) Duration

III. History of Psychiatric Illness

IV. Contributing Medical Illness

V. Brief Family History

VI. Social History: (a) Marital Status, (b) Employment, (c) Current Living Arrangements

VII. DSM-5 Diagnosis/ICD-10 and Relevant Assessments

VIII. Wellness Focus: (a) Physical, (b) Spiritual, (c) Occupational, (d) Social, (e) Emotional, (f) Intellectual

IX. Prognosis: (a) Poor, (b) Fair, (c) Good

X. Treatment Goals in Specific and Measurable Terms

XI. Student Counselor's Supervision Questions, Needs, and Wants

References

Ashen, A. (1977). *Psycheye: Self-Analytic Consciousness.* New York, NY: Brandon House.

American Psychiatric Association. (2013a). *Desk Reference to the Diagnostic Criteria from DSM-5.* Washington, DC: American Psychiatric Association.

American Psychiatric Association. (2013b). *Diagnostic and Statistical Manual of Mental Disorders: DSM-5.* Washington, DC: American Psychiatric Association.

Beck, A.T., Steer, R.A., & Brown, G.K. (1996). *Manual for the Beck Depression Inventory-II.* San Antonio, TX: Psychological Corporation.

Bergman, J.S. (1985). *Fishing for Barracuda.* New York: WW Norton & Company.

Buckley, M.A. (2014). Back to basics: Using the DSM-5 to benefit clients. *The Professional Counselor*, 4, 3, 159–165. NBCC and Affiliates. doi:10.15241/mrb.4.3.159

Ginter, G. (2002). Treatment planning guidelines for children and adolescents. In R.R. Erk (ed.), *Counseling and Treatment for Children and Adolescents with DSM-IV-TR Disorders.* Upper Saddle River, NJ: Prentice Hall.

Ginter, G. (2014). Case Formulation with DSM-5 [PowerPoint slides]. Retrieved from http://www.lacounseling.org/images/lca/Conference/DSM-5%20LCA%20Case%20Formulation%20Rev..pdf

Hathaway, S.R. & McKinley, J.C. (1989). *Minnesota Multiphasic Personality Inventory-2.* Minneapolis: University of Minnesota; National Computer Systems.

Ivey, A. & Ivey, M. (2003). *Intentional Interviewing and Counseling.* Belmont, CA: Brooks-Cole.

Ivey, A.E. & Ragazio-Digilio, S. (2009). Developmental counseling and therapy: The basics of why it might be helpful and how to use it. *Turkish Psychological Counseling and Guidance Journal*, 4 (32), 1–11.

Ivey, A., Ivey, M., & Zalaquett, C. (2014). *Intentional Interviewing and Counseling: Facilitating Client Development in a Multicultural World* (8th edn). Belmont, CA: Brooks-Cole/Cengage.

Kaplan, D.M., Tarvydas, V.M., & Gladding, S.T. (2014). 2020: A vision for the future of counseling. *Journal of Counseling and Development*, 92, 366. American Counseling Association.

Millon, T. (1994). *Millon Clinical Multiaxial Inventory-III.* Minneapolis, MN: National Computer Systems.

Millon, T., Grossman, S., & Millon, C. (2015). Millon Clinical Multiaxial Inventory-IV. Psychcorp, Pearson.

Nussbaum, A. (2013). *A Pocket Guide to DSM-5 Diagnostic Exam.* Arlington, VA: American Psychiatric Publishing.

Ratey, J.J. (2008). *Spark: The Revolutionary New Science of Exercise and the Brain.* New York, NY: Little Brown.

Ratey, J.J. & Manning, R. (2014). *Go Wild: Free Your Body and Mind from the Afflictions of Civilization.* New York, NY: Little Brown.

Russell-Chapin, L.A. (2016, in press). The power of neurocounseling and self- regulation. In J. Edwards, S. Young, & H. Nikels (eds.), *Handbook of Strengths-based Clinical Practices: Finding Common Factors.* London: Routledge.

World Health Organization. (2015). *International Classification of Diseases* (ICD-10 Version 2015). Geneva, Switzerland: WHO.

Section II

KNOWLEDGE NEEDED TO GROW

Issues in Professional Practice

Chapter 6 is the beginning of Section II and presents a third case study for you to analyze. The entire module addresses the myriad of issues facing a new helping professional. By the time you have completed Section II and the remaining five chapters, you can expect to demonstrate:

- KNOWLEDGE AND COUNSELING SKILLS INVOLVED IN PRACTICING CULTURAL COMPETENCY.
- ATTITUDES AND BEHAVIORS NECESSARY FOR PROFESSIONAL AND ETHICAL COUNSELING.
- AN UNDERSTANDING OF OUTCOME RESEARCH AND ITS CORRELATION TO EFFECTIVE COUNSELING.
- A PHILOSOPHY OF WELLNESS, CREATING A PERSONAL AND PROFESSIONAL BALANCE.
- ADVOCACY FOR YOURSELF AND THE HELPING PROFESSION.

6

BECOMING A CULTURALLY COMPETENT HELPING PROFESSIONAL

Appreciation of Diversity in Action

Knowing yourself well and becoming a culturally competent helping professional is a never-ending journey. It is a proactive and mindful process.

—Lori Russell-Chapin

Counseling and psychotherapy are multicultural. Both the client and you as counselor or therapist bring many voices from the past and present to the session

—Paul Pedersen

Overview

Chapter 6 focuses on the need for multicultural competencies and encourages you to move from tolerance of differences to an appreciation of differences to actively working with inclusivity. Helping professionals must understand that diversity encompasses race, age, gender, sexual orientation, socioeconomic status, religious affiliation, and life experiences, and how each of these and other factors may impact the counseling process.

This chapter has several main emphases. The first goal is to provide you with a better understanding of your beliefs and attitudes about living in a diverse society. Being aware of your personal worldview will affect how you engage in counseling. It is also imperative that you understand how stereotypes and prejudices occur. Several conceptual frameworks will be presented to assist you in comprehending the cross-cultural dynamics involved in counseling relationships (Kwan, 2001). Finally, you need to be aware of the many resources available to you in your diversity journey whether that be a diversity simulation or interacting with those who are different than you, as in the Case of Darryl. Another self-regulation skill will be introduced by teaching the biofeedback technique of skin temperature control.

Goals

1. Practice the self-regulation skill of skin temperature control.
2. Be aware of the Multicultural Competencies written for the helping professions.
3. Identify individual racial identities and prejudices.
4. Learn several Racial Identity Models.
5. Understand how multicultural dimensions affect diversity concerns.

6. React and respond to a Diversity Simulation.
7. Analyze the Case of Darryl.

Key Concepts: A Continuum for Multicultural Development

It is crucial for you as a helping professional to have the awareness, knowledge, and skills to understand your own racial and cultural beliefs, values, and biases (Sue, Arredondo, & McDavis, 1992). If you understand yourself well, then you may be able to assist better in your client's development (Kwan, 2001). Helms (1995) noted that positive client change is more likely to occur if you are at a more advanced stage of racial identity development status than your client.

Once you understand your racial development, you can apply the same three-stage model to your clients. According to Sue and Sue (1999), the first stage is Awareness. You must be aware that there are individual differences and be clear what your beliefs and values are. The second stage is Knowledge. You must gain needed information and knowledge about your client to help your client grow successfully. You must be able to "enter into the world of those you are trying to help by learning their unique cultures, family histories, languages, customs, values, and priorities" (Kottler, 2000, pp. 6–7). The third stage is Skills. There may be specific skills that work more sensitively and effectively with different types of concerns. However, awareness, knowledge, and skills are not enough. You must be able to put these stages into action with words and behaviors.

As we work to understand better the issues surrounding multiculturalism, sometimes cognitive dissonance occurs along with symptoms of anxiety. To understand others may make us look at our beliefs with a different set of lenses and perspectives. In a previous chapter, you learned about the importance of breathing to reduce anxiety. Another self-regulation skill that assists in calming bodily functions is the regulation of skin temperature.

Skin Temperature Control

Of all the biofeedback interventions, teaching and practicing peripheral skin temperature control is one of the easiest and most rewarding. Sometimes within ten minutes clients can learn to increase their skin temperature. The typical response is, "Wow, I didn't know I could manage and raise my skin temperature!" Almost immediately clients have a new sense of personal control.

This form of direct biofeedback for self-regulation once again relies on operant conditioning of the autonomic nervous system. This involves the voluntary control of peripheral skin temperature (Schwartz & Andrasik, 2003). When stressed, the smooth muscles surrounding blood vessels become constricted, rerouting blood to internal organs and large muscle groups in preparation for a flight or fight response. This vasomotor response, once constricted, reduces the amount of blood flow to the periphery and the surface skin temperature decreases (Criswell, 1995). Normal peripheral skin temperature is 86 plus or minus two degrees for women and 88 plus or minus two degrees for men. Less than these amounts suggests a stress reaction and more suggests a relaxation response. Often the goal is to reach around 90 degrees. The relaxed response has begun, and at that temperature you can remain focused and alert. Too much higher will trigger too much relaxation and even a sleep response.

A script for skin temperature training is as follows:

1. Acquire an inexpensive digital or handheld temperature thermometer. A digital unit can be purchased for around twenty dollars and handheld thermometers for less than a dollar each. See www.cliving.org for details on skin temperature equipment.
2. Hold the thermometer or attach the digital sensor with gauze tape to palm side, large finger of your non-dominant hand.
3. Sit normally until the reading stabilizes. This is your pre-baseline peripheral skin temperature. If your hands are cold from outdoors, let them first adjust to the room temperature.
4. Then close your eyes and focus on "letting go" and replacing anxious thoughts with calming thoughts. Imagine a relaxing place. Repeat to yourself, "I am . . . calm. I am . . . relaxed. I am . . . warm. My arms . . . are calm. My arms . . . are relaxed. My arms . . . are warm. My hands . . . are calm. My hands . . . are relaxed. My hands . . . are warm."
5. Take time to allow your imagination to recreate all the beautiful aspects of your relaxing place. Notice what you see, hear, feel, smell, and taste. Let the picture in your mind become a movie and enjoy it as it plays out in mind's theater.
6. If the temperature decreases, you may be trying too hard. Take a few deep breaths. Remind yourself to let go and allow the imagery to unfold. If you are still having problems, it may be more helpful to follow along with a relaxation CD.
7. Sometimes it is also helpful to have the client use imagery when learning biofeedback. Imagine the smooth muscles of the blood vessels beginning to

relax, the blood flowing more easily through your arms, hands, and fingers, and your skin beginning to feel warmer.

8. Now open your eyes and notice your temperature reading. This is your treatment induced reading. Congratulations on learning how to increase your peripheral skin temperature.

9. Next, return to normal non-imagery activity and after a few minutes notice your post-baseline peripheral skin temperature. This is a measure of how much your training has generalized to your usual state.

10. Practice skin temperature training for five to eight days in a row so it becomes your normal state of arousal (Chapin & Russell-Chapin, 2014, pp. 73–74).

Practical Reflection 1: Skin Temperature Control

Practice this script for at least five days. Right now measure your baseline skin temperature and begin to chart where you are during the day. How does your body feel after the script is completed? What have you discovered?

_____

_____

_____

_____

Cross-cultural Dimensions in Counseling

Cultural issues have become so broad that many believe all counseling is multicultural or cross-cultural. Ivey, Pedersen, and Ivey (2001, pp. 2–3) classify the following factors to assist you in identifying essential multicultural dimensions.

Family Context

- Nuclear
- Extended family
- Adoptive
- Gay/lesbian
- Divorced
- Alcoholism/drugs

Social Systems Context

- Language
- Gender
- Ethnicity/race
- Religion and spirituality

Demographic Context

- Age
- Sexual orientation
- National origin
- Region of the Nation
- Community of origin and present community

Status Context

- Past and present socioeconomic background
- Education
- Key group affiliations (living group, fraternities, service agencies, athletics)

Life Experience Context

- Major physical issues
- Major emotional issues
- Experiences of discrimination or prejudice
- Experiences of trauma (rape, divorce, accident, serious illness, war)

Nwachuku and Ivey (1991) also believe that asking individuals from specific cultures to examine their own culture and describe the culture's values and helping styles is a beginning strategy for developing training materials for all helping professionals. As a student in field experience, you can generalize this to working with individual clients, as well as better understanding your personal helping style.

The Multiplicity of Multicultural Understanding

Another way to view the multicultural dimensions is to see the multiplicity of multicultural understanding. You are a unique human being with a background and experience that no one else in the world has had. Your client is equally unique. Both of you constantly change as you encounter new experiences and gain new knowledge (Ivey, Ivey, & Zalaquett, 2016).

> **Multicultural counseling:** Two or more persons who are working together in a counseling relationship presenting differing ways of perceiving the world and environment.

When we say the word "multicultural," we historically have used a White perspective, assuming that culture only belongs to those different from the "majority group." In truth, there is a White culture just as there are African, Asian, Latina/o, and Native American Indian cultures. There are also Australian, US, Canadian, and an array of international cultures. Regional differences can be profound. In Canada, the culture of Edmonton differs significantly from Toronto, Montreal, and Inuvik. Southern regions, New England, and California all differ markedly and influence who we are and how we think.

Some of us are deeply committed to a religious/spiritual orientation while for others this is less important. Lesbians/gays/bi-sexual/transgendered/queer/intersexed (LGBTQI) all share the challenge of discrimination and oppression, but each of these six groups has its issues. Moreover, the individual within each group has a unique life experience.

Let us assume that you have a client who is White, male, straight, economically privileged, and a member of a majority church in your region or nation. You are also educated, have had no significant experience of life trauma. Now, change any one of those dimensions and we have a client whose background is already quite different. Change to a Person of Color, a woman, and poor, then the world and personal worldview is even more distinct from so-called "majority culture" and clients are likely to have endured discrimination, disrespect, and oppression.

The RESPECTFUL Cube: Individual Culture and the Ownership of Privilege

What is your multicultural background and how privileged has been your life experience? Just because clients are White and male or Black and female, obviously the first thing to do is avoid stereotyping. Again, what voices are they bringing to their time with you?

The RESPECTFUL Cube of Figure 6.1 presents a visual representation of many of the multicultural variants that counselors and therapists may expect to encounter. At this point, we ask you to take out a sheet of paper and identify yourself on the dimensions of the multicultural cube, but there may be additional things that you wish to add.

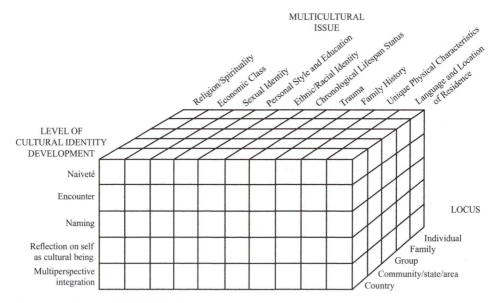

Figure 6.1 **The RESPECTFUL Cube shows multicultural variants. © 2015 Allen E. Ivey.**

Most of the terms of the top line are self-explanatory, but additional information below may be useful. Identify yourself on each dimension.

Personal style and education refer first to your personality characteristics such as openness, warmth, or perhaps more formal and distant. Educational level should be apparent.

Chronological lifespan status means age-relevant issues ranging from childhood to teenage years, young adulthood, maturity/middle age, and elderly (which itself is now considered as young old, old (75–85), and those over 85).

Trauma is defined broadly. War, rape, assault, a major accident, abuse, and poverty come immediately to mind, but estimates are that 95% of the population experiences some form of trauma. These can range from losing a child, divorce or being a child of divorce, suffering bullying, losing a limb, having one's home foreclosed, and becoming homeless. For some, not getting into the college of one's choice or failing an important exam can be traumatic and bring the person to counseling.

Unique physical characteristics range from ability/disability to false standards of appearance and strength, or even lack of flexibility and balance.

The level of cultural identity development is typically defined on a five-point scale:

Naiveté. The individual is unaware of one or more of the RESPECTFUL dimensions being important in personal identity. This can be a general lack of awareness of the importance of social class, religion, or another dimension. A White person may deny racism or sexism while being totally unaware that Whiteness in many countries represents a certain cultural privilege. A Person of Color denies or ignores discrimination and oppression, particularly if their life is going well and they feel acculturated to majority standards.

Encounter. An early stage of awareness often represents a breakthrough, often surprising. An immigrant from Pakistan or a refugee from Syria may experience a honeymoon period on arrival (naiveté), but gradually encounters subtle and obvious forms of discrimination in a predominantly English speaking country. The result can be active, passive acceptance of the situation and a marked increase in awareness of prejudice.

Naming. This is a more advanced form of encounter in which the person actively names and starts more action against oppression, perhaps through protest or community action. The emotion of anger may become predominant. The person is often defined in opposition to the privileged and dominant system.

Reflection of self as a cultural being—the development of pride and self-respect. Here the person may withdraw from protest and focus on her or his cultural background and history developing a positive view of strengths. Examples include taking pride in one's ethnic/racial background, accepting one's own minority religion or spirituality as a life center, or an Afghanistan or Iraq veteran coming to terms with what they did within a most confusing and unsupportive political context.

Multiperspective integration. All four dimensions above are seen as potentially useful and viable depending on the situational context.

Locus should be clear. Here you want to identify these dimensions, as each interact with each other and impact you and your clients individually. However, where does your family stand in terms of their identity development? Your primary groups, community, and even your country? Do all these interact with your views of self and system in challenging ways?

Practical Reflection 2: Examining Your Multicultural Self and Environment

Examine your multicultural development using the cube as a framework. First, identify yourself in each RESPECTFUL area. Next, think about your awareness of each and their impact on your life. What level of cultural identity do you have for each? Mark with an X on the intersection of these two.

You obviously cannot fill in the locus, so you can make a three column chart that enables you to see the patterns.

If you wish, add other areas to the Cube.

_____
_____
_____
_____

Intersectionality Within the Cube

It has been a tendency within the multicultural movement to focus on multicultural issues, particularly that of oppression from a single focus, often that of race/ethnicity or gender. While both of these are central issues and, in fact, the foundations of multicultural awareness, each person, male or female, of any race or ethnicity also comes from a socioeconomic class, has varying levels of interest or knowledge in a spiritual tradition, and is at varying stages of the lifespan.

For example, considerable attention has been given to the intersection between race and class. Consider just African American and White: being upper class and wealthy makes a large difference from the working or poorer classes, regardless of race. And, the differences in privilege between upper, middle, or lower class Whites and African Americans remain substantial.

Privilege and Power

In counseling, we also need to be constantly aware of privilege. Privilege almost inevitably brings power with it. Just being a counselor brings some power and privilege into each session. The importance of privilege was first identified by Peggy McIntosh (1988) in her seminal work. Each of the dimensions of the multicultural cube brings with them varying degrees of privilege and power. McIntosh first identified White male power, but soon the concept expanded in many ways throughout the multicultural world.

Whiteness is just one of the many variables that you can look at, starting with, for example, your place in the birth order, or your body type, or your athletic abilities, or your relationship to written and spoken words, or your parents' places of origin, or your parents' relationship to education and to English, or what is projected onto your religious or ethnic background. We're all put ahead and behind by the circumstances of our birth. We all have a combination of both. And it changes minute by minute, depending on where we are, whom we're seeing, or what we're required to do (Rothman, 2014). When working with people different from you, privilege is always in the background, and can make developing a working relationship more challenging. In general, people feel more comfortable with those who share common experiences continuing in many ways beyond the multicultural cube. If you have not experienced drugs or been in prison, you already have a position of power and privilege over the client, which can beget mistrust.

How to work with an unbalanced situation of privilege and power is explored in the remainder of this chapter. But, we highly recommend that you understand where your experience places you on the multiple dimensions of privilege.

Practical Reflection 3: Privilege and You

You can learn about your privilege and obtain a "privilege score" at: http://www.buzzfeed.com/regajha/how-privileged-are-you#.vugz P6DOMT. Follow that by reading the *New Yorker* about the origins of the concept of privilege and Peggy McIntosh at http://www.newyorker.com/ books/page-turner/the-origins-of-privilege. If you are willing, share your privilege score with your classmates. List it below.

_____

_____

_____

_____

You and Multicultural Competence

For years helping professionals have discussed the importance of using special skills when working with clients who are culturally different than the helper. It wasn't until the early 1990s that concerned multicultural leaders developed the Multicultural Competency Standards (Sue, Arredondo, & McDavis, 1992).

The importance of multicultural differences in counseling and therapy was first brought to the field's attention by Clemmont Vontress in the late sixties (Moodley, Epp, & Yusuf, 2012). For the most part, not much happened until Derald Wing Sue chaired a committee of the Society of Counseling Psychology, which presented the first definitive set of competencies in 1981. The report was not endorsed until 15 years later. Even following that, committed professionals met strong resistance to the ideas that you now know as basic, and this extended to picketing conferences at times. It wasn't until the early 2000s that the American Psychological Association and American Counseling Association formally approved the idea of multicultural guidelines and competencies, the result of the work of many individuals building on Sue's original thought.

The actual implementation of the broadly based competencies still meets considerable resistance, most of it now quietly behind the scenes. The competencies defined below are adaptions of written work by many authors and are best reviewed in Derald and David Sue's 2012 *Counseling the Culturally Diverse*. As you review our discussion below, please consider the complex context of the Foci of Cultural Competence below, as well as the multicultural cube. There you see many of the challenges that remain from the time of earlier confrontation and picketing.

Practical Reflection 4: Examining Your Cultural Beliefs about Helping

What is your culture's existing way of helping? Answering that question is a start in understanding your beliefs about helping. Discuss among your classmates.

_____

_____

_____

_____

The competencies presented below have been endorsed by many professional helping groups, among them the Association for Multicultural Counseling and Development, the Association for Counselor Education and Supervision, and the Counseling Psychology Division of the American Psychological Association. The competencies are used by the American Psychological Association as guidelines for professional practice, research, and teaching. Social work and human services have their approaches to these key issues.

Using the Multicultural Competency Standards developed by Sue, Arredondo, and McDavis (1992), Kwan (2001) developed the following guidelines to assist you in exploring your personal multicultural journey. Read through each of the bold, italicized competency sentences and first decide whether you agree or disagree with the guideline and what it means to you. If you believe the guideline is true or useful for you, then begin to dissect how it might play a role in your work with clients.

Multicultural Counseling Competencies and Standards: A set of standards for working with clients of minority populations.

Attitudes and Beliefs Guidelines

Culturally skilled counselors believe that cultural self-awareness and sensitivity to one's own cultural heritage are essential. Every person has a culture. Examine your

culture and begin to recognize what influences it may have on your development. For example, when Lori's children were in elementary school, they went
to a school where diversity was valued. She remembers one birthday party of
her nine-year-old at the time. Lori told him he could invite four other children.
He invited his best buddy who was African American and his second best buddy
who was Vietnamese. Jaimeson's worldview as a child was very different than
Lori's as a child. She grew up in a small, western state with little diversity.

*Culturally skilled counselors are aware of how their own cultural background and
experiences have influenced attitudes, values, and biases about psychological processes.*
Look at yourself as a multicultural being—race/ethnicity, spirituality, gender,
sexual orientation, and so on. All these variables play a role in how you see
the world. It is easy to depict all counseling as multicultural when defining the
world in this manner.

One of Lori's most pivotal experiences as a teenager was to travel to New York
City and be a part of the annual United Nations Pilgrimage! It was then that she
realized that the world is vast and made up of many different populations and
traditions. As she interacted with others who were different than she was, the
realization hit her that still we are more alike than different!

*Culturally skilled counselors can recognize the limits of their multicultural compe-
tency and expertise.* As you think about the varying cultural groups reviewed, how
much knowledge and experience have you had with each group? Recognizing
your limitations in certain areas is important. Asking others to help you learn
more is a compliment to that group. Most people love to share information
about their beliefs and cultural traditions.

Knowledge Guidelines

*Culturally skilled counselors have specific knowledge about their own racial and cul-
tural heritage and how it personally and professionally affects their definitions of and
biases about normality/abnormality and the process of counseling.*
If you haven't already done so, this is a great opportunity to learn more about
your cultural heritage. Dissect your cultural dimensions and see how they have
affected you, positively and negatively. How has your ethnic background influenced you? What has your religious/spiritual background given you? Are your
beliefs yours alone, or do you share them with your parents and grandparents?

A favorite anecdote demonstrates how traditions and beliefs are passed down
through the ages. It goes something like this. A newlywed couple is preparing
their first Sunday afternoon dinner. It is a pot roast with tasty vegetables. The
husband carefully observes his wife's detailed preparation. Just before placing
the roast in the pan, she takes a large knife and cuts off the end of the meat.
In conversation, the husband asks his wife why she cut off the end of the meat.

She replies, "I don't truly know, but my mother always does that!" The curious wife calls her mother and inquires. Her mother says, "I don't truly know, but my mother always does that!" Luckily for our story, the grandmother is still living! Grandmother is asked why she cuts off the end of the meat. The grandmother begins to laugh, "Honey, I cut off the end of the meat because my pan was way too little for the roast!"

**Practical Reflection 5: Influential Experiences Impacting
Your Cultural Identity**

You need to familiarize and assess your personal ideas about all of the attitudes and beliefs, knowledge, and skills guidelines. For now, please select at least one personal response that you would be willing to share with your classmates. For example, what cultural background and experiences have influenced you and your beliefs about people and the psychological processes?

_____

_____

_____

_____

Culturally skilled counselors possess knowledge and understanding about how oppression, racism, discrimination, and stereotyping affect them personally and in their work. It is important for you to discuss and understand your situations with oppression, stereotyping, and so on. All of us have experienced some aspect of discrimination.

The frequency of the events and your responses and reactions to them help you to understand better the process of oppression. Understanding is the first step; acting and choosing to intervene in the process is another phase.

Culturally skilled counselors possess knowledge about their social impact on others. They are knowledgeable about communication style differences, how their style may clash with or foster the counseling process with persons of color or those different from themselves, and how to anticipate the impact it may have on others. In several of the previous chapters, you have been encouraged to ask for feedback during your supervision sessions. Your supervision is a wonderful opportunity to ask others you trust about your social impact on others. Supervision provides a relatively safe environment to discuss your reactions and responses to those who are different. Each of us does tend to react in our style to differences.

Practical Reflection 6: Stereotype Development

Based on the knowledge from this chapter and your personal experiences, how have many of your stereotypes developed? Everyone has biases and prejudices. Try discussing yours with your classmates and supervisor.

_____

_____

_____

_____

_____

Skill Guidelines

Counselors seek out educational, culturally skilled consultative, and training experiences to improve their understanding and effectiveness in working with culturally different populations. If you believe this guideline is true, then demonstrate your belief through your actions by doing something to improve your understanding and effectiveness.

By this time in your graduate education, most of you have taken a course on diversity. If you have not taken a course on diversity, this is the time. Attending a diversity fair, going out to lunch with someone who is different from you, and having a party with a diverse group of people are steps in the right direction.

Culturally skilled counselors are constantly seeking to understand themselves as racial and cultural beings and are actively seeking a nonracist and nonoppressive identity. You have a chance to demonstrate your opposition to discrimination of any type. Be sure to work with others to fight against it. You can begin small by not laughing at an insensitive joke or asserting your thoughts during a meeting where an oppressive statement was made. Again begin with small gestures to spread the word against discrimination.

Awareness, knowledge, and skills are not enough. None of these components is important if those beliefs are not practiced. For example, most of us know how important exercise and proper nutrition are but do neither. Clients understand what could be done to create new possibilities and effect success and yet do not do it. Here is a website that was developed to increase awareness, knowledge, and skills, and to recognize the knowing–doing gap and promote action to close this gap: http://www.coedu.usf.edu/zalaquett/kdg.html. We need to focus more on how knowing can be transformed into doing (Zalaquett & Akdogan, 2011).

**Practical Reflection 7: Proactive Experiences in
Multicultural Development**

What have you done in the past and what are you doing presently to
become skilled as a multicultural helping professional?

_____

_____

_____

_____

_____

Models of Racial Identity Development

Three models will be presented to assist you in better understanding the manner
in which racial identities may be developed. As you read each model, integrate
the previous information into this material on racial identity development.

People of Color Racial Identity Developmental Model: Helms described
five ego identity statuses in the People of Color Racial Identity Developmental
Model (POC/RID):

1. Conformity, where you believe that other cultures are superior;
2. Encounter/dissonance, when a racial situation causes dissonance of previ-
    ously held beliefs;
3. Immersion/emersion, when identified culture is idealized and White cul-
    ture is criticized;
4. Internalization, when reappraisals of selective cultures are organized; and
5. Integration, when you become less reactive and the identity comprises the
    benefits of cultures involved. Integration allows you to make a commitment
    to advocate against any racial discrimination.

White Racial Identity Developmental Model: In the White Racial Identity
Developmental Model (W/RID) you would go through a series of ego statuses
or expressions of current racial identity. Each status has an Information Processing Strategy (IPS) that allows you to reflect on the information given that
is race related. The information could be attitudinal, behavioral, or affective.
If you are White, Helms stated that moving through the six statuses requires an
awareness first that racism does exist and then "abandonment of entitlement"
and personal superiority must be addressed (Helms, 1995, p. 184).

During Abandonment of Racism, there are three statuses involved on the continuum:

1. Contact with others and recognition of racism;
2. Disintegration of current beliefs about diversity and guilt surrounding racial issues; and
3. Reintegration, which includes idealization of White status and confusion with racial issues.

In the second phase, you become more actively involved in Defining a Nonracist Identity. There are three statuses in which you must evolve:

1. Pseudo-independence from your race but still a cognitive commitment to your race;
2. Immersion/emersion, which may include racial activism; and
3. Autonomy, which allows you to move away from your privileged status and work toward the benefits of a diverse society.

Helms' Racial Identity Interaction Process Model (Helms, 1995) emphasizes even more the importance of your knowing your racial identity status because it does interact with the racial identity status of your client. Helms and Cook (1999) believe that the "counselor's expression of her or his underlying racial identity statuses influences his or her reaction to the client, and the client's underlying statuses, in turn, influence his or her reactions to the counselor" (p. 180). Pederson (2002) articulates that you have thousands of "culture teachers" such as friends, family, enemies, and images that continually influence your racial identity. It is a mistake not to recognize these internalized influences.

Thompson and Carter (2012) applaud the ground-breaking work of Helms (1995) who postulates that there are three possible, distinct counseling relationships that can occur as racial identity statuses emerge: (1) parallel, (2) regressive, and (3) progressive. Parallel relationships occur when the helping professional and client have similar worldviews. The opposite happens in regressive counseling relationships, where the client has a more mature racial identity than the counselor and conflicts continue to erupt.

The final progressive relationship occurs when the helping professional has a more advanced racial identity than the client. Although this counseling relationship can still involve challenges and conflict, the counselor can more readily facilitate growth in the client.

Practical Reflection 8: Racial Identity Development

Read the three racial identity models and select one model that fits you
and then discuss your racial development.

_____

_____

_____

_____

An Example Approach for Enhancing Diversity Appreciation:
A Diversity Simulation

According to a seminal article by Russell and Berger (1993), diversity simulations can be powerful and effective tools for teaching people to discover
personal attitudes toward inclusivity. Often when you engage in multicultural
training, much-needed information is given, but there seem to be few "activating events" to get you out of the intellectual viewing of diversity and into your
personal worldview (Russell-Chapin & Stoner, 1995).

One of the main reasons simulations work is that you are given no verbal
instructions or information about the experience, so you must use your worldview to make meaning of the simulation. Frequently, the only way to make
meaning is to enter the experience with preconceived perceptions from prior
life experiences and filters.

There is a simulation that we use in the classroom and during consultations,
and every time people react in the same way. They are surprised, angry, curious,
confused, and embarrassed! A classic diversity simulation is called "The Albatross"
created by Batchelder and Warner (1977). Russell-Chapin and Stoner (1995)
emphasize the need for ambiguity when presenting "The Albatross" simulation.
The less information that is provided, the more you have to rely on your filters
to understand this ambiguous situation.

Imagine this experience for yourself.

You walk into a dimly lit room where a woman dressed in an ornate gown is
sitting on the floor. A man is sitting in a chair next to her. There are four more
empty chairs arranged in a semi-circle. A candle and incense are burning, and
unusual music is playing quietly. The entire environmental setup is different
and out of character and context.

The man rises and begins to select male participants. There are no verbal
instructions or words spoken. The men are individually directed to sit in chairs.
The head male grunts to each man to sit. He then sits and makes four clicking
noises. The woman rises to her feet, and she begins to select women to join the

group. Each woman is nonverbally asked to come, but before sitting on the floor, shoes must be removed and placed in front of the chairs.

The head male grunts again and demonstrates how to place their hands on the women's heads and push the heads to the floor. The participants imitate the facilitator and push the head to the floor of the female kneeling to their right.

Another set of clicking noises is heard, and the head woman rises and brings a bowl of water. Each man must wash their hands, but the women do not.

There is a head pushing at the end of each aspect of the tradition.

Next the head facilitator clicks and the head woman quickly responds by feeding each male an unfamiliar edible food with a toothpick. It is served by the head female. Then the women all eat but they serve themselves.

A similar round of events happens with drinking from one chalice.

The head female serves the cup to the lips of the males while the females all drink the liquid one by one. The final component of the simulation occurs when the male clicks and both rise. The women are directed to display their feet and the two facilitators walk around observing the women's feet. One woman is selected and directed to rise. She is joined by the head male, and they walk outside!

Following the simulation, the processing of the experiences begins.

The facilitators offer a four-tiered system of organizing the activating event. First you are asked to describe what each of you observed.

Inevitably people respond by interpreting what the performance meant, not describing what they saw or observed. For example, you might say the performance was an example of subservience of women rather than describing that men sat on chairs, and the women sat on the floor.

Once the group understands how to describe actual events and not first react with emotions and assumptions, then the facilitators move to the second tier.

In this next part of the discussion, you are asked to share how the performance made you feel. Typically, many people from the group, whether they are participants or observers, are uncomfortable, angry, and confused.

The third tier asks for a discussion of meaning. Usually, the group states that it is a ritual of some sort where men are dominant and women are inferior.

Finally, the facilitators reveal that this simulation represents a demonstration of a matriarchal society, not a patriarchal one. Uniformly, there is surprise, confusion, and embarrassment! According to Russell-Chapin and Stoner (1995), most individuals desire immediate answers to unfamiliar events and ascribing interpretation or meaning from individual perceptual sets provides more comfort and security. What they do not acknowledge or realize is that this interpretation is filtered from personal perceptual sets and frequently is not accurate for another culture or person. When participants take the risk to describe accurately what was seen, they are ready to take the next step by asking questions about possible meanings.

The facilitators assist each of you to then go through the first three tiers of the organization system to describe what you saw and make that perceptual switch, now that you know it is an example of a matriarchal system. Each observation can be taken one by one and processed. For example, why would men be fed with toothpicks and not the women? Possibly, the men must be fed first to ensure that the food is safe so that the women can eat it! The perceptual switch can be made for each observation.

Practical Reflection 9: The Albatross Simulation

As you read the Albatross script, what were your first impressions? How were you feeling? How are you responding once you understand that perceptual switch?

_____

_____

_____

_____

_____

The Albatross Simulation is just one category of activating events, but any activity that can assist you or others to "get out of your heads and into your personal belief system" is a powerful mechanism to learn and integrate diversity into your life. These types of experiences can become a catalyst for change and are a must if diversity is to be lived and acted upon (Russell-Chapin & Stoner, 1995). In the next section, your second case study will unfold. Take risks as you read the case study. Begin to see how understanding diversity will assist you in better serving this client.

Example Interview: The Case of Darryl

Darryl was introduced to you in the Preface. You may want to review his history again. He entered Lori's life much later in her professional counseling career. Their first counseling encounter had Darryl in a dissociative state with only a small amount of the initial counseling interview occurring.

Lori did join Darryl on the floor, and toward the end of the session they processed the happenings of the first meeting. Darryl requested a second appointment two days later. Darryl is a 45-year-old African American man.

We are presenting your third case study in this chapter for two reasons.

Begin viewing the Case of Darryl with a cumulative perspective from Chapters 1 through 5, plus add to your worldview the ideas of additional related multicultural issues.

You may want to use another CIRF and continue to classify and process the interviewing skills. There is a blank copy of the CIRF in Resource R. Again, you are welcome to compare your classifications with our CIRF in Resource S. See Resource T for the entire script with skill identifications. Be sure to begin to view the Cases of Stephen and Rachel from a multicultural aspect as well.

The Case of Darryl

(1) LORI: *Hi, Darryl, I am glad you came today.*

(2) DARRYL: *Me, too, I guess.*

(3) LORI: *From your voice and posture, you sound a bit ambivalent about being here.*

(4) DARRYL: *I do want to be here because I have so much to share, but I can't believe I was so scared that I began talking in tongues. I do that sometimes. My father was an evangelist. I am glad I didn't scare you off.*

(5) LORI: *You didn't scare me off. I know very little about talking in tongues. You may have to teach me more, but the two of us can make this a safe place to discuss anything you want. Last time I didn't take the time to explain how I do counseling. Perhaps this would be a good time.*

(6) DARRYL: *Yes, I want to know more about the way you do counseling. So far, you are doing OK. You know, I have seen lots of other professionals, so I probably know the scoop. I like the fact you were sitting on the floor with me last time, though.*

(7) LORI: *I appreciate you giving me feedback, Darryl. As I will do the same with you. The more the two of us can become a team and build a counseling relationship, the better your counseling will go.*

(8) DARRYL: *You want me to work with you? Maybe I don't know the scoop, cuz most of the time people just tell me what to do.*

(9) LORI: *Darryl, I will not tell you what to do. My job is to listen to your concerns and assist you with your desired changes. I do not have the answers, but I can help you through the process of change.*

(10) DARRYL: *I thought you would have the answers!*

(11) LORI: *You have the answers, Darryl, to your problems. I can help you discover the needed answers by guiding you to the many possible solutions.*

(12) DARRYL: *I would like to find some solutions. I seem to have lots of problems.*

(13) LORI: *We all have problems, Darryl. Let's talk about your problems today, and by the end of this session, we will set several counseling goals to give us some counseling direction. How does that sound to you?*

(14) DARRYL: *Strange, but good.*

(15) LORI: *Darryl, what do you want to work on today in counseling?*

(16) DARRYL: *My life seems to be falling apart. I am struggling in my marriage, and I am having a difficult time keeping my job intact. The most frustrating thing is that I have been in this place before.*

(17) LORI: *You are explaining to me that your marital problems and job difficulties are not new experiences. How discouraging that must be.*

(18) DARRYL: *Yes, it is. It is deeper than discouragement, though, this time it seems hopeless.*

(19) LORI: *I am sorry, Darryl, that you are in such a desperate place in your life. (Reflection of Meaning)*

(20) DARRYL: *Thanks for being so kind and understanding. My wife, Sophia, thinks I am a bum. This is the third job I have had since our marriage of seven years. Our son, Michael, is four, and he loves to draw pictures. He drew a picture of me. I don't know exactly what it means, but his depiction of me made me very sad. He drew me shouting with a mouthful of teeth.*

(21) LORI: *Whatever is happening in your life is keeping you from having a healthy marriage and job. Sophia finds your work history unreliable, and Michael thinks you are angry some of the time. Is that correct?*

(22) DARRYL: *Absolutely correct.*

(23) LORI: *What do you want to do about all this, Darryl?*

(24) DARRYL: *I don't know. You are the counselor, you tell me.*

(25) LORI: *It probably would be easier if I could tell you what to do, but I can't, Darryl. Remember I don't have the answers to your life.*

(26) DARRYL: *Now you are not helpful.*

(27) LORI: *Help comes in many forms. If all your old ways of thinking and feelings have not worked, then let's try a different approach. Darryl, tell me the last time your life was not falling apart.*

(28) DARRYL: *(There is a long pause, and Darryl begins to stare. I thought he might go into another trance-like, dissociative state.)*

(29) LORI: *Darryl, it is okay if you need to go away. I will be here when you get back. You need to know that you are safe in here.*

(30) DARRYL: *(After several minutes of silence) I have been going away for many years. Sophia hates it and screams at me.*

(31) LORI: *My guess is that Sophia may be scared too and doesn't know what to do either.*

(32) DARRYL: *I think she just hates me because I am a no good bum.*

(33) LORI: *Darryl, I appreciate your choosing, on some level, not to dissociate. That makes our work here easier. You will be okay in here. Let's focus again on a time when your life was not falling apart.*

(34) DARRYL: *Well, it was many years ago. I had decided that I would be single forever. I had my dog, Alex, and a good job as a nurse practitioner. My past was behind me. I felt good helping others and working in a doctor's office.*

(35) LORI: *I want to make sure I understand. Years ago, you remembered a time when your life was together. You enjoyed your single lifestyle, your dog, Alex, and your nursing job. Helping other people seemed the right thing to do. Is that accurate?*

(36) DARRYL: *Yes. Even hearing you talk about my old life makes me happy and sad.*

(37) LORI: *There are those ambivalent feelings again, Darryl. Life has both happy and sad times doesn't it?*

(38) DARRYL: *Yes, but I hate sad times.*

(39) LORI: *What do you hate about sad times, Darryl?*

(40) DARRYL: *In my life there have been more sad times than not.*

(41) LORI: *(I decided to be silent for at least two minutes!) What were some of your saddest times, Darryl?*

(42) DARRYL: *(Tears were welling in his eyes.) My sad times are too sad to share!*

(43) LORI: *You do not have to share them, Darryl. (We sat in silence.)*

(44) DARRYL: *I want to share them with you, though.*

(45) LORI: *You are very brave, Darryl. Tell me about your sad times.*

(46) DARRYL: *I was a medic in Viet Nam. I saw such devastation, but I honestly was doing okay. Knowing I was helpful seemed to make the atrocities a little better. I helped many people, and I saw many men die.*

(47) LORI: *I can't imagine what you saw and lived through, but the fact that you saved so many people helped you through many difficult times.*

(48) DARRYL: *I guess so. One night my best friend, Stan, and I were together. Stan didn't have many friends, and he was kind of little. The other guys made fun of him. I really liked Stan. His friendship made the war more tolerable.*

(49) LORI: *Sounds as if you were a very good friend and that you helped people in many different ways.*

(50) DARRYL: *NO! I was not a good friend. I am done here. I need to go!*

(51) LORI: *Darryl, if you need to go, you can. Before you go, I want to give you an observation. When you were talking about Stan initially, your voice was soft and almost dreamy. When I suggested that you were a good friend to Stan, your voice became loud and aggressive. What are those voice changes about?*

(52) DARRYL: *I really need to go away.*

(53) LORI: *It is okay that you go. We will see each other again.*
There are many ways of "going away," aren't there, Darryl?

(54) DARRYL: *You are really a pain in the neck.*

(55) LORI: *I can be a pain in the neck. I believe I am in good hands, though.*

(56) DARRYL: *Okay, I won't go away, but you are not in good hands.*

(57)   LORI: *You sound like a very competent nurse and friend, Darryl. Tell me why I am not in good hands.*

(58)   DARRYL: *(Darryl begins shouting.) You are not in good hands because these hands did not stop things I should have stopped. Are you happy now!*

(59)   LORI: *I am not happy, Darryl, but I truly appreciate you continuing to talk to me about such difficult times.*

(60)   DARRYL: *I don't like to talk about my past. I haven't spoken a word of it to anyone, not even to my wife, Sophia.*

(61)   LORI: *Then many memories are buried very deep.*

(62)   DARRYL: *(Darryl begins to weep.)*

(63)   LORI: *This must be very painful and devastating.*

(64)   DARRYL: *It is more than devastating. It should not have happened.*
       For years I wished I had been able to stop the hurt that we caused so many people.

(65)   LORI: *So for all these past years, you have carried the burdens that you saw.*

(66)   DARRYL: *Yes, I feel guilty for living. I have moments when I am happy with Sophia and Michael, but they are fleeting.*

(67)   LORI: *Tell me what you should have stopped.*

(68)   DARRYL: *One night, Stan and I were in a village, and we heard sobbing and screaming. We approached the huts carefully and saw our own soldiers raping the village women. Stan and I told them to stop, but several of the men yelled at us to get lost and mind our own business. That night I went back to our temporary quarters, and I began having horrible nightmares! Those dreams still haunt me.*

(69)   LORI: *That must have been frightening. And I would like to hear about your dreams, Darryl.*

(70)   DARRYL: *That is just it. I am not sure they were dreams.*

(71)   LORI: *What do you mean you are not sure they were dreams?*

(72)   DARRYL: *This is so difficult to say . . . I have been trying to piece together things.*

(73)   LORI: *Tell me about those things, Darryl.*

(74)   DARRYL: *Well, I believe someone close to me sexually hurt me as a child. Bits and pieces come back to me, whether it be in dreams or vivid pictures in my head. I just don't know.*

(75)   LORI: *There are so many of the dreams and pictures in your head that you believe they might be connected to a time when someone may have sexually hurt you. Is that right?*

(76)   DARRYL: *I think so.*

(77)   LORI: *Is it possible that the night in Viet Nam triggered some of your current behaviors and feelings?*

(78)   DARRYL: *I hadn't put the two together, but it makes some sense, as that is when the dreams began. I just don't want to believe that someone close could sexually harm me.*

(79)   LORI: *You and I do not know if that is true or not. We may never know the truth, but that is not the issue here. Whether the sexual abuse occurred or not is not the*

problem. We need to create a way for you to handle your present situation and your many perceptions about your past. Since we cannot change the past, one of our counseling goals is to change your perceptions of that past. That we can do.

(80) DARRYL: *That doesn't sound easy.*

(81) LORI: *It is not easy, but we can do it together as a team. How does that sound to you?*

(82) DARRYL: *Nothing else has been working, so it is worth a try. Where do we start?*

(83) LORI: *You and I have already started, Darryl. You will never be the same again, you have bravely faced the beast today in whatever form it appears.*

(84) DARRYL: *It feels like such a long haul.*

(85) LORI: *It will be worth your effort, Darryl. The outcome may be that you learn new coping mechanisms to deal with your past and present.*

(86) DARRYL: *I want my life to be different. I want Sophia and Michael to have a husband and father who can cope better with whatever life brings.*

(87) LORI: *I believe you can do that, Darryl. You even coped differently here. Talk to me about how you coped differently today.*

(88) DARRYL: *(long silence) I guess I did cope differently today. I felt strong enough to tell you things I have never shared . . . And I somehow did not "go away" when you asked me difficult questions.*

(89) LORI: *So you have at least two new coping skills to take with you to assist in the week to come. As a homework assignment for the next week, please share with Sophia whatever comes into your mind. I have a feeling she will appreciate sharing more than "going away." Also please spend at least 15 minutes a day with Michael doing some fun activity.*

(90) DARRYL: *What if I shout at Michael again?*

(91) LORI: *You will shout again, but this time Michael will also have quality time to remember. Darryl, how committed are you to these two homework goals?*

(92) DARRYL: *I believe I can accomplish these two goals by sharing with Sophia and playing more with Michael.*

(93) LORI: *So you are committed to these goals. Before we go, I want to ask one more question. What kind of nurse were you in counseling today?*

(94) DARRYL: *That is a funny question . . . But I guess I was a helpful and brave medic and nurse.*

(95) LORI: *You applied your skills as a helping nurse practitioner to yourself! Wow! You shared and faced your fears. Darryl, when do you want to come back to counseling?*

(96) DARRYL: *Do you have something available early in the week?*

(97) LORI: *There's an opening on Tuesday. See you at 10:00. Enjoy those competent nursing skills.*

Darryl and Lori continued to counsel together over a period of two years. During that time, Darryl was hospitalized once for severe depression.

Working conjointly with a psychiatrist, Darryl was placed on an antidepressant, and then continued in counseling with Lori. His prognosis was good, and he went back to work as a nurse practitioner.

The Case of Darryl: A Multicultural Perspective

As you begin to analyze the Case of Darryl, many of the dimensions suggested in this chapter come to life. Darryl and Lori had to understand the differences of race, gender, age, life experiences, religion, and coping strategies.

It has been suggested that you need to address the racial differences soon after developing a counseling relationship (Sanders-Thompson, 1994). Notice that Lori did address the differences between religious experiences at the beginning of the session. Review the script beginning with statement number 5.

Practical Reflection 10: Response to the Case of Darryl

After reading the script from the Case of Darryl, describe your thoughts and feelings concerning the cultural differences between Darryl and Lori. Share your responses with your colleagues.

_____

_____

_____

_____

Soon after, Lori chose to begin working on the symptoms that were debilitating Darryl the most. Once Darryl's symptoms of depression and dissociation were addressed and maintained, Lori and Darryl began work on racial identity concerns together.

Summary and Personal Integration

In this chapter, you were introduced to several approaches to assist you in becoming a culturally competent helping professional:

• Multicultural dimensions and multicultural competencies were presented to assist you in better understanding yourself and counseling others.
• The RESPECTFUL Cube was diagrammed to integrate you into the environment.
• Models of racial identity and the interaction process between client and helping professional were described.

- An example of an educational diversity simulation was presented.
- The third case study of the book was presented to continue demonstrating the variety of issues facing you on your helping professional journey.

Taking the information from this chapter into your daily practice will not happen all at once. Rather it is best to select one or two areas, focus on them, and see what it says to you when you see clients. Remember these key components when putting your awareness, knowledge, and skills into action:

1. Warmth and listening are basic to the relationship.
2. Be open and willing to discuss multicultural differences.
3. Avoid stereotyping and recognize the important of the intersection of multiple cultural identities. We are all cultural beings with many dimensions, and many voices have influenced us.
4. Perhaps most important, avoid the constant emphasis on problem-solving and "what's wrong with you and your situation." Yes, hear the problems and concerns fully and carefully encourage emotional understanding.
5. Always search for strengths within and without the session. Help the client use those strengths as they build the future. Optimism and the hope factor need to become much more central to the helping professions.
6. In short, don't just search for a return to normal. Always seek to send your clients out with awareness of their strengths and their ability to become themselves in the future.

Practical Reflection 11: Integration

Which Chapter 6 constructs, models, and techniques will assist you the most in becoming a culturally competent helping professional?

_____
_____
_____
_____

Resource R

Counseling Interview Rating Form

Counselor: _____	Date: _____
Observer: _____	Recording Number: _____
Observer: _____	Audio or Video; please circle
Supervisor: _____	Session Number: _____

For each of the following specific criteria demonstrated, make a frequency marking every time the skill is demonstrated. Then assign points for consistent skill mastery using the ratings scales below. Active mastery of each skill marked by an X receives a score of 2 and should be seen consistently on every recording. List any observations, comments, strengths, and weaknesses in the space provided. Providing actual counselor phrases is helpful when offering feedback.

Ivey Mastery Ratings

3   Teach the skill to clients (teaching mastery only)
2   Use the skill with specific impact on client (active mastery)
1   Use and/or identify the counseling skill (basic mastery)

To receive an A on a recording at least 52–58 points must be earned.
To receive a B on a recording at least 46–51 points must be earned.
To receive a C on a recording at least 41–45 points must be earned.

Specific Criteria	Frequency	Comments	Skill Mastery Rating
A. OPENING/DEVELOPING RAPPORT			
1. Greeting X			
2. Role Definition/Expectation			
3. Administrative Tasks			
4. Beginning X			
B. EXPLORATION PHASE/DEFINING THE PROBLEM MICRO SKILLS			
1. Empathy/Rapport			
2. Respect			
3. Nonverbal Matching X			
4. Minimal Encourager X			
5. Paraphrasing X			
6. Pacing/Leading X			
7. Verbal Tracking X			
8. Reflect Feeling X			
9. Reflect Meaning X			
10. Clarifications X			
11. Open-ended Questions X			
12. Summarization X			
13. Behavioral Description X			
14. Appropriate Closed Question X			
15. Perception Check X			
16. Silence X			
17. Focusing X			
18. Feedback X			

(Continued)

Specific Criteria	Frequency	Comments	Skill Mastery Rating

C. PROBLEM-SOLVING SKILLS/ DEFINING SKILLS

1. Definition of Goals
2. Exploration/Understanding of
   Concerns   X
3. Development/Evaluation of
   Alternatives   X
4. Implement Alternative
5. Special Techniques
6. Process Counseling

D. ACTION PHASE/CONFRONTING INCONGRUITIES

1. Immediacy
2. Self-disclosure
3. Confrontation
4. Directives
5. Logical Consequences
6. Interpretation

E. CLOSING/GENERALIZATION

1. Summarization of Content/
   Feeling   X
2. Review of Plan   X
3. Rescheduling
4. Termination of Session
5. Evaluation of Session   X
6. Follow-up   X

F. PROFESSIONALISM

1. Developmental Level Match
2. Ethics
3. Professional (punctual, attire, etc.)

G. Strengths:

Area(s) for Improvement

TOTAL _____

Resource S: Author's Quantification of CIRF Summarization and Processing Skills of the Case of Darryl

Counseling Interview Rating Form

Counselor: __Lori Russell-Chapin__ Date: __November, 2015__

Observer: _____ Recording Number: __2__

Observer: _____ Audio or Video; please circle

Supervisor: __Allen Ivey__ Session Number: __II__

For each of the following specific criteria demonstrated, make a frequency marking every time the skill is demonstrated. Then assign points for consistent skill mastery using the ratings scales below. Active mastery of each skill marked by an X receives a score of 2 and should be seen consistently on every recording. List any observations, comments, strengths, and weaknesses in the space provided. Providing actual counselor phrases is helpful when offering feedback.

Ivey Mastery Ratings

3   Teach the skill to clients (teaching mastery only)
2   Use the skill with specific impact on client (active mastery)
1   Use and/or identify the counseling skill (basic mastery)

To receive an A on a recording at least 52–58 points must be earned.
To receive a B on a recording at least 46–51 points must be earned.
To receive a C on a recording at least 41–45 points must be earned.

Specific Criteria	Frequency	Comments	Skill Mastery Rating
A. OPENING/DEVELOPING RAPPORT			
1. Greeting X	I	"Hi Darryl, I am glad you came today"	2
2. Role Definition/Expectation	I	"I appreciate your giving me feedback, Darryl. As I will do the same with you. The more the two of us can become a team and build a counseling relationship, the better your counseling will go."	2
3. Administrative Tasks			
4. Beginning X	I	"Darryl, what do you want to work on today in counseling?"	2

(Continued)

Specific Criteria	Frequency	Comments	Skill Mastery Rating
B. EXPLORATION PHASE/ DEFINING THE PROBLEM MICRO SKILLS	III	"Darryl, it is okay if you need to go away. I will be here when you get back. You need to know that you are safe in here."	2
1. Empathy/Rapport			
2. Respect			
3. Nonverbal Matching X			
4. Minimal Encourager X			
5. Paraphrasing X	III	"So for all these past years, you have carried around the burdens that you saw."	2
6. Pacing/Leading X	II	"We all have problems, Darryl. Let's talk about your problems today, and by the end of this session, we will set several counseling goals to give us some counseling direction. How does that sound to you?"	
7. Verbal Tracking X	III	"You didn't scare me off. The two of us can make this a safe place to discuss anything you want. Last time I didn't take the time to explain how I do counseling. Perhaps this would be a good time."	2
8. Reflect Feeling X	III	"You are explaining to me that your marital problems and job difficulties are not new experiences. How discouraging that must be."	2
9. Reflect Meaning X	III	"I am sorry, Darryl, that you are in such a desperate place in your life."	2
10. Clarifications X			
11. Open-ended Questions X	IIII	"What do you want to do about all this, Darryl?"	2
12. Summarization X	II	"I want to make sure I understand. Years ago, you remembered a time when your life was together. You enjoyed your single lifestyle, your dog, Alex, and your nursing job. Helping other people seemed the right thing to do. Is that accurate?"	2
13. Behavioral Description X	I	"From your voice and posture, you sound a bit ambivalent about being here."	2

(*Continued*)

(Continued)

Specific Criteria	Frequency	Comments	Skill Mastery Rating
14. Appropriate Closed X Question	I	"It is okay that you go. We will see each other again. There are many ways of 'going away,' aren't there, Darryl?"	2
15. Perception Check X	I	"Whatever is happening in your life is keeping you from having a healthy marriage and job. Sophia finds your work history unreliable, and Michael thinks you are angry some of the time. Is that correct?"	2
16. Silence X	I	(I decided to be silent for at least 2 minutes) "What were some of your saddest times, Darryl?"	2
17. Focusing X	I	"Darryl, I appreciate your choosing, on some level, not to dissociate. That makes our work here easier. You will be okay in here. Let's focus again on a time when your life was not falling apart."	2
18. Feedback X	I	"There are those ambivalent feelings again, Darryl. Life has both happy and sad times, doesn't it?"	2
C. PROBLEM-SOLVING SKILLS/ DEFINING SKILLS			
1. Definition of Goals	I	"So you have at least two new coping skills to take with you to assist in the week to come. As a homework assignment for the next week, please share with Sophia whatever comes into your mind. I have a feeling she will appreciate sharing more than 'going away.' Also please spend at least 15 minutes a day with Michael doing some fun activity."	2
2. Exploration/Understanding of Concerns X	II	"What do you hate about sad times, Darryl?"	2

(*Continued*)

Specific Criteria	Frequency	Comments	Skill Mastery Rating
3. Development/Evaluation of Alternatives X	I	"You will shout again, but this time Michael will also have quality time to remember. Darryl, how committed are you to these two homework goals?"	2
4. Implement Alternative			2
5. Special Techniques	I	"You do not have to share them, Darryl"	2
6. Process Counseling	I	"You and I have already started, Darryl. You will never be the same again, you have bravely faced the beast today in whatever form it appears."	2
D. ACTION PHASE/ CONFRONTING INCONGRUITIES			
1. Immediacy			
2. Self-disclosure			
3. Confrontation			
4. Directives	I	"Help comes in many forms. If all your old ways of thinking and feelings have not worked, then let's try a different approach. Darryl, tell me the last time your life was not falling apart."	2
5. Logical Consequences			
6. Interpretation	I	"My guess is that Sophia may be scared too and doesn't know what to do either."	2
E. CLOSING/ GENERALIZATION			
1. Summarization of Content/ Feeling X	I	"You applied your skills as a helping nurse practitioner to yourself! Wow! You shared and faced your fears. Darryl, when do you want to come back to counseling?"	2
2. Review of Plan X			
3. Rescheduling	I	"When do you want to come back to counseling?"	
4. Termination of Session			

(*Continued*)

(Continued)

Specific Criteria	Frequency	Comments	Skill Mastery Rating
5. Evaluation of Session X	I	"You even coped differently here. Talk to me about how you coped differently today."	2
6. Follow-up			
F. PROFESSIONALISM			
1. Developmental Level Match	I	"You are being very brave, Darryl. Tell me about your sad times."	2
2. Ethics			
3. Professional (punctual, attire, etc.)			

G. Strengths:
1. Your microcounseling skills were accomplished with intention and mastery.
2. You took your client's strengths as a medic and applied those skills to his current concerns.

Area(s) for Improvement:
1. Be sure to deal with the multicultural issues as soon as your client is developmentally ready.
2. Continue to attend supervision sessions for added resources and assistance.

Total: 56

Resource T: The Case of Darryl with Skill Identification

The Case of Darryl

(1)   LORI: *Hi, Darryl, I am glad you came today.* (Greeting)

(2)   DARRYL: *Me, too, I guess.*

(3)   LORI: *From your voice and posture, you sound a bit ambivalent about being here.* (Behavioral description)

(4)   DARRYL: *I do want to be here because I have so much to share, but I can't believe I was so scared that I began talking in tongues. I do that sometimes. My father was an evangelist. I am glad I didn't scare you off.*

(5)   LORI: *You didn't scare me off. I know very little about talking in tongues. You will have to teach me more, but the two of us can make this a safe place to discuss anything you want. Last time I didn't take the time to explain how I do counseling. Perhaps this would be a good time.* (Verbal tracking; role definition)

(6) DARRYL: *Yes, I want to know more about the way you do counseling. So far, you are doing OK. You know, I have seen lots of other professionals, so I probably know the scoop. I like the fact you were sitting on the floor with me last time, though.*

(7) LORI: *I appreciate your giving me feedback, Darryl. As I will do the same with you. The more the two of us can become a team and build a counseling relationship, the better your counseling will go.* (Role definition/expectation)

(8) DARRYL: *You want me to work with you? Maybe I don't know the scoop, cuz most of the time people just tell me what to do.*

(9) LORI: *Darryl, I will not tell you what to do. My job is to listen to your concerns and assist you with your desired changes. I do not have the answers, but I can help you through the process of change.* (Role definition)

(10) DARRYL: *I thought you would have the answers!*

(11) LORI: *You have the answers, Darryl, to your problems. I can help you discover the needed answers by guiding you to the many possible solutions.* (Role definition)

(12) DARRYL: *I would like to find some solutions. I seem to have lots of problems.*

(13) LORI: *We all have problems, Darryl. Let's talk about your problems today, and by the end of this session, we will set several counseling goals to give us some counseling direction. How does that sound to you?* (Pacing; goal-setting; open-ended question)

(14) DARRYL: *Strange, but good.*

(15) LORI: *Darryl, what do you want to work on today in counseling?* (Beginning)

(16) DARRYL: *My life seems to be falling apart. I am struggling in my marriage, and I am having a difficult time keeping my job intact. The most frustrating thing is that I have been in this place before.*

(17) LORI: *You are explaining to me that your marital problems and job difficulties are not new experiences. How discouraging that must be.* (Paraphrasing; reflection of feeling)

(18) DARRYL: *Yes, it is. It is deeper than discouragement, though, this time it seems hopeless.*

(19) LORI: *I am sorry, Darryl, that you are in such a desperate place in your life.* (Reflection of meaning)

(20) DARRYL: *Thanks for being so kind and understanding. My wife, Sophia, thinks I am a bum. This is the third job I have had since our marriage of 7 years. Our son, Michael, is 4, and he loves to draw pictures. He drew a picture of me. I don't know exactly what it means, but his depiction of me made me very sad. He drew me shouting with a mouthful of teeth.*

(21) LORI: *Whatever is happening in your life is keeping you from having a healthy marriage and job. Sophia finds your work history unreliable, and Michael thinks you are angry some of the time. Is that correct?* (Paraphrase; perception check)

(22) DARRYL: *Absolutely correct.*

(23) LORI: *What do you want to do about all this, Darryl?* (Open-ended question)

(24) DARRYL: *I don't know. You are the counselor, you tell me.*

(25) LORI: *It probably would be easier if I could tell you what to do, but I can't, Darryl. Remember I don't have the answers to your life.* (Focusing; role definition)

(26) DARRYL: *Now you are not being helpful.*

(27) LORI: *Help comes in many forms. If all your old ways of thinking and feelings have not worked, then let's try a different approach. Darryl, tell me the last time your life was not falling apart.* (Directive)

(28) DARRYL: *(There is a long pause, and Darryl begins to stare. I thought he might go into another trance-like, dissociative state.)*

(29) LORI: *Darryl, it is okay if you need to go away. I will be here when you get back. You need to know that you are safe in here.*
(Empathy/rapport; respect)

(30) DARRYL: *(After several minutes of silence) I have been going away for many years. Sophia hates it and screams at me.*

(31) LORI: *My guess is that Sophia may be scared too and doesn't know what to do either.* (Reflection of feeling; interpretation)

(32) DARRYL: *I think she just hates me because I am a no-good bum.*

(33) LORI: *Darryl, I appreciate your choosing, on some level, not to dissociate. That makes our work here easier. You will be okay in here. Let's focus again on a time when your life was not falling apart.* (Focusing)

(34) DARRYL: *Well, it was many years ago. I had decided that I would be single forever. I had my dog, Alex, and a good job as a nurse practitioner. My past was behind me. I felt good helping others and working in a doctor's office.*

(35) LORI: *I want to make sure I understand. Years ago, you remembered a time when your life was together. You enjoyed your single lifestyle, your dog, Alex, and your nursing job. Helping other people seemed the right thing to do. Is that accurate?* (Summarization; perception check)

(36) DARRYL: *Yes. Even hearing you talk about my old life makes me happy and sad.*

(37) LORI: *There are those ambivalent feelings again, Darryl. Life has both happy and sad times, doesn't it?* (Feedback; verbal tracking)

(38) DARRYL: *Yes, but I hate sad times.*

(39) LORI: *What do you hate about sad times, Darryl?* (Open-ended question; exploration/understanding of concerns)

(40) DARRYL: *In my life there have been more sad times than not.*

(41) LORI: *(I decided to be silent for at least 2 minutes!) What were some of your saddest times, Darryl?* (Silence; open-ended questions; exploration)

(42) DARRYL: *(Tears were welling in his eyes.) My sad times are too sad to share!*

(43) LORI: *You do not have to share them, Darryl. (We sat in silence).*
(Special technique—going with the resistance; rapport)

(44) DARRYL: *I want to share them with you, though.*

(45) LORI: *You are being very brave, Darryl. Tell me about your sad times.* (Feedback; directive; developmental match)

(46) DARRYL: *I was a medic in Viet Nam. I saw such devastation, but I honestly was doing okay. Knowing I was being helpful seemed to make the atrocities a little better. I helped many people, and I saw many men die.*

(47) LORI: *I can't imagine what you saw and lived through, but the fact that you saved so many people helped you through many difficult times.* (Reflection of meaning)

(48) DARRYL: *I guess so. One night my best friend, Stan, and I were together. Stan didn't have many friends and he was kind of little. The other guys made fun of him. I really liked Stan. His friendship made the war more tolerable.*

(49) LORI: *Sounds as if you were a very good friend and that you helped people in many different ways.* (Reflection of meaning)

(50) DARRYL: *NO! I was not a good friend. I am done here. I need to go!*

(51) LORI: *Darryl, if you need to go, you can. Before you go, I want to give you an observation. When you were talking of Stan initially, your voice was soft and almost dreamy. When I suggested that you were a good friend to Stan, your voice became loud and aggressive. What are those voice changes about?* (Feedback; behavioral description)

(52) DARRYL: *I really need to go away.*

(53) LORI: *It is okay that you go. We will see each other again.*
There are many ways of "going away," aren't there, Darryl?
(Rapport/empathy; closed question)

(54) DARRYL: *You are really a pain in the neck.*

(55) LORI: *I can be a pain in the neck. I believe I am in good hands, though.* (Verbal tracking)

(56) DARRYL: *Okay, I won't go away, but you are not in good hands.*

(57) LORI: *You sound like a very competent nurse and friend, Darryl.*
Tell me why I am not in good hands. (Verbal tracking; directive)

(58) DARRYL: *(Darryl begins shouting.) You are not in good hands, because these hands did not stop things I should have stopped. Are you happy now!*

(59) LORI: *I am not happy, Darryl, but I truly appreciate you continuing to talk to me about such difficult times.* (Feedback)

(60) DARRYL: *I don't like to talk about my past. I haven't spoken a word of it to anyone, not even to my wife, Sophia.*

(61) LORI: *Then many memories are buried very deep.* (Reflection of meaning)

(62) DARRYL: *(Darryl begins to weep.)*

(63) LORI: *This must be very painful and devastating.* (Reflection of feeling)

(64) DARRYL: *It is more than devastating. It should not have happened.*
For years I wished I had been able to stop the hurt that we caused so many people.

(65) LORI: *So for all these past years, you have carried around the burdens that you saw.* (Paraphrase)

(66) DARRYL: *Yes, I feel guilty for living. I have moments when I am happy with Sophia and Michael, but they are fleeting.*

(67) LORI: *Tell me what you should have stopped.* (Directive)

(68) DARRYL: *One night, Stan and I were in a village and we heard sobbing and screaming. We approached the huts carefully and saw our own soldiers raping the village women. Stan and I told them to stop, but several of the men yelled at us to get lost and mind our own business. That night I went back to our temporary quarters, and I began having horrible nightmares! Those dreams still haunt me.*

(69) LORI: *That must have been frightening. And I would like to hear about your dreams, Darryl.* (Reflection of feeling; verbal tracking)

(70) DARRYL: *That is just it. I am not sure they were dreams.*

(71) LORI: *What do you mean you are not sure they were dreams?* (Open-ended question; exploration)

(72) DARRYL: *This is so difficult to say . . . I have been trying to piece together things.*

(73) LORI: *Tell me about those things, Darryl.* (Directive)

(74) DARRYL: *Well, I believe someone close to me sexually hurt me as a child. Bits and pieces come back to me, whether it be in dreams or vivid pictures in my head. I just don't know.*

(75) LORI: *There are so many of the dreams and pictures in your head that you believe they might be connected to a time when someone may have sexually hurt you. Is that right?* (Paraphrase; reflection of meaning)

(76) DARRYL: *I think so.*

(77) LORI: *Is it possible that the night in Viet Nam triggered some of your current behaviors and feelings?* (Interpretation)

(78) DARRYL: *I hadn't put the two together, but it makes some sense, as that is when the dreams began. I just don't want to believe that someone close could sexually harm me.*

(79) LORI: *You and I do not know if that is true or not. We may never know the truth, but that is not the issue here. Whether sexual abuse occurred or not is not the problem. We need to create a way for you to handle your present situation and your many perceptions about your past. Since we cannot change the past, one of our counseling goals is to change your perceptions of that past. That we can do.* (Goal-setting; development/evaluation of alternatives)

(80) DARRYL: *That doesn't sound easy.*

(81) LORI: *It is not easy, but we can do it together as a team. How does that sound to you?* (Open-ended question)

(82) DARRYL: *Nothing else has been working, so it is worth a try.*

Where do we start?

(83) LORI: *You and I have already started, Darryl. You will never be the same again, you have bravely faced the beast today in whatever form it appears.* (Feedback)

(84) DARRYL: *It feels like such a long haul.*

(85) LORI: *It will be worth your effort, Darryl. The outcome may be that you learn new coping mechanisms to deal with your past and present.* (Goal-setting)

(86) DARRYL: *I want my life to be different. I want Sophia and Michael to have a husband and father who can cope better with whatever life brings.*

(87) LORI: *I believe you can do that, Darryl. You even coped differently here. Talk to me about how you coped differently today.*
(Feedback; directive)

(88) DARRYL: *(a long silence) I guess I did cope differently today. I felt strong enough to tell you things I have never shared . . . and I somehow did not "go away" when you asked me difficult questions.*

(89) LORI: *So you have at least two new coping skills to take with you to assist in the week to come. As a homework assignment for the next week, please share with Sophia whatever comes into your mind. I have a feeling she will appreciate sharing more than "going away." Also please spend at least 15 minutes a day with Michael doing some fun activity.* (Paraphrase; goal-setting)

(90) DARRYL: *What if I shout at Michael again?*

(91) LORI: *You will shout again, but this time Michael will also have quality time to remember. Darryl, how committed are you to these two homework goals?* (Rapport; open-ended question)

(92) DARRYL: *I believe I can accomplish these two goals by sharing with Sophia and playing more with Michael.*

(93) LORI: *So you are committed to these goals. Before we go, I want to ask one more question. What kind of nurse were you in counseling today?* (Paraphrase; open-ended question; evaluation of session)

(94) DARRYL: *That is a funny question . . . but I guess I was a helpful and brave medic and nurse.*

(95) LORI: *You applied your skills as a helping nurse practitioner to yourself! Wow! You shared and faced your fears. Darryl, when do you want to come back to counseling?* (Summarization of content and feeling; rescheduling)

(96) DARRYL: *Do you have something available early in the week?*

(97) LORI: *There's an opening on Tuesday. See you at 10:00. Enjoy those competent nursing skills.* (Rapport; feedback, rescheduling)

Darryl and Lori continued to counsel together over a period of two years. During that time Darryl was hospitalized once for severe depression.

Working conjointly with a psychiatrist, Darryl was placed on an antidepressant, and then continued in counseling with Lori. His prognosis was good, and he went back to work as a nurse practitioner.

References

Batchelder, D. & Warner, E. (eds.). (1977). *Beyond Experience: The Experiential Approach to Cross-cultural Education.* Brattleboro, VT: Experiment Press.

Criswell, E. (1995). *Biofeedback and Somatics.* Cotati, CA: Free Person.

Helms, J.E. (1995). An update of Helms' white and people of color racial identity models. In J.G. Ponterotto, J.M. Casas, L.A. Suzuki, & C.M. Alexander (eds.). *Handbook of Multicultural Counseling* (pp. 181–191). Thousand Oaks, CA: Sage.

Helms, J.E. & Cook, D.A. (1999). *Using Race and Culture in Counseling and Psychotherapy: Theory and Process.* Needham Heights, MA: Allyn Bacon.

Ivey, A., Pedersen, P., & Ivey, M. (2001). *Intentional Group Counseling.* Pacific Grove, CA: Brooks/Cole.

Ivey, A., Ivey, M., & Zalaquett, C. (2016) *Essentials of Intentional Interviewing.* San Francisco: Brooks/Cole/Cengage.

Kottler, J. (2000). *Nuts and Bolts of Helping.* Boston, MA: Allyn & Bacon.

Kwan, K.K. (2001). Models of racial and ethnic identity development: Delineation of practical implications. *Journal of Mental Health Counseling, 23,* 269–277.

McIntosh, P. (1988). Working Paper 189. *White Privilege and Male Privilege: A Personal Account of Coming to See Correspondences through Work in Women's Studies.* Wellesley, MA: Wellesley College Center for Research on Women.

Moodley, R., Epp, L., & Yusuf, H. (2012). *Across the Cultural Divide: A Clemmont E. Vontress Reader.* Monmouth, UK: PCCS Books.

Nwachuku, U.T. & Ivey, A.E. (1991). Culture-specific counseling: An alternative training model. *Journal of Counseling and Development,* 70, 106–111.

Pederson, P. (2002). In F.D. Harper & J. McFadden (eds.). *Culture and Counseling: New Approaches.* New York, NY: Pearson Education.

Rothman, K. (2014). The origins of privilege. (www.newyorker.com/books/page-turner/the-origins-of-privilege)

Russell, L.A. & Berger, S. (1993). Learning about diversity: A multicultural simulation. *Journal of College Student Development,* 34, 438–439.

Russell-Chapin, L.A. & Stoner, C. (1995). Mental health consultants for diversity training. *Journal of Mental Health Counseling,* 17, 146–155.

Sanders-Thompson, V. (1994). A preliminary outline of treatment strategies with African Americans coping with racism. *Psychological Discourse,* 25, 6–9.

Schwartz, M.S. and Andrasik, F. (2003). *Biofeedback: A Practitioner's Guide* (3rd edn). New York, NY: Guilford.

Sue, D.W. & Sue, D. (1999). *Counseling the Culturally Different: Theory and Practice* (3rd edn). New York: Wiley.

Sue, D.W., Arredondo, P., & McDavis, R.J. (1992). Multicultural competencies/standards: A call to the profession. *Journal of Counseling and Development,* 70, 477–486.

Thompson, C.E. & Carter, C.E. (2012). *Racial Identity Theory: Applications to Individuals, Groups and Organizational Interventions.* Mahwah, NJ: Lawrence Erlbaum.

Zalaquett, C. & Akdogan, G. (2011) http://www.coedu.usf.edu/zalaquett/kdg.html.

7

WORKING WITH ETHICS, LAWS, AND PROFESSIONALISM

Best Practice Standards

Professional and ethical codes for the helping professions serve as guidelines defining good practice and standards of care.

RESOURCE U: WEB ADDRESSES FOR PROFESSIONAL ORGANIZATIONS AND CODES OF ETHICS

RESOURCE V: ACA CODES OF ETHICS AND STANDARDS OF PRACTICE

Overview

Students, faculty, and supervisors must be able to foster a sense of ethical behaviors and professionalism. Distinguishing these two elements and demonstrating appropriate behaviors is essential. Ethical guidelines for many of the helping professions will serve as resources. This chapter will also present landmark case law and the needed knowledge base to assist in decision making during the counseling process. Having a solid foundation about the origins of ethics, basic ethical guideline frameworks, and appropriate professional behavior will directly impact you and the way you practice in the helping professions. The mandated Health Insurance Portability and Accountability Act (HIPAA) requirements will also be introduced.

The seventh self-regulation skill of Heart Rate Variability will be discussed.

Goals

1. Define and practice the skill of heart rate variability (HRV).
2. Recognize and describe ethical and professional behaviors.
3. Express and acknowledge issues of social justice.
4. Be aware of the ethical guidelines for helping professionals.
5. Understand the varying elements dictating ethical responsibility from codes and case law to professional organizations.
6. Identify specific case law that directly influences counseling decision making.
7. Comprehend the impact of the Health Insurance Portability and Accountability Act of 1996 (HIPAA) requirements for the helping professions.
8. Integrate the Case of Darryl into ethical and professional behaviors.

Key Concepts: Standards of Care

When you go to any professional as a consumer of services, you expect a certain standard of care, whether it is a physician, lawyer, accountant, or other professional. You expect your chosen expert to have expertise and knowledge in the services you desire. You expect to be treated respectfully and competently. These are the same expectations for any consumer seeking out mental health services.

Embedded in these expectations is also the concept of social justice.

Social justice is a standard of care concerning issues of human rights, fairness, and equity. Many clients will come to you having suffered from economic, racial/ethnic, gender-related, and other forms of oppression. A fundamental value of social work is to attend "to the environmental forces that create, contribute to, and address problems in living" (NASW, 2008). Historically, counseling and mental health professions have not become directly involved in helping clients cope with cultural/environmental/contextual concerns; rather they focused on individual counseling and therapy.

The Code of Ethics of the National Association of Social Workers (2008) challenges the emphasis on the individual. Their ethical code states that many clients develop their problems because of external pressures of poverty, abuse, and prejudice.

It is vital to help clients understand how their problems relate to their social context (Ivey & Ivey, 2003).

One ethical principle for social workers stipulates that social workers must challenge social injustice. "Social workers pursue social change, particularly with and on behalf of vulnerable and oppressed individuals and groups of people. Social workers' social change efforts are focused primarily on issues of poverty, unemployment, discrimination, and other forms of social injustice. These activities seek to promote sensitivity to and knowledge about oppression and cultural and ethnic diversity. Social workers strive to ensure access to needed information, services, and resources; equality of opportunity; and meaningful participation in decision-making for all people" (NASW, 2008).

The American Counseling Association (ACA) focuses the Preamble to its Code of Ethics on issues of diversity as an ethical matter. The ACA is an educational, scientific, and professional organization whose members are dedicated to the enhancement of human development throughout the lifespan. ACA members recognize diversity in our society and embrace a cross-cultural approach in support of the worth, dignity, potential, and uniqueness of each individual (ACA, 2014). In its Ethical Principles of Psychologists and Code of Conduct (2010), the American Psychological Association (APA) also views diversity from an ethical viewpoint.

The Ethical Standards of Human Service Professionals (National Organization for Human Services, 2015) includes the following assertions:

STANDARD 10 Human service professionals provide services without discrimination or preference in regards to age, ethnicity, culture, race, ability, gender, language preference, religion, sexual orientation, socioeconomic status, nationality, or other historically oppressed groups.

STANDARD 11 Human service professionals are knowledgeable about their cultures and communities within which they practice. They are aware of multiculturalism in society and its impact on the community as well as individuals within the community. They respect the cultures and beliefs of individuals and groups.

STANDARD 16 Human service professionals advocate for social justice and seek to eliminate oppression. They raise awareness of the underserved population in their communities and with the legislative system.

As a helping professional, it is your counseling responsibility and duty to behave ethically, fairly, and professionally. These behaviors will be addressed throughout this chapter.

Before we dive into ethics and ethical behaviors, your seventh self-regulation skill, heart rate variability, will be discussed.

Ethical practice: Professional behaviors that are guided by written organizational guidelines set forth through professional mandates.

Heart Rate Variability

Heart rate variability (HRV) is a biofeedback technique that focuses on heart rhythm feedback (beat to beat changes in heart rate) for improved self-regulation (Chapin & Russell-Chapin, 2014). HRV is derived from the electrocardiogram (ECG). The Institute of HeartMath and its researchers have conducted research and discovered that people have the ability to regulate and control breathing through and with the heart (McCarthy, Atkinson, & Tomasino, 2001). As a student, you can learn and practice an optimal level of beat-to-beat variability for healthier functioning, flexibility, and adaptability. You know that your negative emotions lead to increased dysregulation in the heart's rhythm and adversely affect your physiological and psychological health.

Although there are many HRV software and hardware packages on the market, there are two we will present in this chapter. EmWave is produced through the Institute of HeartMath. It uses a plethysmograph that slides into a small cuff on the big finger of the non-dominant hand or an ear sensor clip to measure heart rate variability. It will also show your pulse and offer you a visual coherence coach to teach proper breathing actions (Childre & Cryer, 2008). Three rules are helpful when trying to control your heart rate variability.

1. Begin by focusing on your heart and its beating.
2. Use the diaphragmatic breathing technique from Chapter 1 and try to breathe with and through your heart.
3. The final rule is the emotional shifting of remembering a positive memory and emotion.

As you practice these skills, your breathing will become slower, the pulse will decrease, and your body will begin to calm down.

Another breathing instrument is RESPeRate (2013), the first Food and Drug Administration (FDA) instrument approved for blood pressure control that allows clients to practice breathing while watching corrective visual feedback. The EmWave gives corrective visual feedback but is not approved for blood pressure control. Clinical trials have proven that RESPeRATE significantly reduced blood pressure without side effects when used for 15 minutes per session and 3 to 4 times per week.

Practical Reflection 1: Breathing Through Your Heart

If you can locate an EmWave or RESPeRate instrument or software program, practice with these systems. If not, follow the HRV rules of focusing on your heart; breathing through your heart and thinking of a pleasant experience. Write down your physiological responses. How does your body feel when you practice HRV?

_____

_____

_____

_____

Ethics And Ethical Behaviors

Ethical behaviors are guided by written organizational mandates adopted by a specific discipline. Later in this chapter you will have the opportunity to examine several codes of ethics. Examples of ethical behaviors that most people easily recognize are clients' rights to privacy, proper counseling relationships, and credentialing. These issues are written specifically in the ethical codes. Arthur and Swanson (1993) state that "acting in an ethical manner can be summarized as emanating from six sources: acts of the United States Congress or state legislation, common or case law, administrative law, professional association ethical standards, personal socio-moral values, and state credentialing bodies providing licensure, certification, or registration which promulgate rules for practice and codes of ethics that become incorporated into law" (p. 6).

Across the continuum of disciplines, the main features and functions of ethical guidelines seem to be similar and consistent. According to Koocher and Keith-Spiegel (2008), the related areas are: an interest in the welfare of clients, practicing within one's competence, avoiding harm, protecting privacy and confidentiality, avoiding discrimination in providing services, and upholding the integrity of the profession by striving for aspirational practice. Kaplan (2003) comments that 80 percent or more of all ethical concerns revolve around a single issue: informed consent.

If that is the case, then it is essential that you have given your clients enough information about the counseling rules and expectations to decide whether or not to enter the therapeutic relationship. A verbal approach to informed consent is not enough. Refer to the earlier example of informed consent. In this chapter, you have several ethical guidelines to peruse.

As you read the guidelines, you begin to notice that the standards do guide you, but they can never tell you the "right" way to make a decision concerning clients. We have discussed that ethical codes are designed to protect the consumer, but they also protect you as the practitioner and your profession (Baird, 2010).

> **Informed consent**: Informed consent typically includes informing clients of the nature and expected duration of counseling, explaining fee policies, providing details about the involvement of third parties, and discussing the limits of confidentiality.

In your program coursework, you were introduced to ethical decision-making models. If you have not already, choose one model and use it faithfully and always consult a supervisor!

> **Confidentiality**: "Confidentiality refers to a general standard of professional conduct that obliges a professional not to discuss information about a client with anyone. Confidentiality may also be based on statutes (i.e. laws enacted by legislatures) or case law (i.e. interpretations of laws by courts).

But when cited as an ethical principle, confidentiality implies an explicit contract or promise not to reveal anything about a client except under certain circumstances agreed to by both parties" (Koocher & Keith-Spiegel, 2008).

Practical Reflection 2: Ethical Behavior

Most ethical behaviors are derived from your organizational ethical codes. Select and discuss at least three ethical behaviors that you must demonstrate in your current placement site.

_____

_____

_____

_____

Code of Ethics

In most graduate mental health curricula, a professor has instructed you to read your discipline's professional organization Code of Ethics. Probably these same instructors have requested that you peruse the Code of Ethics from other professions as well. Many of these ethical guidelines are included in the resources at the end of this chapter, and each document has been written by members of that professional organization to assist you in providing quality treatment to your clients and always to do no harm (Baird, 2010).

You may view these codes and others online through the associations' homepages. Many web addresses are listed in Resource U. Resource V provides a link to the entire Code of Ethics from the American Counseling Association (ACA). Two additional sources of excellent ethical materials are Corey, Corey, and Callanan (2011) and Zuckerman (2008).

Practical Reflection 3: Comprehending Your Profession's Code of Ethics

Read through the ethical guidelines in the resource section at the end of this chapter. How will these guidelines serve you during your field experiences?

_____

_____

_____

_____

Case Notes, Record Keeping, and HIPAA Information

All ethical standards mention some aspect of keeping accurate counseling case notes; however, there seems to be a controversy surrounding what should be included in the notes and where they can be stored. It is essential that you enter information from the counseling session into the record as soon as possible.

We like to write our case notes as soon as the client has left the appointment, that way the material is fresh in your mind. Date your entries, and try to be as concise as possible and do not offer impressions, assumptions, or clichés about your client.

On some issues, particularly in the first interview, it may be wise to take notes during the session, but only if the client approves. One major advantage of a pre-session written history is that you do not have to take notes. Sometimes it is imperative to jot down notes. Try to remember what that may feel and look like to your client. We find that it usually distracts the client and does not help in building rapport. If you must take notes, let your client know that your notes are open records to that particular client and can be seen with you when requested. You could also tell your client what you have written. Sharing case notes with your clients can be an integral part of therapy.

Mitchell (2002) offers excellent examples of the need for clarity. A frequent goal may be, "Increase self-esteem," which is difficult to measure. A clearer version may be, "Will not be critical of self or personal decisions about disciplining children." Another example is, "Darryl is depressed." Again, how do we know Darryl is depressed? Mitchell suggests that we add a clarifying statement: "Darryl is depressed because he lost his job" (pp. 29–30).

It is also essential to focus on counseling goals for the client and list any session achievements and setbacks. Use behavioral and measurable terms. We have a standard form for case notes, which is attached to the intake form. Your form or agency form might look something like this:

Date: 6/10/2015. Goal: To introduce one new or old activity back into C.'s life. Demeanor: C. had shaved and was dressed in a clean and pressed company uniform. Outcome: C. did one random act of kindness for an anonymous person. Discussed stages of grief and loss.

Remember these two helpful rules for writing case notes: Write as if your work is being subpoenaed for court, and always store your notes in a locked and safe file. Many codes of ethics stipulate these points, but they are also mandated by the Health Insurance Portability and Accountability Act of 1996 (HIPAA). The U.S. Congress recognized the importance of protecting the privacy of patient and client health records, so uniform privacy standards were established. Privacy regulations include privacy, security, and electronic transmission standards. The HIPAA requires providers and others who maintain health information to design and implement security measures to safeguard the integrity and confidentiality of patient information (Tomes, 2001).

These are very serious regulations and persons or agencies in noncompliance may have fines up to $100 per person per violation or $250,000 and/or ten years' imprisonment, depending on the maliciousness of the crime. For many large companies, getting into compliance was a costly and timely maneuver. For smaller counseling practices, compliance may be as simple as developing a security plan and locking client files. There are seven basic steps for developing and implementing a security system (Tomes, 2001):

1. Get management's commitment.
2. Appoint key personnel.
3. Perform a gap analysis of your agency's system for privacy.
4. Write and adopt a security policy and statement of information practices.
5. Perform a risk analysis of your agency methods and threats to confidentiality such as electronic records, and so on.
6. Implement security elements as necessary.
7. Test and revise your security system when needed.

Health Insurance Portability Accountability Act: This 1996 Act requires helping professionals to ensure privacy and confidentiality of client information. The final security rule was put into place in 2003.

Contact the Department of Health and Human Services (DHHS) for questions concerning interpretation and application of the rules via e-mail at OCR Privacy@hhs.gov or see their website at http://www.hhs.gov/ocr/privacy/. You may also inquire through your professional organization for updated information.

Practical Reflection 4: Writing Concise Case Notes Focusing on HIPAA Compliance

Practice entering a short and valid case note. Be sure to make your goals measurable, describing behaviors, not impressions. Describe where and how your case notes are stored. Share this information with your classmates.

_____

_____

_____

_____

The Process of Referring Clients to Other Practitioners

All ethical standards address the importance of referring clients when appropriate, and many guidelines stipulate that helping professionals must treat only those clients for whom they have qualified skills and competencies. Moursand and Kenny (2002) believe there are two basic questions that you must ask yourself when accepting or deciding to refer any client: 1. Will the client benefit from your services and area of expertise? 2. Do you and your client agree on similar counseling goals?

If the answer is yes to both these questions, then your decision to begin a counseling relationship has a solid foundation. Schuyler (1991) stated there are several aspects that create the necessary building blocks toward successful counseling outcomes. The client must want to seek help, have a readiness for change, and be open to communicating about personal concerns. The counselor must be able to instill a sense of hope, trust, and the need for commitment to the counseling process. The counselor must also be seen as confident, competent, and be able to create a counseling relationship that is warm and safe. If these conditions are not present, Schuyler believes a referral may be necessary.

Practical Reflection 5: The Referral Process

Which clients, if any, have been assigned to your caseload that you believe should be referred? Ethically why should you refer them? Discuss.

_____

_____

_____

_____

Utilizing Case Law

In addition to utilizing the ethical codes, there are several landmark case laws that you need to understand to make solid ethical decisions; two will be presented. It is our hope that you will find these case laws interesting and challenging. Please continue to search out additional state and national case law that may assist you in your ethical decision making.

Case law: State and federal laws that set precedence for many helping professionals to follow.

Confidentiality and Duty to Warn

Tarasoff v. Regents of the University of California 551 P.2d 334 (Cal.1976). This suit occurred when Tatiana Tarasoff's parents sued their daughter's psychologist and the university with which he was affiliated for her wrongful death. Tatiana's boyfriend, Prosenjit Poddar, was the psychologist's patient. Mr. Poddar revealed in a counseling session that he wanted to kill Tatiana when she returned home from a trip. Dr. Moore, the psychologist, felt that hospitalization was needed, but he had to consult with others prior to such a decision. Poddar was examined by two additional psychiatrists, and a letter was sent to local police requesting their assistance in detaining Poddar. The police did interview Poddar, but by then he denied his threats against Tatiana. Poddar was released. Two months later, Poddar attacked and killed Tatiana Tarasoff (CL 551 P.2d 334 Cal, 1976).

This case ruling of duty to warn has molded the very manner in which we explain confidentiality to our clients or patients. It is essential that you understand the importance of this ruling, the limits of confidentiality, and your duty to warn. The exceptions to confidentiality are numerous. Read about your duty to warn potential victims and proper authority when your client may be a danger to self or others, including drug use and criminal activity that has or may endanger human life. Maintaining confidentiality is your ethical counseling responsibility. It is specifically written and delineated in every helping profession's Code of Ethics. Arthur and Swanson (1993) list thirteen limits to confidentiality (pp. 19–20).

Exceptions to Confidentiality

1. The client is a danger to self and others.
2. The client requests the release of information and waives privacy.
3. A court orders the release of information.
4. The client gives up the right to confidentiality when the counselor is receiving clinical supervision and client has been informed.
5. The client must be informed when office personnel will have access to billing and record keeping.
6. The client must be informed if legal and clinical consultation is needed.
7. Client raises the issue of their mental health in a legal proceeding.
8. A third party is present in the room.
9. Clients are under the age of 18. Check each state for the age limit.
10. The client must be informed if informational sharing is a part of the treatment process.
11. Sharing of information is required in a penal system.

12. The client's purpose in disclosing information was to seek advice in the furtherance of a crime or fraud.
13. The counselor has reason to suspect child abuse.

> **Release of Information**: A written contract signed by the client and a witness designating particular information that may be shared with stated professionals.

Privileged Communication

Jaffee v. Redmond 518 U.S. 1 (1996). The case of Jaffee v. Redmond originated when a police officer shot and killed a man. The police officer entered into counseling with a licensed social worker. The deceased's family brought about a federal civil suit against the police officer for wrongful death. During the trial, the family's attorney requested the social worker's counseling case notes to see what comments were made about the incident. The legal question arose whether there was "psychotherapist privilege" that would prevent the disclosure of the needed information (CL 518 U.S., 1996).

This Supreme Court decision has major implications for you as a helping professional. This landmark ruling establishes a new standard for privileged communication that prevents counseling communications from being shared in a court of law without written client or patient consent.

For years only licensed psychiatrists and psychologists had psychotherapist privilege. After Jaffe v. Redmond, this privilege was expanded to include licensed psychotherapists in general, and all 50 states, as well as the District of Columbia, have passed into law some aspect of psychotherapist privilege (Falvey, 2002). In a computerized search of all U.S. jurisdictions, 98 percent of the jurisdictions that credentialed professional counselors showed evidence of granting privileged communications to the counselor–client relationship (Glosoff, Herlihy, & Spence, 2000). You are responsible for locating and understanding your state's statutes.

> **Privileged communication**: A client's legal right that confidences originating in a therapeutic relationship will be safeguarded during certain court proceedings (Arthur & Swanson, 1993).

Practical Reflection 6: Understanding Case Law

Describe how these case laws will be relevant to your field experiences and future counseling sessions.

_____

_____

_____

_____

Professionalism and Professional Behaviors

How do ethical behaviors differ then from professional behaviors? We often hear students say that certain behaviors are unethical. When encouraged to clarify the actions that are unethical, many times the behaviors are not unethical but unprofessional. For example, where do you learn about the importance of punctuality and dressing appropriately for your counseling setting? We learn about confidentiality in our ethical guidelines. Do our guidelines spell out specifically that we should not talk about clients with other counselors in elevators or over lunch? None of these behaviors are unethical; they are not spelled out in any ethical guidelines. However, they are critical, unprofessional, and related to the outcome of counseling.

Professional behaviors are dictated by your professional workplace and address job norms and expectations. Often professional behaviors are those that are spoken but unwritten norms of a particular agency or counseling culture, but you may find clarifications in workplace manuals and handbooks.

Be sure to check your agency handbooks for any rules and expectations that may be addressed in a policy manual. If these types of questions are not spelled out, please ask your supervisor or a colleague about special etiquette and professional behaviors. Remember that professionalism and the need for appropriate professional behaviors are as important as ethical behaviors. Be sure to discuss these professional behaviors with your supervisors. Adherence to these behaviors demonstrates standards of care for your clients, the profession, and you.

Professionalism: Counseling behaviors that are expected although often are unwritten norms and cultures of agencies and disciplines.

Practical Reflection 7: Recognizing Professional Behaviors

List several examples of professional behaviors that may be specific to your placement site. Discuss with your classmates.

_____

_____

_____

_____

Professional Organizations

Another aspect of professionalism is belonging to a professional organization. Many of the same professors who requested that you read and understand the ethical guidelines may also encourage you to join a discipline-specific parent, division, and state organization. There are many professional organizations for you to join, including the American Counseling Association (ACA), the American Mental Health Counseling Association (AMHCA), the American Psychological Association (APA), the National Association of Social Workers (NASW), the Canadian Counseling Association, the Canadian Psychological Association, and the British Association for Counselling and Psychotherapy. These are parent organizations, and there are divisions within each of the above that emphasize inclusive concentrations, such as the American School Counselor Association (ASCA), the Association of Specialists in Group Work (ASGW), the Association for Multicultural Counseling and Development (AMCD), and many more.

The first, and perhaps the most important responsibility of membership is a commitment to the profession. By becoming a member, you agree to abide by the organization's ethical guidelines. This commitment assists you in adhering to competency requirements of the discipline, but it also helps you in advocating for the needs of your clients and your discipline through your association's lobbying efforts. It was these same state, grassroots efforts that brought all the important licensing needs to the attention of your state legislature!

There are numerous other benefits to membership, such as refereed journals mailed to your home, library resources, insurance protection, and up-to-date information about the mental health profession. This information assists you in keeping informed and learning about what your colleagues are practicing throughout the state, region, nation, and world. Consider joining through the mail or online—student membership rates are greatly reduced!

Ethical and Professional Behaviors: The Case of Darryl

As you review the Case of Darryl from Chapter 6, begin to think of the possible ethical and professional dilemmas that could occur. For example, when Darryl first goes into a dissociative state, did Lori have adequate skills to deal with Darryl? Is that an ethical and professional concern?

Another possible controversy concerned Lori's actions when she chose to sit on the floor with her client. Would that be considered an ethical and professional violation, if any? What are the potential privacy issues from HIPAA that need to be addressed?

Practical Reflection 8: Dilemmas in the Case of Darryl

Go over the script in the Case of Darryl. Write down any potential ethical and professional concerns that you observe. Also write any of Lori's behaviors that were ethical and professional. Share your ideas with your classmates.

Summary and Personal Integration

The information in Chapter 7 defines your standards of care and offers good practice methods. Many ethical and professional issues were covered, but not everything you need to know about professional and ethical decision making can be covered. Keep your Code of Ethics and agency manuals handy, continue to refer to them whenever you come across a professional and ethical dilemma, and consult your supervisor.

In this chapter, you were introduced to guidelines and knowledge to assist you in becoming an ethical and professional mental health worker.

- Ethical and professional behaviors were defined and examples given.
- Sources and origins of ethical and professional practices were presented.
- Relevant landmark case laws were offered.
- HIPAA was introduced to assist in keeping client information confidential.
- The Case of Darryl was integrated into the chapter.

Practical Reflection 9: Integration

After you review Chapter 7, outline the key ethical and professional issues
that you would like to examine further. Discuss those with your classmates
and supervisors.

_____

_____

_____

_____

Resource U

Web Addresses for Professional Organizations and Codes of Ethics

American Association of Christian Counselors: Code of Ethics: http://www.
aacc.net/about-us/code-of-ethics/

American Association of Marriage and Family Therapy: http://www.aamft.org/
iMIS15/AAMFT/Content/Legal_Ethics/Code_of_Ethics.aspx

American Association of Pastoral Counselors: http://www.aapc.org/about-us/
code-of-ethics/

American Counseling Association: http://www.counseling.org/resources/code
ofethics.htm

American Group Psychotherapy Association: http://www.agpa.org/home/prac
tice-resources/ethics-in-group-therapy

American Medical Association: http://www.ama-assn.org/ama/pub/physician-
resources/medical-ethics.page?

American Psychiatrists Association: http://www.psychiatry.org/practice/ethics

American Psychological Association: http://www.apa.org/ethics/code.html

American School Counseling Association: http://www.schoolcounselor.org/
asca/media/asca/Resource%20Center/Legal%20and%20Ethical%20
Issues/Sample%20Documents/EthicalStandards2010.pdf

Australian Psychological Society: http://www.theaca.net.au/documents/
ACA%20Code%20of%20Ethics%20and%20Practice%20Ver%2010.pdf

Association for Addictions Professionals: http://www.naadac.org/code-
of-ethics

British Association for Counselling: http://www.bacp.co.uk/ethical_framework/

Canadian Counselling Association: http://www.ccpa-accp.ca/en/ethics/

Canadian Psychological Association: http://www.cpa.ca/aboutcpa/committees/
ethics/

Commission on Rehabilitation Counselor Certification: http://www.crccertifi
   cation.com/pages/crc_ccrc_code_of_ethics/10.php
National Association of Social Workers: http://www.socialworkers.org/pubs/
   code/default.htm
National Board for Certified Counselors: http://www.nbcc.org/Interactive
   CodeOfEthics/
National Organization for Human Service Education: http://www.national
   humanservices.org/ethical-standards-for-hs-professionals
Neurocounseling Interest Network: www. neurocounselinginterestnetwork.com

Resource V

The complete ACA Ethical Standards can be found at:
   http://www.counseling.org/Resources/aca-code-of-ethics.pdf

References

American Counseling Association. (2014). *American Counseling Association Code of Ethics and Standards of Practice.* Alexandria, VA: American Counseling Association.
American Psychological Association. (2010). Ethical principles of psychologists and code of conduct. Retrieved from: http://www.apa.org/ethics/code/.
Arthur, G.L. & Swanson, C.D. (1993). *The ACA Legal Series: Confidentiality and Privileged Communication,* vol. 6. Alexandria, VA: American Counseling Association.
Baird, B.N. (2010). *The Internship, Practicum, and Field Placement Handbook: A Guide for the Helping Professions* (6th edn). Upper Saddle River, NJ: Prentice Hall.
Chapin, T. & Russell-Chapin, L. (2014). *Neurotherapy and Neurofeedback: Brain-based Treatment for Psychological and Behavioral Problems.* New York, NY: Routledge.
Childre, D. & Cryer, B. (2008). *From Chaos to Coherence: The Power to Change Performance.* Boulder Creek, CA: Institute of HeartMath.
Corey, G., Corey, M., & Callanan, P. (2011). *Issues and Ethics in the Helping Professions* (6th edn). Pacific Grove, CA: Brooks/Cole.
Falvey, J.E. (2002). *Managing Clinical Supervision: Ethical Practice and Legal Risk Management.* Pacific Grove, CA: Brooks/Cole.
Glosoff, H.L., Herlihy, B., & Spence, E.B. (2000). Privileged communication in the counselor–client relationship. *Journal of Counseling & Development,* 78, 454–461.
Ivey, A. & Ivey, M. (2003). *Intentional Interviewing and Counseling: Facilitating Client Development in a Multicultural Society.* Pacific Grove, CA: Brooks/Cole.
Jaffee v. Redmond, CL 518 U.S. 1 (1996).
Kaplan, D. (2003). Excellence in ethics. *Counseling Today,* 45(10), 5.
Koocher, G.P. & Keith-Spiegel, P. (2008). *Ethics in Psychology and the Mental Health Professions: Standards and Cases* (3rd edn). New York: Oxford University Press.
McCarthy, R., Atkinson, M., & Tomasino, D. (2001). *Science of the Heart: Exploring the Role of the Heart in Human Performance.* Boulder Creek, CA: Institute of HeartMath.
Mitchell, R.W. (2002). *The ACA Legal Series: Documentation in Counseling Records* (2nd edn), vol. 2. Alexandria, VA: American Counseling Association.
Moursand, J. & Kenny, M. (2002). *The Process of Counseling and Therapy* (4th edn). Upper Saddle River, NJ: Prentice Hall.

National Association of Social Workers (NASW). (2008). *Code of Ethics.* Washington, DC: NASW.

National Organization for Human Services. (2015). *Ethical Standards of Human Service Professionals.* Retrieved from standards-for-hs-professionals.

Schuyler, D. (1991). *A Practical Guide to Cognitive Therapy.* New York: W.W. Norton & Company.

Tarasoff v. Regents of the University of California, 551 P.2d 334 (Cal. 1976).

Tomes, J.T. (2001). *The Compliance Guide to HIPAA and the HHS Regulations.* Leawood, KS: Veterans Press.

Zuckerman, E. (2008). *The Paper Office: Forms, Guidelines, and Resources to Make Your Practice Work Ethically, Legally and Profitably* (4th edn). New York: Guildford Press.

8

COUNSELING RESEARCH OUTCOMES

Discovering What Works

Using evidence-based research will ensure that you are conducting quality counseling. As counselors our goal is to change some type of (problematic) behavior, thought, or feeling. Measuring behavioral change is one accountable way of assessing whether change has occurred.

—Vickie White (2002)

Overview

Much of the research on counseling effectiveness has been theoretically based and historical. This chapter discusses action research that is outcome based and efficacious and summarizes the need for quality evaluation procedures for the counseling and supervision process. You will be asked to integrate approaches and evaluations that will make your counseling more accountable and effective. Self-regulation skills used in neurotherapy and neurofeedback will be addressed.

Goals

1. Research the efficacy of neurotherapy and neurofeedback interventions.
2. Understand the need for counseling outcome research or evidence-based counseling practices.
3. Differentiate between outcome research and efficacy research.
4. Examine differing methods for conducting your own outcome research.
5. Evaluate consistently your counseling effectiveness and that of your supervisors and clients.
6. Commit to consistent use of personal, clinical, and client evaluations.

Key Concepts: Practicing Evidence-based Counseling

It is our ethical and professional responsibility to understand what makes counseling effective. These days of managed care have made us more aware of our efficacy and called for accountability of our services (Hayes, Barlow, & Nelson-Gray, 1999; Whiston, 1996). It is also important that you investigate not only the efficacy of counseling but also the validity of psychotherapy (Mace & Moorey, 2001).

Clients must be given the highest standards of care by receiving the best practices. As a new helping professional, you must be able to determine if, how, and when your clients change (Snyder & Ingrams, 2000). You must be realistic in what outcome research has to offer and know the difference between outcome research and efficacy research (Chapin & Russell-Chapin, 2014; Lambert, 2003).

Self-regulation Skills of Neurotherapy and Neurofeedback

Many of the self-regulation skills practiced in neurotherapy (NT) and neurofeedback (NFB) are perfect for adding to your self-regulation repertoire and knowledge base. A brief definition of each will be helpful. Neurotherapy is any change to the neurons, neuromodulation, that may alter neuronal functioning. You have already figured out that the previous self-regulation skills you are practicing are a type of neurotherapy and neuromodulation. Neurofeedback is a type of neurotherapy that requires a brain–computer interface to map certain aspects of a client's neurophysiology. Neurofeedback, a noninvasive intervention, uses an electroencephalogram (EEG) and the principles of operant and classical conditioning to assist in treating the dysregulation of the brain waves. Sometimes NFB is labeled biofeedback for the brain. After a careful EEG assessment and other paper-pencil inventories for depression, anxiety, insomnia, ADHD, and head injuries, treatment is created. Depending on the severity of the dysregulation, typically 30–40 twenty-minute sessions are administered (Russell-Chapin, 2015).

Often the goal is to regulate the brain waves by reinforcing brain waves that need to be strengthened, and inhibiting brain waves that need to be lessened. This is accomplished through the use of visual puzzles, games, and watching a favorite movie. Neurofeedback requires specialized education, mentoring, and additional certification to practice. Understanding its many benefits allows practitioners another referral source for chronic symptoms and peak performance (Chapin & Russell-Chapin, 2014).

A brief discussion of the brain wave categories is needed to assist you in better understanding how NFB works. When teaching NFB to students, Lori often gives a mnemonic to help remember the categories: Do Think About Brain Growth. The D stands for the delta waves that are slow, cycling at 0.5–3.5 hertz (Hz) per minute; T stands for theta waves between 4.0 and 4.7 Hz; A represents the alpha category of 8.0–12.0 Hz; B represents the beta category of low beta at 13–21 Hz and high beta at 22–35 Hz. The final category defined is G for gamma waves from 35 to 45 Hz per minute. See Figure 8.1 to comprehend the brain wave functions and morphology.

Practical Reflection 1: Your Brain Wave Type

Look closely at the brain wave chart. Think about you and the brain waves you predominantly use during the waking hours. Are you the under-aroused person who is typically calm and laid back; over aroused with a busy brain or unstable with some difficulty transitioning through the needed brain states?

We could assess that accurately through a 5- or 19-channel EEG. You probably already know your dominant brain style.

_____
_____
_____
_____

Band	Description	Waveform
Electroencephalography 0.16–45.0 Hz	The EEG is composed of many electrical frequencies produced by the cortex and driving mechanisms. The EEG is most commonly measured from 0.16–45.0 Hz or similar range of frequencies.	
Delta 0.5–3.5 Hz	The Delta frequencies are predominant during sleep and recovery in healthy adults.	
Theta 4.0–7.7 Hz	The Theta frequencies are predominant during drowsing or are associated with creative states.	
Alpha 8.0–12.0 Hz	The Alpha frequencies are predominant during an awake and alert state yet not during cortical arousal. They are often referred to as the idle rhythm.	
Low Beta 13.0–21.0 Hz	The lower Beta frequencies are present during times of focus and engagement.	
High Beta 22.0–35.0 Hz	The higher Beta frequencies are predominant during concentration and higher levels of cortical activation.	
Gamma 35.0–45.0 Hz	The Gamma frequencies represent higher levels of cognition and are often representative of learning processes.	

Figure 8.1 **This depicts EEG brain band ranges, descriptions, and morphology. © 2015 Leslie H. Sherlin.** All EEG samples are filtered at 0.16–45 Hz. Gain = 70µV. Time = 2 seconds.

A Brief History of Counseling Effectiveness and Change

One day a discussion in our counseling internship class evolved concerning client termination. Lori was emphasizing the importance of creating a therapeutic atmosphere that encourages the setting of client counseling goals, evaluation of those goals, and appropriate termination, all at the very beginning of the counseling relationship. A brave intern stammered, "I never seem to get to the termination phase, and exactly how do you know when a client has completed counseling?" The class was very quiet, and soon other students nodded their heads as if to thank the student for asking a question that was on all their minds! From that conversation came the foundation for understanding the essentials of client change, action research, and program evaluation.

For many years, researchers have been discussing whether counseling interventions have been effective. Do you remember hearing about the Eysenck debates in the 1960s? Eysenck (1966) stated that counseling was not effective, causing much controversy in the helping professions and sparking the need for better research.

In *The Benefits of Psychotherapy*, Smith, Glass, and Miller (1980) used a meta-analysis to evaluate the effectiveness of counseling interventions. They found that counseling interventions were more effective in 80 percent of subjects when compared to a control group. In this study, theoretical orientation did not seem to make a difference, but empathy in the counseling relationship did.

Lambert and Cattani-Thompson (1996) researched counseling effectiveness and change. They found that client variables accounted for 64 percent of the change. Client variables were described as severity of disturbances, motivation, the capacity to relate, ego strength, psychological mindedness, and ability to clearly identify problems. Relationship factors, such as therapeutic relationships and past and present personal relationships, accounted for approximately 30 percent of change. Specific interventions chosen to address specific problems and concerns accounted for 6 percent of change.

Outcome-based counseling research is becoming more common, expected, and accessible (Chapin & Russell-Chapin, 2014; Mace, Moorey, & Roberts, 2001). There appear to be three counseling outcome research questions that need to be consistently addressed (Elliott, 2002b). First, you must ask yourself, "Has my client changed?" (Elliott, 2002b; Strupp, Horowitz, & Lambert, 1997). If the answer is yes, a second outcome research question needs to be addressed: Was it the actual counseling that was responsible for my client's change? (Elliott, 2002b; Haaga & Stiles, 2000). If the answer to the first question is no, then you must ask, "Why was there no change?" Then a final question needs to be analyzed: What direct or indirect factors or evidence are responsible for the change? (Elliott, 2002b; Greenburg, 1986).

Counseling outcome research: Investigations of counseling problems that lead to causal, relational, and attitudinal answers about counseling effectiveness.

For example, changes may be attributed to statistical and research biases, counseling relationship biases, client expectations, client self-correction, events that occurred outside of counseling, and medication benefits. See Resource W for more detail of the eight indirect evidence methods evaluating the possible nontherapy explanations.

Whether these questions are researched qualitatively, quantitatively, or both may not be realistic for your counseling agency or practice. However, you owe it to yourself and your clients to at least ask these questions in supervision by taking the skeptic's position that counseling was not responsible or the affirmative side that counseling did make a difference (Elliott, 2002b). That would be a beginning for you in evidence-based counseling practice.

Evidence-based counseling practice: Best practice techniques and measures that come from counseling outcome research.

Types of Outcome Research

There are many different types of available outcome research for you to choose and utilize (Heppner, Kivlighan, & Wampold, 1999). Your task is to find the kinds that are best suited for your counseling practice and client populations. In a survey designed by Sexton (1996), the five most popular types of research presented are descriptive fields, quantitative/experimental designs, program evaluations, meta-analysis, and qualitative analysis. Let's take a brief look at those five selected methods of conducting outcome research. These descriptions will be skeletal in nature and very selective. There are numerous additional types of research, so be sure to go back to your basic research and statistics coursework for a more thorough review.

Practical Reflection 2: Beginning to Practice Outcome Research

Describe what you are currently doing to integrate outcome research into your counseling interventions. What research questions are you asking about your counseling effectiveness?

_____

_____

_____

_____

Descriptive Research

Research studies that use descriptive fields offer readers information concerning measures of central tendencies. Statistics on the mean, mode, median, standard deviations, and more are usually presented. Describing the population being studied is the main function of descriptive studies. In your counseling practice, you might use descriptive fields to count the number of times your client attended his or her scheduled interviews. Perhaps you wanted to target a certain symptomatic behavior and count the number of times your client reported a decrease or increase in that targeted behavior.

Using descriptive fields is an endless method of collecting essential information and demographics. If nothing else, you might use descriptive statistics to list the type of clients you are seeing, the ratio of males to females, the average age of your clientele, or even the types of problems you see the most. You could also use descriptive research to tell if you are seeing women for ten sessions, but you only see men for three. You could track whether your culturally different clients drop out sooner than others. By now you can tell that this method of data collection is essential to your counseling practice.

Quantitative Designs

Through the scientific method, quantitative research designs surmise that possible answers to research hypotheses or questions can be discovered. There are two types of quantitative research: experimental and nonexperimental. Experimental research searches for cause and effect by manipulating the treatment variables. Nonexperimental research often looks at relationships between variables (Corty, 2013; Neukrug, 1999).

> **Quantitative research:** Research designed to obtain information by collecting numerical data that are analyzed using mathematically based methods.

One example of a quantitative, experimental method relevant to counseling is the single subject/case design. Single-case and N = 1 designs are natural units for most clinical practices because they are practical and applicable to clients. Because you cannot generalize from group research to individual clients, the use of single-case designs has rationality and clinical utility (Elliott, 2002a; Lundervold & Belwood, 2000).

> **Single-case designs:** A method of quantitative research where only one subject is studied.

You could take almost any one of your clients and develop a single-case study. If your client came to you with the presenting problem of anxiety and procrastination in completing work projects, you would follow three basic steps. First a baseline would need to be measured using a valid and reliable instrument for anxiety and procrastination, labeled (A). Then a treatment for anxiety and procrastination would be offered over the next few weeks, labeled (B). Measurements during the treatment would be taken.

Finally, after the treatment is over, the same measurements (A) would be taken to see if the treatment had, in fact, reduced the anxiety and procrastination over completing work projects. If you wanted to extend your study you may prefer to use the ABAB model. This is one of many examples of a quantitative, experimental method using a single-case design. Elliott's (2002a) essential research questions can be applied to this ABA or ABAB single-case study as well.

Program, Client, Counselor, and Supervision Evaluations

Evaluations are crucial to the effectiveness of your counseling practice and your counseling skills. Evaluations are another method of determining whether or not a program or intervention has been an effective counseling strategy for change.

There are several ways to accomplish program evaluations. Once you have determined the specific concern, you could select a pre- and post-test method using a valid and reliable instrument such as the Beck Depression Inventory (Beck et al., 1996) that measures the diagnosed problem of depression in your client.

It is also essential to evaluate your individual and group clients. Patterson and Basham (2002) conducted a study creating graphs for weekly group evaluations to track individual and group results with promising results. Other researchers have found group evaluations informative with women's issues and career concerns (Sullivan & Mahalik, 2000; Marotta & Asner, 1999).

As counselors, we do not perform enough of this type of evaluation. This evaluation is easy to accomplish though, as you can and should be evaluating at the end of every counseling session! Individual counseling goals should be assessed at the end of every three sessions. Both methods assist you and the client in determining the efficacy of the counseling sessions.

These evaluations do not determine whether it was the actual counseling that caused change, but they will assist you in gathering the client's perceptions about change that occurred during the counseling period. Be sure to allow time for you and your counseling supervisor to assess your progress. One effective way to conduct evaluations is to examine your use of skills. In previous chapters, you used the Counseling Interview Rating Form (CIRF) to rate and classify your counseling skills, one method of using process research to analyze your skills. You may want to review periodically your interviewing style and submit it to colleagues and supervisors at least annually. Both of these evaluations will keep you fresh and challenged!

Ask your supervisor if she or he will be willing to receive feedback from you on a regular basis. Ask your supervisors and instructors for examples to guide you. Some supervisors may have little experience and education in supervision and may be reluctant and naïve about the supervision process (Magnuson, Wilcoxen, & Norem, 2000). You may want and need to develop your evaluations that will better reflect personal needs relevant to your counseling practice.

Meta-analysis

The positive attribute of meta-analysis is clear: it allows you to synthesize research data from many projects over time in an aggregate manner. Recently the methods of meta-analysis have become more discriminating and useful (Mace & Moorey, 2001). In your counseling work, you could look to see whether the effect size of a certain program on substance abuse has proven effective over its 10-year history.

Qualitative Designs

Qualitative research presumes that there are many different ways to experience and interpret the world. The scientific method may not be able to answer all the different realities that a person may perceive, such as abstractions and meanings. The qualitative researcher becomes a careful observer of a phenomenon and begins to describe and interpret attitudinal and sociological contexts (Corty, 2013; Kopala & Suzuki, 1999; Neukrug, 1999; Schumacher & McMillan, 1993).

Qualitative research: Research discoveries that have a naturalistic phenomenological approach.

One type of qualitative study is the Behavioral Observation Plan. This method can be very helpful to you in determining client change. There are many unique types of behavioral observations, but the eight steps to this plan can be used for a variety of purposes (Hayes, Barlow, & Nelson-Gray, 1999).

1. Conduct a preliminary assessment.
2. Determine the target behaviors.
3. Decide what and how many behaviors to record.
4. Decide who will observe and record the behaviors: client, counselor.
5. Decide when and where to record.
6. Train the observer.
7. Look at the concern in a systematic fashion.
8. Begin collecting baseline behavior.

Behavioral observations: A type of qualitative research where observations are noted, reviewed, and interpreted.

For example, in the Case of Darryl, Step 1 was conducted by investigating his past and current behaviors. As the case was conceptualized, and many problems surfaced, the goal of working on two coping skills was determined. Step 2 required that a target behavior be selected. For Darryl, because he had kept his secrets for a very long time, sharing even everyday thoughts and feelings was a challenge. The targeted behaviors for Darryl were to share at least two thoughts and feelings with his wife, Sophia, and his son, Michael. Darryl was asked to spend at least 15 minutes per day playing with Michael and sharing thoughts with Sophia. In Steps 3, 4, 5, and 6, Darryl recorded in a daily journal how he shared with his family.

Steps 7 and 8 began at the next counseling session. Information collected acts as a beginning phase determining Darryl's baseline behaviors and their outcomes. This same method could be used to track Darryl's nightmares and depressive symptoms.

Practical Reflection 3: Selecting the Most Efficient Research Type for You

Of the outcome research types mentioned, which method could you see yourself actually implementing in your counseling work? For example, could you see yourself using evaluations, the CIRF, single-case designs, or behavioral observation plans?

_____

_____

_____

_____

Efficacy Research

Often efficacy and outcomes research are words used interchangeably. Although they both are looking at the effect of clinical interventions, the perspectives are very different. As helping professionals, we tend to understand outcome research more than efficacy research. Remember this difference. Efficacy research has the main goal of clarifying how effective a specific intervention or skill is on the outcome. Outcome research has the main goal of how this intervention or treatment benefits the client, patient, or population (Chapin & Russell-Chapin, 2014).

Research Criteria for Clinical Efficacy Levels

Two main professional association guidelines provide the majority of the standards for efficacy levels and ratings: the American Psychological Association (APA, 2002) and the Association for Applied Psychophysiology and Biofeedback (AAPB; LaVaque et al., 2002) guidelines. Both guidelines have their highest efficacy ratings mandating empirical evidence demonstrating efficacy and specificity.

Here are the five efficacy levels with corresponding ratings and narratives from strongly efficacious to weakly efficacious (La Vaque et al., 2002).

Level 5 Efficacious and Specific: Shown to be superior to a sham, medication, or bona fide treatment in at least two independent settings.

Level 4 Efficacious: Involves a non-treatment, alternative treatment, or sham using a randomized assignment with sufficient statistical power and analysis, and valid and reliable outcomes measures.

Level 3 Probably Efficacious: Involves multiple observational studies, wait list controls, within subject, and intra-subject replication.

Level 2 Possibly Efficacious: One study with sufficient statistical power and outcome measures without random assignment to a control group.

Level 1 Not Empirically Supported: Involves anecdotal and case study evidence.

Searching the literature for efficacy ratings on interventions is very helpful to you and your clients. Imagine being able to state to clients and professionals that this intervention has been given an efficacy rating of a 4 or 5! That is a very impressive and powerful piece of evidence for espousing the effectiveness of a counseling intervention. Here is such an example. Using neurofeedback (NFB) and the standard protocol for children with ADHD has been given an efficacy rating of a 4, Efficacious, and a 5, Efficacious and Specific, depending upon the guidelines used and the evaluators. That information is beneficial to potential clients, their families, and other professionals.

Here is an example of a research study that Lori conducted adding to the Level 4–5 Efficacy Levels. She worked with a team researching and validating a NFB protocol called Sensorimotor Motor Rhythm of 12–15 hertz with children diagnosed with Attention Deficit Hyperactivity Disorder (ADHD). The design used an experimental, randomized control group and a treatment group. The results validated that 40, twenty-minute NFB sessions over a period of three and a half months allowed the treatment group to raise the amplitude of their low beta, 12–14 hertz, and decrease the amplitude of their theta and high beta. The research also discovered that the default mode of the treatment group was activated after the NFB session. This was illustrated through the pre-post fMRI tests

(Russell-Chapin et al., 2013). Remember that counselors have much to add to the research base. Start researching!

Research Practitioner Models

Now that you have had a review of some of the available types of outcome research, two theoretical models may help solidify your opinions and guide you through future research of your own. Here are two major models that can be used to assist the helping professions in becoming researchers as well as counselors. The first is the scientist/practitioner model and the second is the teacher/scholar paradigm.

Scientist/Practitioner Model

In this model, you as the helping professional must believe there are certain interventions that will assist your client in changing thoughts and behaviors. You must also believe that you can discover more about client change through research. Also, as a counselor, you must have confidence in your skills to implement those discoveries into your therapy interventions.

Scientist/practitioner model: A model where clinicians use outcome-based research and integrate into the world of counseling practice.

Practical Reflection 4: Clarifying Your Strengths and Liabilities

What would be your biggest challenge in implementing the scientist/practitioner model? How would this affect your counseling?

_____

_____

_____

_____

To use research in practice three things need to occur (Sexton & Whiston, 1996). Practitioners must be aware of what research is available. This statement reinforces how important it is that you join and maintain your professional affiliations. As you know, most of these associations provide you with newspapers and journals that keep abreast of the latest research, observations, and trends. Again your thoughts turn to time constraints.

Just remember that you and your clients will benefit if you keep current in your specific discipline. The second skill is the ability to determine what the research you are reading means or what the implications are. You do not have to be an expert statistician, but you do need to know the basics related to quality research, whether the research is quantitative or qualitative. Last, you must make a commitment to yourself that you will consistently integrate your findings into your actual practice. If your current skills did not allow you to do so, be sure to get the skill training you may need to update your counseling interventions.

Teacher/Scholar Model

Many years ago I read the compelling, seminal work of Ernest Boyer (1990) entitled *Scholarship Reconsidered: Priorities of the Professoriate.* His ideas about the expanded functions of scholarship helped to crystallize the idea that counselors too can and must use scholarship to advance the profession of counseling. Boyer stated that scholarship had four unique but overlapping functions: the scholarship of discovery, the scholarship of integration, the scholarship of application, and the scholarship of teaching (Boyer, 1990, p. 19).

Teacher/scholar model: Boyer's (1990) model of diverse scholarly functions including discovery, integration, application, and teaching.

The scholarship of discovery is the traditional meaning of research and asks the question, "What is yet to be known, what is yet to be found?" It adds to the knowledge base of the intellectual world. The scholarship of integration asks the question, "What do already existing findings mean?" Integration tends to be collaborative in nature and seeks to expand what past research has discovered. The scholarship of application moves even further and asks the question, "How can knowledge be applied to consequential problems?" (Boyer, 1990, p. 21). Finally, the scholarship of teaching urges professors to ask the question, "How can we transmit knowledge creatively and in a challenging fashion?"

Lori molded her university teaching career around these four separate functions, and believes it has assisted her in becoming a well-rounded, dynamic, and versatile professor. These same scholarly functions can be used easily as a practicing counselor. Sometimes it seems that, as a practicing counselor, there is no time for research and scholarly production. We have to complete so many direct services hours to clients that the paperwork can be overwhelming! Using Boyer's expanded use of scholarship, you have many more options available to be a scholar as well as a counselor.

Practical Reflection 5: Choosing Your Best Fit Scholarly Function

Which of Boyer's scholarly functions would best fit you and be compatible with your life as a new counseling practitioner? Choose one of the four and offer an example: scholarship of discovery, integration, application, or teaching.

_____

_____

_____

_____

Summary and Personal Integration

In this chapter, you were introduced to models and measures that could assist you in integrating outcome research into your counseling practice:

- The beginning step toward research awareness is to develop a commitment to evidence-based counseling practice or at least an orientation toward using it in your counseling practice.
- Incorporate neurofeedback into your knowledge base and referral resources.
- Knowing strengths and limitations of the research methods and studies chosen is essential.
- Being realistic in your expectations about what outcome research has to offer was recommended.
- Locating studies most similar to your particular counseling concern was recommended.
- The benefits of the scientist/practitioner and teacher/scholar models to your counseling practice were presented.
- Continue supervision whether it be individual or group counseling.

Practical Reflection 6: Integration

Which of the constructs presented in this chapter will assist you in integrating research outcomes into your counseling practice?

_____

_____

_____

_____

Resource W

Indirect Evidence: Methods for Evaluating the Presence of Nontherapy Explanations

NONCHANGE/NONTHERAPY POSSIBILITY

- Nonimprovement:
  A. Apparent changes are trivial.
  B. Apparent changes are negative.
- Statistical artifacts:
  A. Apparent changes reflect measurement error.
  B. Apparent changes reflect outlier or regression to the mean.
  C. Apparent change is due to experimental error.
- Relational artifacts: Apparent changes are superficial attempts to please therapist/researcher.
- Apparent changes are result of client expectations or wishful thinking.
- Self-correction: Apparent changes reflect self-help and self-limiting easing of short-term or temporary problems.
- Apparent changes can be attributed to extra therapy life events (changes in relationships or work).
- Psychobiological factors: Apparent changes can be attributed to medication or herbal remedies or recovery from illness.
- Apparent changes can be attributed to reactive effects of research, including relation with research staff, altruism, etc.

References

American Psychological Association. (2002). Criteria for evaluation of treatment guidelines. *American Psychologist, 57*(12), 1052–1059.

Beck, A.T., Steer, R.A., & Brown, G.K. (1996). *Manual for Beck Depression Inventory II*. San Antonio, TX: Psychological Corporation.

Boyer, E.L. (1990). *Scholarship Reconsidered: Priorities of the Professoriate. Carnegie Foundation for the Advancement of Teaching*. San Francisco, CA: Jossey-Bass.

Chapin, T. & Russell-Chapin, L. (2014). *Neurotherapy and Neurofeedback: Brain-based Treatment for Psychological and Behavioral Problems*. New York, NY: Routledge.

Corty, E.W. (2013). *Using and Interpreting Statistics* (2nd edn). New York, NY: Worth Publishers.

Elliott, R. (2002a). Hermeneutic single-case efficacy design. *Psychotherapy Research*, 12, 1–21.

Elliott, R. (2002b, May). Evaluating the effectiveness of therapy in your own practice: Hermeneutic single-case efficacy design. Paper presented at the British Association of Counselling and Psychotherapy Research Conference, London, England.

Eysenck, H. (1966). *The Effects of Psychotherapy*. New York: International Science Press.

Greenburg, L.S. (1986). Change process research. *Journal of Consulting and Clinical Psychology*, 54, 4–9.

Haaga, D.A. & Stiles, W.B. (2000). Randomized clinical trials in psychotherapy research: Methodology, design, and evaluation. In C.R. Snyder & R.E. Ingram (eds.). *Handbook of Psychological Change* (pp. 14–39). New York: John Wiley & Sons.

Hayes, S.C., Barlow, D.H., & Nelson-Gray, R.O. (eds.). (1999). *The Scientist-Practitioner: Research and Accountability in the Age of Managed Care* (2nd edn). Boston: Allyn & Bacon.

Heppner, P.P., Kivlighan, D.M., & Wampold, B.E. (eds.). (1999). *Research Design in Counseling*. New York: Brooks/Cole.

Kopala, L.A. & Suzuki, M. (1999). *Using Qualitative Methods in Psychology*. Thousand Oaks, CA: Sage Publications.

La Vaque, T.J., Hammond, D.C., Trudeau, D., Monsastra, V., Perry, J., Lehrer, P., Matheson, D., & Sherman, R. (2002). Template for developing guidelines for the evaluation of the clinical efficacy of psychophysiological interventions. *Applied Psychophysiology and Feedback*, 27(4), 273–281.

Lambert, M.J. (2003). Bergin and Garfield's *Handbook of Psychotherapy and Behavior Change* (5th edn). New York, NY: John Wiley & Sons, Inc.

Lambert, M.J. & Cattani-Thompson, K. (1996). Current findings regarding the effectiveness of counseling: Implications for practice. *Journal of Counseling and Development*, 74, 601–608.

Lundervold, D.A. & Belwood, M.F. (2000). The best kept secret in counseling: Single-case (*N*–1) experimental designs. *Journal of Counseling and Development*, 78, 92–102.

Mace, C. & Moorey, S. (2001). Evidence in psychotherapy: A delicate balance. In C. Mace, S. Moorey, & B. Roberts (eds.), *Evidence in the Psychological Therapies* (pp. 1–11). Hove, UK: Brunner-Routledge.

Mace, C., Moorey, S., & B. Roberts, B. (2001). *Evidence in the Psychological Therapies*. Hove, UK: Brunner-Routledge.

Magnuson, S., Wilcoxen, A.S., & Norem, K. (2000). A profile of lousy supervision: Experienced counselors' perspectives. *Counselor Education and Supervision*, 39, 189–202.

Marotta, S.A. & Asner, K.K. (1999). Group psychotherapy for women with a history of incest: The research base. *Journal of Counseling and Development*, 77, 315–323.

Neukrug, E. (1999). *The World of the Counselor*. Pacific Grove, CA: Brooks/Cole.

Patterson, D. & Basham, R. (2002). A data visualization procedure for the evaluation of group treatment outcomes across units of analysis. *Small Group Research*, 33, 209–332.

Russell-Chapin, L.A. (2015). Neurofeedback. In E.S. Neukrug (ed.), *The SAGE Encyclopedia of Theory in Counseling and Psychotherapy* (2nd edn). Los Angeles, CA: Sage.

Russell-Chapin, L.A., Kemmerly, T., Liu, W.C., Zigardo, M., Chapin, T., Dailey, D., & Dinh, D. (2013). The effects of neurofeedback in the default mode network: Pilot study results of medicated children with ADHD. *Journal of Neurotherapy*, 17(1), 35–42.

Sexton, T.L. (1996). The relevance of counseling outcome research: Current trends and practical implications. *Journal of Counseling and Development*, 74, 590–599.

Sexton, T.L. & Whiston, S.C. (1996). Integrating counseling research and practice. *Journal of Counseling and Development*, 74, 588–589.

Schumacher, S. & McMillan, J.H. (1993). *Research in Education* (3rd edn). New York: HarperCollins.

Smith, M.L., Glass, G.V., & Miller, T. (1980). *The Benefits of Psychotherapy*. Baltimore, MD: The John Hopkins University Press.

Snyder, C.R. & Ingrams, R.E. (eds.). (2000). *Handbook of Psychological Change: Psychotherapy Processes and Practices for the 21st Century*. New York: John Wiley & Sons.

Strupp, H.H., Horowitz, L.M., & Lambert, M.J. (eds.). (1997). *Measuring Patient Changes in Mood, Anxiety, and Personality Disorders: Toward a Core Battery*. Washington, DC: American Psychological Association.

Sullivan, R.K. & Mahalik, J.R. (2000). Increasing career self-efficacy for women: Evaluating a group intervention. *Journal of Counseling and Development*, 78, 54–62.

White, V. (2002). Personal communication.

Whiston, S. (1996). Accountability through action research: Research methods for practitioners. *Journal of Counseling and Development*, 74, 616–625.

9

STAYING WELL

Guidelines for Responsible Living

We often look at the world not as it is, but as we think it is. You are responsible for the life you create, regardless of the demands around you.

Overview

Awareness of wellness and a balanced lifestyle are critical to the success of your field experience, supervision in general, and your new professional life to come. Earlier in the book you looked at the importance of self-analysis.

Understanding that you can only take your clients as far as you have gone yourself motivates you to continue self-reflection and maintenance of personal mental health. This chapter provides reflections and a lifestyle assessment to assist you with necessary skills and ideas for your own wellness.

Goals

1. Understand that healthier helping professionals make for healthier clients.
2. Focus on a new model for integration of balance and wellness.
3. Be aware of wellness and its corresponding components.
4. Assess your personal wellness.
5. Set individual goals toward prevention and wellness.

Key Concepts: A Balanced Lifestyle
With Proportion, Not Equity

As work began on this chapter, the concept of integrating a balanced lifestyle into our personal and professional life was to be the main theme. Once the chapter key concepts were formulated, and Lori continued to think about your life as graduate students and her life as a mother, professor, and wife, the idea of achieving balance seemed so difficult and complicated. Adding to this difficulty are the results from a study of mental health providers. In a seminal piece of research, one-third of a large sample had experienced emotional exhaustion, poor sleep, chronic fatigue, loneliness, anxiety, or depression (Mahoney, 1997). Chronic stress continues to be evident with the statistic that over 90% of the symptoms presented to physicians are stress related (Salleh, 2008).

You want to have a balanced lifestyle, but trying to juggle all those pieces is so difficult and discouraging. Even the presumption of balance suggests equity and relatively equal parts on some level. However, if you were to create a formula for the amount of time you eat, intervene in life problems, play, sleep, study, and work, there would not be equal parts of time or energy. So perhaps there may be no such thing as a balanced lifestyle with equity of parts. If this is the case, the days of superwomen and supermen need to be banished. Instead you need to replace the old theory with a new model. This formula for responsible living achieves balance with proportional, not equitable, parts!

In class, Lori often uses boxes that fit inside each other to demonstrate the idea of proportional parts. Once you know your most important values, then each box represents your values in order of priorities. Your most important value is shown and labeled using the biggest box. It is your foundation on which all other values stand. Value number two, represented by a smaller box, is important to your overall well-being, but it would not receive as much of your attention as value number one. This visual aid continues until you have at least five top values, and the boxes look like a stable tower with each value/box adding to the next!

Personal health and wellness are firmly founded on your own lifestyle.

A classic piece of research stated that 20 percent of our lives are controlled by heredity, 19 percent by environment, and 10 percent by available health care (United States Public Health Service, 1979). Often you cannot control these percentages, but you can still make healthy choices around those things you cannot control. For example if there is heart disease in your family, you can still choose to eat heart healthy foods and practice the self-regulation skills presented in your text. Epigenetics teach that how you live today can impact your genes, gene activation of certain diseases, and aging (D'Aquila et al., 2013).

That still leaves 51 percent of your life that you can shape by the choices you make! Listed in the next section are several guidelines for choosing to live wisely, responsibly, and intentionally. If you can live a healthy and balanced lifestyle, odds are you will not be at such risk for professional burnout and enjoy a long and satisfying career.

Burnout: Emotional and physical exhaustion due to excessive personal demands and depletion of resources.

Before examining the Rules for Responsible Living, your ninth self-regulation skill of harmonics will be presented. This skill, as all the previous skills, provides added value and benefit to your personal and professional wellness.

Harmonics

The technique of harmonics has been utilized for years in the biofeedback, neurofeedback, and counseling fields. According to Swingle (2010), therapeutic harmonics offer a self-regulation tool that operates on the principles of entrainment. Swingle described entrainment as instruments or materials that present subliminal sounds below the threshold of hearing, influencing mood, thoughts, and physiological functions, even brainwave activity. The main component of harmonics is that subliminal sounds are embedded in filtered pink or white noises. These sounds could be in the form of music that sounds somewhat like running water and is played at a very low volume. It is essential that the sounds or music are not too loud to interfere with the desired activity that the client or you may be needing, from studying to sleep (Chapin & Russell-Chapin, 2014).

> **Harmonics:** Entrainment instruments or materials presenting subliminal sounds below the threshold of hearing, influencing mood, thoughts, and physiological functions, even brainwave activity.

Oster conducted some of the earliest research in acoustic brainwave entrainment in 1993 by demonstrating that binaural beats, two slightly different tones, would cause the brain to entrain and alter its state of consciousness or brainwave activity. The two hemispheres of the brain become synchronized as the binaural beats send neural signals through both ears to the sound processing centers, olivary nuclei, in both hemispheres of the brain.

Swingle's (2008) research has expanded this knowledge to investigate the use of blended subliminal harmonics as a supplementary and helpful treatment in neurotherapy (Swingle, 2010). He has developed several therapeutic harmonic CDs for specialized clinical applications. You can purchase his CDs to work with your clients for a variety of symptoms. The CDs include the Alert CD for ADHD that decreases theta wave activity, the Serene CD for anxiety that reduces fast beta wave activity and increases slow theta wave activity, the Sweep CD for trauma that increases theta and alpha wave activity, and the Harmonic Sleep CD for insomnia that increases slow theta and delta wave activity (see www.ToolsforWellness.com for details on therapeutic harmonics) (Chapin & Russell-Chapin, 2014). Often using these types of harmonics as counseling homework assignments helps consolidate the work you have accomplished in counseling.

One of the harmonics useful in counseling is a package of harmonic CDs developed by Dr. Jeffrey Thompson, PhD of the Center for Neuroacoustic Research. The BrainSuite package, purchased in any bookstore or at www.neu roacousticresearch.com, has brainwave audio processes layered into rich, ambient musical soundtracks.

These CDs have been used in class to demonstrate harmonics, counseling sessions, and personality. Individually, headsets can be used and after listening for only a few minutes the brain becomes entrained to the needed brainwave. Thompson (2007) has harmonics for delta for sleep and rejuvenation, theta for insight and intuition, alpha-theta for an awakened mind (deep meditation), alpha for relaxation and quiet meditation, beta for energy and focus, and gamma for enhanced perception, openness to compassion, insight, and personal transformation (Chapin & Russell-Chapin, 2014).

You have experienced the effects of harmonics in many different settings. The first time Lori became aware of entrainment was driving down a very long road in Wyoming. Her mood was excited as she was going back home. Suddenly a country and western song came on the radio. It had sadness and melancholy in its lyrics and harmony. Lori began to cry and her mood changed dramatically.

Probably you have also experienced this phenomenon in church. Your mood may be altered by the music. Of course we know from looking at the Head Map of Functions in Chapter 2 that the temporal lobes in the brain house music and emotion and are closely correlated.

Even without the use of commercial harmonics, you can begin to observe what types of music, sounds, and environments help you with your emotional regulation. When Lori's son, Jaimeson, was in middle and high school, he would automatically go downstairs and play his drums. This would regulate and center his moods. What do you do? Do you enjoy the rhythmic nature of the rain, or the gentle rhythm of the ocean? Everything around us influences and entrains the brain.

Practical Reflection 1: How Harmonics Influence You

Reflect back on some of your preferred, perhaps even unconscious, songs, sounds, and environments. Describe below examples of harmonics that can help or harm your emotional regulation.

_____

_____

_____

_____

Rules for Responsible Living

Try these rules to see if they are a good match for you. If not, there are other methods and perspectives for helping you create a sense of balance.

It truly doesn't matter what model you adopt, as long as you are working on living healthfully.

Rule One: Clarify Your Values and Personal Expectations. This must be accomplished with intentionality and the forethought of possible consequences.

You have spent considerable time learning about intentional counseling. Intentional and responsible living are very similar. It is essential that you purposefully understand the why, the how, and the impact of the personal choices you make.

Understanding these choices will make you a healthier counselor. If you know the why behind many of the personal choices you make, the odds are greater that you will better understand the decisions you make as a counselor!

A guess is that you don't spend as much time on your top values as you want and need! Remember in counseling we often tell clients that a value is something we must act upon. In other words, what we say must be congruent with what we do!

Practical Reflection 2: Clarifying Your Values

There are three interrelated aspects of this exercise. On a piece of paper write down the top five values in your life. Once you have listed them, determine the amount of time you spend with each of your top five values. Finally, use an asterisk to mark which value(s) you would like to devote more time to. Share your discoveries with your classmates.

_____

_____

_____

_____

Rule Two: Understand Your Personal Locus of Control. In your counseling classes, many of you learned about Rotter's Locus of Control. This is useful information for our clients' well-being, but it can very easily generalize to your wellness, too. According to Rotter's early work (1973), *locus of control* is the ability and belief about how much control you have over the events around you. Sometimes history and certain social events may determine your discourse and some of who you are, but you still have control over how you perceive events.

External locus of control suggests that others' opinions and influence, chance, and fate determine your destiny. *Internal locus of control* suggests that your own choices mainly determine your life and actions. Rotter believed you need both internal and external locuses of control. You need to have a ratio of three to one internal control to external control in order to have the skills necessary for healthy decision making (Brammer, Shostrum, & Abrego, 1992).

Those of you "who have a high degree of internality tend to be free thinkers, have the ability to critically evaluate the opinions of others and do not interject other points of view" (Neukrug, 1999, p. 12). If you can achieve high internal locus of control, there is evidence that you tend to be more respectful and have more empathy toward others with different points of view. Obviously the more internally controlled you are, the easier responsible living will be!

Practical Reflection 3: Assessing Your Locus of Control

Complete Rotter's Locus of Control Scale located in Resource X at the end of this chapter. Be as honest and spontaneous as you can. Try not to analyze each of the given paired statements too long! Score the scale according to the instructions to discover your total number of agreements. How might your results influence your ability to live responsibly and the manner in which you counsel others?

_____

_____

_____

_____

Rule Three: Seek Understanding of Wellness and Personal Choices. One of the methods for understanding your personal choices is to examine the needed dimensions of wellness and your choices within each category. When you search the literature on wellness, typically many of the same categories are repeated with minor variations: physical, emotional, intellectual, occupational/ life work, social, and spiritual (Adams, Bezner, & Steinhardt, 1997; Chapin & Russell-Chapin, 2004; Depken, 1994; Sackney, Noonan, & Miller, 2000; Thompson, 2001). As you read about the wellness dimensions, begin thinking about your personal wellness and lifestyle choices. The following dimensions are similar to the Therapeutic Life Changes (TLC) developed by Ivey, Ivey, and Zalaquett (2014). Ivey (et al.) conducted a review of the research on wellness and TLCs and found that practicing TLCs was "as effective or more effective than medication" (p. 331).

Wellness: An individualized experience using six dimensions to define wellness and balance: emotional, intellectual, physical, life work satisfaction, social, and spiritual.

Physical Health

The dimension of physical health is essential to your personal wellness because it relates to your perceptions and expectations about physical health.

Researchers have concluded that good or optimistic perceptions about physical health correlate positively with greater levels of actual physical activity (Fylkesnes & Forde, 1991; Rejeski et al., 2001). Remember, if you don't have your physical health, overall wellness is often more difficult to obtain. However, the physical health dimension is not the biggest predictor of overall wellness. Can you guess which two dimensions hold the greatest predictive weight? Read on!

Emotional Well-being

Being secure with who you are, the emotions you allow yourself to have, and your stated values are essential elements in overall wellness. *Emotional well-being* is multifaceted, but two major elements are strong self-esteem and a positive regard for who you are. Researchers have discovered that positive self-esteem is correlated to internal locus of control, physical activity, and a principle-centeredness (Adams, Bezner, & Steinhardt, 1995). Your time in graduate school may sometimes work against this wellness dimension. Professors are constantly offering important feedback about your counseling skills and giving you earned grades.

You must remember the feedback guidelines we wrote about in Chapter 1 of this book. Feedback is just about your skills, not about you as a whole person!

Intellectual Enrichment

Intellectual enrichment is a fascinating category in the wellness formula. It is defined as your perception of just the right amount of intellectually stimulating information (Adams et al., 1997). Finding that "right amount" is important; researchers have found that too much or too little intellectual stimulation can negatively affect your health (Antonovsky, 1988.) This dimension is a difficult one for most graduate students. You must be careful not to experience the intellectual overload at the expense of the other wellness dimensions.

Life Work Satisfaction

Life work satisfaction is often associated with your choice of occupation as well. We prefer *life work satisfaction* because it denotes the idea of passion and satisfaction for all that your life entails (Chapin & Russell-Chapin, 2004). As you began to contemplate your graduate education, there was something about the helping professions that gave you pleasure and a sense of meaning and significance. Hopefully as you have learned new skills and techniques and gained more confidence as a person, your satisfaction and passion for life continues to grow.

Social Effectiveness

Social effectiveness or *social wellness* is one of the two dimensions that holds the highest predictive weight for overall wellness! You may have guessed correctly or perhaps you have experienced the need for a strong social network of friends and family. One definition of social effectiveness is the individual perception of having and providing support to self and others (Adams et al., 1997). Studies have shown that social support is positively correlated with physical and psychological well-being (Manning & Fullerton, 1988). The wellness dimension of social effectiveness is another difficult one to emphasize while in graduate school, because your time is filled with studying and other responsibilities. However, in the helping disciplines much of your graduate work may force you into groups and working teams. Some of your social support may actually be derived from your colleagues.

Spiritual Awareness

Spiritual awareness is emerging as the most fascinating dimension of wellness. It is the other wellness dimension that holds the highest predictive weight for overall wellness! There are many definitions of spiritual awareness, but the one that has the most empirical support is the positive perception and belief that every life has purpose, meaning, and significance (Crose, Nicholas, & Gobble, 1992). Researchers have discovered that a healthy spiritual life is associated with better physical and psychological health outcomes and overall well-being (Seybold & Hill, 2001; Zika & Chamberlain, 1992). Dr. Harold Koenig believes that our society is getting close to convincing people that religion and spirituality can help you stay healthy. Koenig and colleagues also write that those of you who are more spiritual experience greater well-being and life satisfaction, have less depression and anxiety, and are much less likely to commit suicide (Koenig, McCullough, & Larson, 2000).

Practical Reflection 4: Your Lifestyle Assessment Score

Resource Y contains The Lifestyle Assessment Survey for you to take (Chapin & Russell-Chapin, 2004). You will be assessing the wellness dimensions described. Read the 60 wellness statements and honestly assess your current lifestyle. There are directions for administration and scoring. When you have calculated your results, write down your insights. Share your ideas with your classmates.

You do not have to share your actual scores! There is also another inventory in Resource Y.1, Therapeutic Lifestyle Change Inventory (Ivey, Ivey, & Zalaquett, 2014), to take as well.

_____
_____
_____
_____

Rule Four: Repeat and Share These Same Steps and Processes with Those Significant Others in Your Social System. We live in a social world. Share your discoveries with significant others. This may include your partner, family members, special friends, work associates, and colleagues/students. The idea of listening to the feedback loop is essential in this phase of the wellness model.

Once the feedback has been heard, a search for a consensus is needed, if the other person truly is a valued member of your life. You will begin to shape or balance your life and decisions by taking into account the resources, demands, and choices in your life.

You are responsible for the life you create, inclusive of the demands around you! You also have a responsibility as a helping professional to maintain your own health for you, your family, and your clients (Iliffe & Steed, 2000; O'Halloran & Linton, 2000). Remember that what you say must be exactly what you do! If something is truly a value to you, then you need to act responsibly and consistently, if at all possible. By practicing a wellness philosophy, you increase your chances of not getting burned out from the stresses and demands involved in counseling. Burnout leads to counseling impairment, but a balanced lifestyle will decrease the odds that you will become impaired (Sheffield, 1998).

Counselor impairment: A compromising condition due to a physical, emotional, or situational stressor that reduces the quality and effectiveness of counseling received by clients.

Practical Reflection 5: Wellness and You: Setting Personal Goals

Using all the information you have gleaned from this chapter and your classmates, begin to formulate at least three individual wellness goals. Use your total score from the Lifestyle Assessment Survey (LAS), items which you scored low, and your reflections to set measureable goals. It could look something like: I, _____ (your name), will begin to _____ (action) for at least _____ (time). I will evaluate my goal at the end of _____ (period of time). Be sure to share at least one of your goals with your classmates.

Summary and Personal Integration

In Chapter 9, you were introduced to wellness constructs that could assist you in developing a personal wellness philosophy. A reframe of balanced living was presented to prevent counselor impairment.

- Rules for Responsible Living were provided.
- Six wellness dimensions were defined with corresponding reflections.
- A Lifestyle Assessment Survey and the Therapeutic Lifestyle Change Inventory were provided as examples to assist you in developing wellness goals.

Practical Reflection 6: Integration

Which of the Chapter 9 ideas will help you the most in becoming a more balanced person and helping professional?

_____
_____
_____
_____

Resource X

*Rotter's Locus of Control Scale**

Each statement has two choices. Select one of the given options.

1a. Children get into trouble because their parents punish
     them too much.   1a. _____

  b. The trouble with most children nowadays is that their
     parents are too easy with them.   1b. _____

2a.   Many of the unhappy things in people's lives are
      partly due to bad luck.   2a. _c___

 b.   People's misfortunes result from the mistakes they make.   2b. _____

3a.   One of the major reasons why we have wars is because
      people don't take enough interest in politics.   3a. _____

 b.   There will always be wars, no matter how hard people
      try to prevent them.   3b. _b___

4a.   In the long run people get the respect they
      deserve in this world.   4a. _____

 b.   Unfortunately, an individual's worth often passes
      unrecognized no matter how hard he tries.   4b. _b___

5a.   The idea that teachers are unfair to students is nonsense. 5a. _b___

 b.   Most students don't realize the extent to which their
      grades are influenced by accidental happenings.   5b. _____

6a.   Without the right breaks one cannot be an effective leader. 6a. _a___

 b.   Capable people who fail to become leaders have not
      taken advantage of their opportunities.   6b. _____

7a.   No matter how hard you try some people just don't like you. 7a. _a___

 b.   People who can't get others to like them don't
      understand how to get along with others.   7b. _____

8a.   Heredity plays the major role in determining one's personality. 8a. _____

 b.   It is one's experiences in life which determine
      what they're like.   8b. _b___

9a.   I have often found that what is going to happen will happen. 9a. _a___

 b.   Trusting to fate has never turned out as well for me as
      making a decision to take a definite course of action.   9b. _____

10a. In the case of the well-prepared student there is rarely
      if ever such a thing as an unfair test.   10a. _____

 b.   Many times exam questions tend to be so unrelated
      to course work that studying is really useless.   10b. _b___

11a. Becoming a success is a matter of hard work; luck
      has little or nothing to do with it.   11a. _____

 b.   Getting a job depends mainly on being in the
      right place at the right time.   11b. _b___

12a. The average citizen can have an influence in
      government decisions.   12a. _a___

 b.   This world is run by the few people in power, and
      there is not much the little guy can do about it.   12b. _____

13a. When I make plans, I am almost certain that I can
      make them work.   13a. _____

b. It is not always wise to plan too far ahead because many things turn out to be a matter of good or bad fortune anyhow. 13b. _____

14a. There are certain people who are just no good. 14a. _____

b. There is some good in everybody. 14b. _____

15a. In my case getting what I want has little or nothing to do with luck. 15a. _____

b. Many times we might just as well decide what to do by flipping a coin. 15b. _____

16a. Who gets to be the boss often depends on who was lucky enough to be in the right place first. 16a. _____

b. Getting people to do the right thing depends upon ability, luck has little or nothing to do with it. 16b. _____

17a. As far as world affairs are concerned, most of us are the victims of forces we can neither understand nor control. 17a. _____

b. By taking an active part in political and social affairs, the people can control world events. 17b. _____

18a. Most people don't realize the extent to which their lives are controlled by accidental happenings. 18a. _____

b. There really is no such thing as luck. 18b. _____

19a. One should always be willing to admit mistakes. 19a. _____

b. It is usually best to cover up one's mistakes. 19b. _____

20a. It is hard to know whether or not a person really likes you. 20a. _____

b. How many friends you have depends upon how nice a person you are. 20b. _____

21a. In the long run the bad things that happen to us are balanced by the good ones. 21a. _____

b. Most misfortunes are the result of lack of ability, ignorance, laziness, or all three. 21b. _____

22a. With enough effort we can wipe out political corruption. 22a. _____

b. It is difficult for people to have much control over the things politicians do in office. 22b. _____

23a. Sometimes I can't understand how teachers arrive at the grades they give. 23a. _____

b. There is a direct connection between how hard I study and the grades. 23b. _____

24a. A good leader expects people to decide for themselves what they should do. 24a. _____

b. A good leader makes it clear to everybody what their jobs are. 24b. _____

25a. Many times I feel that I have little influence over
      the things that happen to me.   25a. _____

  b. It is impossible for me to believe that chance or luck
      plays an important role in my life.   25b. _____

26a. People are lonely because they don't try to be friendly.   26a. _____

  b. There's not much use in trying too hard to please
      people, if they like you, they like you.   26b. _____

27a. There is too much emphasis on athletics in high school.   27a. _____

  b. Team sports are an excellent way to build character.   27b. _____

28a. What happens to me is my own doing.   28a. _____

  b. Sometimes I feel that I don't have enough
      control over the direction my life is taking.   28b. _____

29a. Most of the time I can't understand why politicians
      behave the way they do.   29a. _____

  b. In the long run the people are responsible for bad
      government on a national as well as on a local level.   29b. _____

Score One Point for Each of the Following

2a, 3b, 4b, 5b, 6a, 7a, 9a, 10b, 11b, 12b, 13b, 15b, 16a, 17a, 18a, 20a, 21a, 22b, 23a, 25a, 26b, 28b, 29a

  A high score = external locus of control

  A low score = internal locus of control

Use the 3 to 1 ratio to determine your level of internal to external locus of control.

I–E Scale Scoring Key

The I–E Scale is scored to indicate the total number of choices toward external locus of control. Read the following answers and check only those responses which agree with yours. Please note there are six filler items that are not scored. Total the number of agreements to determine your relative level of external locus of control. The smaller the total number of agreements, the less externally controlled you are.

_____	1.	_____	11. B	_____	21. A
_____	2. A	_____	12. B	_____	22. B
_____	3. B	_____	13. B	_____	23. A
_____	4. B	_____	14.	_____	24.
_____	5. B	_____	15. B	_____	25. A
_____	6. A	_____	16. A	_____	26. B
_____	7. A	_____	17. A	_____	27.
_____	8.	_____	18. A	_____	28. B
_____	9. A	_____	19.	_____	29. A
_____	10. B	_____	20. A		

Total number of agreements or degree of external control: _____

*Reprinted from *Measures of Personality and Social Psychological Attitudes,* 2nd Edition, 1973, pp. 227–234, Rotter et al., Internal/External locus of control scale only. Copyright 1973 with permission from Elsevier.

Resource Y

The Lifestyle Assessment Survey, Form C

Directions. The following survey lists 60 statements reflective of a positive lifestyle. These statements are organized in six categories of wellness or optimal personal effectiveness. They include physical health, emotional well-being, intellectual enrichment, life work satisfaction, and spiritual awareness. For each section, read each statement and circle the number that best describes your behavior. Use the number code below. Then add the numbers you have circled to determine your score for that section. At the end of the survey, write the score from each section in the space provided and compute your total wellness score. The highest possible score is 300. Then interpret your wellness score with the key that is provided.

Number Code: 5_Almost Always; 4_Very Often; 3_Often; 2_Sometimes; 1_Almost Never.

Physical Health Satisfaction

1. Complete 1/2 hour of daily aerobic exercise. 5 4 3 2 1
2. Eat a balanced diet from the four food groups. 5 4 3 2 1
3. Limit intake of caffeine, sugar, salt, and cholesterol. 5 4 3 2 1
4. Seek periodic health examinations. 5 4 3 2 1
5. Drive within traffic safety codes. 5 4 3 2 1
6. Avoid use of tobacco and other dangerous drugs. 5 4 3 2 1
7. Schedule time to relax each day. 5 4 3 2 1
8. Maintain ideal body weight. 5 4 3 2 1
9. Avoid drinking alcohol to intoxication. 5 4 3 2 1
10. Have deep and restful sleep. 5 4 3 2 1

Emotional Well-being Effectiveness

11. Have a sense of humor and enjoy life. 5 4 3 2 1
12. Able to solve personal problems. 5 4 3 2 1
13. Enthusiastic about the future. 5 4 3 2 1
14. Accept responsibility for own actions. 5 4 3 2 1

15. Express feelings openly and genuinely. 5 4 3 2 1
16. Feel that you are loved. 5 4 3 2 1
17. Assertively communicate thoughts and feelings. 5 4 3 2 1
18. Able to avoid previous mistakes. 5 4 3 2 1
19. Comfortable with sexual behavior. 5 4 3 2 1
20. Accept and like yourself. 5 4 3 2 1

Intellectual Enrichment Awareness

21. Attend cultural events (music, art, drama). 5 4 3 2 1
22. Read books, papers, or magazines. 5 4 3 2 1
23. Enjoy learning new information. 5 4 3 2 1
24. Have opportunities to be creative. 5 4 3 2 1
25. Interested in scientific breakthroughs. 5 4 3 2 1
26. Aware of social issues and current events. 5 4 3 2 1
27. Attend workshops or classes for personal benefit. 5 4 3 2 1
28. Exchange ideas and opinions with others. 5 4 3 2 1
29. Seek a variety of entertainment. 5 4 3 2 1
30. Enjoy science or historical museums. 5 4 3 2 1

Life Work

31. Enjoy my life work (school, work, or retirement). 5 4 3 2 1
32. Able to handle stress of life's work. 5 4 3 2 1
33. Motivated to make a meaningful contribution. 5 4 3 2 1
34. Feel a balance between life work and leisure. 5 4 3 2 1
35. Interested in life work. 5 4 3 2 1
36. Feel appreciated for my efforts. 5 4 3 2 1
37. Have plenty of opportunities to learn. 5 4 3 2 1
38. Feel challenged by my life's work. 5 4 3 2 1
39. Accept new or extra responsibilities. 5 4 3 2 1
40. Receive and accept feedback about life work. 5 4 3 2 1

Social

41. Enjoy intimate relationships. 5 4 3 2 1
42. Involved in the local community. 5 4 3 2 1
43. Provide help and support to others. 5 4 3 2 1
44. Enjoy friendships. 5 4 3 2 1
45. Comfortable with authority figures. 5 4 3 2 1
46. Accept others of different race, gender, or faith. 5 4 3 2 1

47. Enjoy family interactions. 5 4 3 2 1
48. Act to keep a clean natural environment. 5 4 3 2 1
49. Participate in group activities. 5 4 3 2 1 5
50. Take pride in personal environment. 5 4 3 2 1

Spiritual

51. Take time for quiet reflection or prayer. 5 4 3 2 1
52. Act out personal beliefs in daily life. 5 4 3 2 1
53. Act to help and care for others. 5 4 3 2 1
54. Respect the beliefs of others. 5 4 3 2 1
55. Search for meaning and value in life. 5 4 3 2 1
56. Support humanitarian causes. 5 4 3 2 1
57. Express values and beliefs to others. 5 4 3 2 1
58. Read inspirational materials. 5 4 3 2 1
59. Experience inner peace. 5 4 3 2 1
60. Follow a personal or group faith. 5 4 3 2 1

Results and Interpretation

SECTION SCORE RANGE DESCRIPTION
Physical Health _____
Emotional Well-being _____
Intellectual Enrichment _____
Life Work Satisfaction _____
Social Effectiveness _____
Spiritual Awareness _____
Total Wellness _____

300–278 You have a healthy lifestyle and it shows!
277–248 Your efforts are paying off.
247–195 More effort and you will feel the difference.
194–168 You have the right idea. Keep at it.
168 There's much you can do!

Resource Y.1 Therapeutic Lifestyle Changes Inventory

HOW HEALTHY IS YOUR LIFESTYLE? Allen Ivey, Mary Bradford Ivey, and Carlos Zalaquett © 2014

Name _____ Gender _____ Age _____
Race/Ethnicity _____

Circle your response

ALIOSTRESS/EUSTRESS/STRESS LEVELS: What is your level of stress?

1	2	3	4	5		1	2	3	4	5
Eustress, life is generally calm and interesting, few major or minor stressors, recover from stress fairly quickly. Pleasant, happy life.	Manageable, stressors can be troublesome, but recover. Some tough stressors time to time. Life is good.	Often feel stressed, sometimes for days, lose some sleep, old stressful events often with me. However, generally life is good.	Constant feeling of stress, pressure, sleep problems, old events still with me. Can blow up, but manage. Life is OK, but	Chronic stress, tired, angry, sleep difficulties, feel sad, easy to blow up, fall apart, out of control. Need to change my life.						

1. **Exercise: How frequently do you exercise (walk, swim, bike, garden, run, rock climb)?**

1	2	3	4	5		1	2	3	4	5
5–7 days weekly	4–5 days weekly	2–3 times weekly	Occasional	Couch potato						

2. **Nutrition: What is your typical diet?**

1	2	3	4	5		1	2	3	4	5
Vegan, vegetarian, fish	Low fat, lean meat, fruit, vegetables	Mediterranean, Paleo	4 (S.A.D.) Standard American Diet	Fast food, fries, sugar						

Figure 9.1 Y.1 Therapeutic Lifestyle Change Inventory assesses healthy lifestyle. © 2014 A.E. Ivey, M.B. Ivey, & C. Zalaquett.

3. Sleep: How many hours nightly, including how restful is your sleep?

1	2	3	4	5
7–9 hours	7 hours	Sleep challenges	Many meds	Serious difficulty

1	2	3	4	5

4. Social Relations: How connected are you to others—close relationships, family, friends, groups?

1	2	3	4	5
Well-connected	Connected	Friends, some groups	Somewhat social	Alone, angry, sad

1	2	3	4	5

4a. Intimacy, Sex Life: How satisfied are you with your sex life?

1	2	3	4	5
Highly	Moderately	Somewhat	Dissatisfied	Do not care

1	2	3	4	5

5. Cognitive Challenge: How actively do you involve yourself in mind-expanding cognitive challenges?

1	2	3	4	5
Joy in constantly learning, searching for the New	Involved, active	Moderately interested, read some books, puzzles	Some, no more than 3 hours	None

1	2	3	4	5

6. Cultural Health and Cultural Identity: Awareness of cultural issues influencing you, including sense of cultural identity.

1	2	3	4	5
Empathy for self & others. Sees self-in-relation, race/ethnicity, etc. awareness, life vision	At least two of the preceding plus life vision	One of the preceding, some life vision	Slightly aware of issues	Oppressive, no real life vision

1	2	3	4	5

Figure 9.1 (Continued)

7. Meditation, Yoga, etc.: How often you engage in this practice?

1	2	3	4	5		1	2	3	4	5
Daily	3–4 weekly	Aware, occasional	Absent	Hyper, cannot do						

8. Drugs, Alcohol: Use of alcohol or other drugs?

1	2	3	4	5		1	2	3	4	5
None	Moderate	Has become part of life	Becomes a focus	Addicted						

9. Medication and Supplements: How aware are you of possible issues plus appropriate contact with physicians?

1	2	3	4	5		1	2	3	4	5
Regular contact with physician, follows directions	Frequent contact	Occasional, some difficulty following directions	Seldom	Never						

10. Positive Thinking/Optimism/Happiness: Do you have resilient positive attitudes and a good level of happiness?

1	2	3	4	5		1	2	3	4	5
Resilient, positive, optimistic	Most of the time	Usually, not always	Seldom	Infrequent						

11. Belief, Values: How engaged are you with living a meaningful life?

1	2	3	4	5		1	2	3	4	5
A life center	Involved	Occasional involvement	Never	Not interested						

11a. Spirituality, Religiosity: Do you participate in spiritual or religious activities?

1	2	3	4	5
Daily	Between 2–4 days	Once a week	Holidays only	Do not believe

	1	2	3	4	5

12. Nature/Green/Garden: How often do you engage in outside/nature activities?

1	2	3	4	5
Get outdoors often	Frequent	Sometimes	Seldom	Almost never

	1	2	3	4	5

13. Smoking: Do you smoke? If yes, how much?

1	2	3	4	5
Never	Never, but exposed to secondary	Stopped smoking	Tries to stop	Still smoking

	1	2	3	4	5

14. Screen Time (TV, Cell, iPad, Computer): Amount of time in front of a screen?

1	2	3	4	5
None	2 hours or less daily	4 hours	6 or more	Never off-line

	1	2	3	4	5

15. Relaxation and Having Fun: How frequently are you involved in leisure or relaxation activities?

1	2	3	4	5
Something every day	5–6 hours weekly	3–4 hours	Limited & stressed	Workaholic and stressed out

	1	2	3	4	5

Figure 9.1 (Continued)

16. Education: What level of education have you completed?

1	2	3	4	5
College, serious hobby	College	Comm. College	High school/GED	Drop out

1	2	3	4	5

17. Money and Privilege: What is your financial situation? Do you benefit from privilege because of race or other factor?

1	2	3	4	5
Have it all, privileged	Comfortable	Making it	On edge, but OK	Poor, oppressed

1	2	3	4	5

18. Helping Others/Community Involvement/Social Justice Action: How frequently do you help others or your community?

1	2	3	4	5
Daily action	Weekly action	Often involved	No time	Destructive

1	2	3	4	5

19. Art, Music, Dance, Literature: How frequently do you release your artistic abilities?

1	2	3	4	5
Daily	Several times weekly	Moderate/frequent	Occasional	None

1	2	3	4	5

20. Joy, Humor, Zest for Living, Keeping it Simple, Not Overdoing: How happy or how much fun do you have?

1	2	3	4	5
Life is a blast	Fun most of the time	Moderately happy	Now and then	Never

1	2	3	4	5

SELF-EVALUATION OF GENERAL LIFESTYLE

Work: What is the level of your work or retirement activities?

1	2	3	4	5		1	2	3	4	5
Fully employed. Retired, never bored	Partial employment. Retired and active	Temporary work. OK, but sometimes bored	Jobless. Bored, less happy	Given up work. Inactive, depressed						

In Control: How much in control of your life are you?

1	2	3	4	5		1	2	3	4	5
In full control of my life	Mostly in control	Somewhat in control	Low control	Out of control						

Health: How healthy are you?

1	2	3	4	5		1	2	3	4	5
Very healthy	Occasional issues	Good, but could be better	Major issue	Very poor						

Stability: How stable is your life currently?

1	2	3	4	5		1	2	3	4	5
Highly stable	Moderately stable	Some ups and downs	Unstable	Chaotic						

Figure 9.1 (Continued)

Resilience: Your ability to bounce back from life challenges

1	2	3	4	5		1	2	3	4	5
Back "at it" soon	Temporarily troubled	Worry a fair amount	Difficult, but do it	Overwhelmed						

Satisfaction: How satisfied are you with your current lifestyle?

1	2	3	4	5		1	2	3	4	5
Highly	Moderately	Somewhat	Dissatisfied	Helpless						

Action: How ready are you to make changes to increase your well-being?

1	2	3	4	5		1	2	3	4	5
Ready to change	Want to change	Thinking about it	Some interest	Not interested						

References

Adams, T., Bezner, J., & Steinhardt, M. (1995). Principle-centeredness: A values clarification approach to wellness. *Measurement and Evaluation in Counseling and Development, 28*, 139–47.

Adams, T., Bezner, J., & Steinhardt, M. (1997). The conceptualization and measurement of perceived wellness: Integrating balance across and within dimensions. *American Journal of Health Promotion*, 11, 208–18.

Antonovosky, A. (1988). *Unraveling the Mystery of Health: How People Manage Stress and Stay Well.* San Francisco: Jossey-Bass.

Brammer, L., Shostrum, E., & Abrego, P. (1992). *Therapeutic Counseling and Psychotherapy* (6th edn). Englewood Cliffs, NJ: Prentice Hall.

Chapin, T. & Russell-Chapin, L. (2004). The lifestyle assessment survey: A self-report wellness survey. *Your Supervised Practicum and Internship: Field Resources for Turning Theory into Practice.* Belmont, CA: Brooks/Cole.

Chapin, T. & Russell-Chapin, L. (2014). *Neurotherapy and Neurofeedback: Brain-based Treatment for Psychological and Behavioral Problems.* New York: Routledge.

Crose, R., Nicholas D., & Gobble, D. (1992). Gender and wellness: A multidisciplinary systems model for counseling. *Journal of Counseling and Development*, 71, 149–56.

D'Aquila, P., Rose, G., Bellizzi, D., & Passarion, G. (2013). Epigenetics and aging. *Maturitas*, 74(2), 130–6.

Depken, D. (1994). Wellness through the lens of gender: A paradigm shift. *Wellness Perspective*, 10, 54–69.

Fylkesnes, K. & Forde, O. (1991). The Tromso study: Predictors of self-evaluated health—has society adopted the expanded health concept? *Social Science Medicine*, 32, 141–6.

Iliffe, G. & Steed, L. G. (2000). Exploring the counselor's experience of working with perpetrators of domestic violence. *Journal of Interpersonal Violence*, 15, 393–412.

Ivey, A.E., Ivey, M.B., & Zalaquett, C.P. (2014). *Intentional Interviewing and Counseling* (8th edn). Pacific Grove, CA: Brooks/Cole.

Koenig, H., McCullough, M., & Larson, D. (2000). *The Handbook of Religion and Health.* New York: Oxford University Press.

Mahoney, M.J. (1997). Psychotherapists' personal problems and self-care patterns. *Professional Psychology: Research and Practice*, 28, 14–16.

Manning, F. & Fullerton, T. (1988). Health and well-being in highly cohesive units of the US army. *Journal of Applied Social Psychology*, 18, 503–19.

Neukrug, E. (1999). *The World of the Counselor: An Introduction to the Counseling Profession.* Pacific Grove, CA: Brooks/Cole.

O'Halloran, T.M. & Linton, J.M. (2000). Stress on the job: Self-care resources for counselors. *Journal of Mental Health Counseling*, 22, 354–64.

Oster, L. (1993). Auditory beats in the brain. *Scientific American*, 229, 94–102.

Rejeski, W.J., Shelton, B., Miller, M., Dunn, A.L., King, C.A., & Sallis, J.F. (2001). Mediators of increased physical activity and change in subjective well-being: Results from Activity Counseling Trials (ACT). *Journal of Health Psychology*, 6, 159–68.

Rotter, J. (1973). Internal/external locus of control scale. In J.P. Robinson and P.R. Shaver (eds.), *Measures of Personality and Social Psychological Attitudes* (2nd edn, pp. 227–34). Ann Arbor, MI: Institute for Social Research.

Sackney, L., Noonan, B., & Miller, C.M. (2000). Leadership for educator wellness: An exploratory study. *International Journal of Leadership in Education*, 3, 41–56.

Salleh, M.R. (2008). Life events, stress and illness. *Malaysian Journal of Medical Science*, 10(4), 9–18.

Seybold, K.S. & Hill, P.C. (2001). The role of religion and spirituality in mental and physical health. *Current Directions in Psychological Science*, 10, 21–4.

Sheffield, D.S. (1998). Counselor impairment: Moving toward a concise definition and protocol. *Journal of Humanistic Education and Development*, 37, 96–106.

Swingle, P.G. (2008). *Basic Neurotherapy: The Clinician's Guide*. Vancouver, Canada: Swingle.

Swingle, P.G. (2010). *Biofeedback for the Brain: How Neurotherapy Effectively Treats Depression, ADHD, Autism and More*. Piscataway, NJ: Rutgers University.

Thompson, J. (2007). *The Brainwave Suite*. www.TheRelaxationCompany.com.

Thompson, K.C. (2001). Dimensions of wellness and the health care matters program at Penn State. *Home Health Care Management and Practice*, 13, 308–11.

United States Public Health Service. (1979). *Preventable Mortality*. Washington, DC: US Department of Health Education and Welfare.

Zika, S. & Chamberlain, K. (1992). On the relation between meaning in life and psychological well-being. *British Journal of Psychology*, 83, 133–45.

10

BECOMING A PROFESSIONAL HELPER

Advocacy for Clients, Self, and the Profession

The ultimate questions of psychotherapy are not a private matter—they represent a supreme responsibility.

—Carl G. Jung (1954)

RESOURCE Z: CHI SIGMA IOTA ADVOCACY THEMES
RESOURCE Z.1: ADVOCACY COMPETENCIES

Overview

Advocacy is the central theme of this chapter, demonstrating that you must advocate for your clients, yourself, and the helping professions. We provide a review of the book chapters, summarizing the essential variables for a successful field experience and how advocacy is an integral part of that experience. This chapter includes a planning program and goal-setting for continuing education, further supervision, and advocacy for the profession.

Goals

1   Comprehend and practice mindfulness in counseling and living.
2. Advocate for your clients, self, and the profession as an integral component of being a professional helper.
3. Review the key components necessary for you to continue having a successful counseling career.
4. Understand the importance of personal and professional advocacy.
5. Realize the benefits of practicing healthy risk management.
6. Set new goals at the end of your field experience.

Key Concepts: Advocacy and Its Relationship to the Ten Essential Principles for Helping Professionals

As you complete your practicum and internship, you must congratulate yourself for your continued growth and risk-taking! Look back and be amazed at all you and your clients have achieved.

Much of what you accomplished came about because of advocacy efforts. Advocacy is offering support and assistance promoting a cause, skills, an individual, and an organization. This advocacy work may be disguised in different ways, but each played an important part in the success of your clients, you, and your profession. As we delve into advocacy further, the final self-regulation skills of mindfulness training will be introduced.

Advocacy: The art of promoting and supporting the efforts and skills of a person, cause, or profession.

Mindfulness

The self-regulation skill of mindfulness always seems easier in theory than in practice. Mindfulness ideas and trainings have been around for a very long time. Much like the other self-regulating skills, though, it is often easier to comprehend the self-regulating theories than to put them into action.

Teaching and illustrating the many benefits of mindfulness to clients is actually fun and meaningful. Siegel defined mindfulness as a specific mental practice of being, "conscientious and intentional in what we do, being open and creative with possibilities or being aware of the present moment without grasping onto judgments" (Siegel, 2010, p. 1). Mindfulness and intentionality go hand in hand. Think how our lives would be easier, healthier, and more efficient if we lived them more intentionally. We discussed being intentional with our counseling skills; now we need to continue that practice and be mindful and intentional in living our lives.

Taking what your clients value and enjoy are often clues for what concepts or foods to first choose to illustrate the self-regulation skills of mindfulness. The use of "the mindful raisin" is always a good 5-minute starter (Williams, Teasdale, Segal, & Kabat-Zinn, 2007). Touch only one raisin between your fingers, then smell the raisin and take in its aromas; next place the raisin in your mouth but do not chew it, begin to sense its taste and let the raisin tease your taste buds. Finally bite into the raisin slowly and allow its juiciness to slide down the throat. Discuss the results in the session. This small exercise on mindful intentionality teaches clients focus and activates the sensory motor cortex and the prefrontal cortex.

Much research has been published on the usefulness of mindfulness and meditation.

Several studies have demonstrated that the use of meditation reduces stressors in our lives and increases healthy gray matter in the amygdala (Hölzel et al., 2011; Ivey et al., 2014). Davis and Hayes (2012) reviewed the mindfulness literature and suggested that the benefits are plentiful, from reducing stress and anxiety to lowering negative ruminations to increasing compassion. Of course, it is best to be well trained in mindfulness and meditation, but there are some self-help methods for beginners. Go to www.mindfulnesstapes.com to locate needed resources.

Lori's favorite demonstration uses her favorite cookie, the chocolate chip cookie, to illustrate mindfulness and neurocounseling concepts. Bring enough chocolate chip cookies for you and your client or graduate students. First have them just hold the cookie in their hands and begin to remember what it takes to make that cookie. Think of the ingredients that went into the creation of the cookie. Ask what chemicals, heat interactions, and electricity had to occur just to make and bake that cookie. Next smell the fragrance of that delicious cookie. Describe each smell that is noticed. Then take one small bite. Let that bite sit in your mouth and feel the saliva in your mouth as it envelops your taste buds. Be sure to think of the chemistry occurring in your mouth. Begin to think about the electrical, chemical, and physical properties of the cookie as it breaks down and metabolizes into the body. Finally ask how the chocolate chip cookie tasted this time compared to the previous time you ate a chocolate chip cookie. A typical response is, "It was the best cookie I have ever eaten!" If life were lived more mindfully and intentionally, would it be the best ever too? (Russell-Chapin, 2016, in press)

Practical Reflection 1: The Best Cookie Ever

Experiment with the above mindfulness exercise. Take the time to intentionally eat that cookie. How was the experience of eating that chocolate chip cookie different than any previous time?

_____

_____

_____

_____

Advocacy for the Client

As we have stated, clients often enter your life in a vulnerable state. Their past efforts at resolving concerns may have been unsuccessful. Once again, it is your ethical and professional responsibility to assist clients in overcoming obstacles, fears, and injustices. That is only the first step, and it may be the least difficult to accomplish. It is not enough to teach individual clients new coping skills. You need to move into the community and work upstream to educate, teach, and prevent oppression and racism and all other dimensions of diversity.

Advocacy for Self

Promotion for self is difficult to do because most helping professionals are very altruistic by nature. You may have learned that advocating may be equivalent to bragging or selfishness. But you will learn that if you don't advocate for yourself, often no one else will. Assertiveness and colleagueship are essential features of advocating for oneself. A wonderful definition of assertiveness includes the concept of mutual respect. You respect yourself enough to share your thoughts, feelings, and behaviors with others in a mutually respectful manner. You teach your clients the importance of healthy communication; now it is time to practice what you preach! It is essential that you let others in the community know what you can do as a professional helper. Don't be afraid to sell your skills and outcomes.

Recently a student of Lori's named Maria wanted to work in a hospital setting. Her credentials and skills were outstanding, but she did not even receive an initial interview. Lori encouraged Maria to share with the interviewer what her skills could do for that particular program. Even if she were not hired, that same supervisor would know more about her skills than before. Maria was brave enough to call again, and the appointment was scheduled, not for a job interview but as an information giving session. The reluctant supervisor listened intently. Lori strongly encouraged Maria to point out her strengths. She had training in counseling diverse populations, was multilingual, and had completed her thesis on eating disorders and adolescence. Maria stated that the interviewer was stunned when she finished, stating how Maria could make a difference in this program. Maria did not get that job, but in a month another position opened up, and Maria was hired! Advocating for self is not bragging, it is respectfully educating others about you, your skills, and the profession!

Another component of advocacy for self is to remember the value of supervision and to listen to critiques. The more trusting feedback you can receive, the more skilled you become. The same is true when your colleagues seek you out for assistance. All of us find ourselves working in oppressive situations in our jobs from time to time. Advocating also means helping others with job-related stressors.

Advocacy for the Profession

You are beginning to understand how advocating for your clients and self is an indirect way of advocating for your profession. There are many reasons why you need to advocate for your profession, but current times are calling for budget cuts in our local communities, the state, and nation.

Counseling centers, community centers, and social service programs have experienced budget cuts to deal with deficits in spending. How can you not sell yourself and your agency to those around you during these times? In Chapter 7, you were strongly encouraged to join professional organizations. Joining is another natural way to be active in necessary lobbying efforts that are constantly underway to ensure that mental health services continue and that you keep updated skills.

As you review the summary of chapters, think about how each chapter and the material presented can assist you in your advocacy efforts. In short, be smart and always think how you can advocate for the clients, yourself, and the profession!

Practical Reflection 2: Your Advocacy Efforts

What are you doing now or can you do to promote the needs of your clients, yourself, and the profession? Be specific.

_____

_____

_____

_____

Ten Essential Chapter Principles for Helping Professionals

1: Transferable Skills, Abilities, and Principles

First, as you begin to complete your practicum and internship experience, there are many skills, abilities, and principles for you to integrate and practice. You might be feeling overwhelmed again, as you leave your structured graduate education. Use this time to review and remember all that you have learned in this clinical experience.

At the beginning of this book, you were asked to accept your fears and insecurities and turn them into facilitative energy to help you move forward. You will need to use that same structure again to ease your way through this next transition, actually graduating and transitioning into a job as a certified and soon-to-be licensed counseling professional!

Go back through Chapter 1, "Turning Theory into Practice: Abilities Needed to Grow." Review your practical reflections and necessary abilities. Remember you have new self-regulation and neurocounseling skills to help with your new transition. All of these skills will assist you in generalizing those ideas and strategies to this new and different stage in your life. This skill of generalizing from one situation to another relevant situation is often exactly what we ask our clients to do!

We hope you better understand what are some of the causes of neurological risks and that you are continuing to practice your diaphragmatic breathing.

Practical Reflection 3: Looking Back and Comparing Feelings

How are feelings about completing your graduate education similar and different from those when you first started your practicum and internship?

_____
_____
_____
_____

2: Creative Interchanges through Core Interviewing Skills

In Chapter 2, "Reviewing and Analyzing Cases: Microcounseling Supervision," you were introduced to the Microcounseling Supervision Model (MSM). You have reviewed and practiced many of the necessary micro- and macrocounseling communication skills as you interviewed each of your clients. You must continue practicing those skills, and soon they will become very natural components of your personality and skill base. You will use those same skills in counseling as well as in everyday living. Those core interviewing skills assist you in having creative interchanges with everyone you meet. What a bonus for you and those around you!

We know you can better comprehend the need for your intentional skills and where those skills are activating in the brain. Using imagery in your counseling will assist your clients in accessing a different brain state than is regularly used.

3: The Path of Right Action

Chapter 3 introduced you to "Becoming Effective as a Supervisee: The Influence of Placement Setting." Discussions of placement sites and their influence were presented as well as the qualities of an effective supervisee. You will continue to use the skills as you set up new supervision schedules in your next counseling position.

Your major task now in the rank of counseling professional will be to make wise and ethical decisions and try to take the path of right action consistently. The term right action encompasses almost everything we do as counselors: human welfare, social justice, and counseling competency.

With that motto, remember the importance of healthy sleep hygiene for you and your clients.

4: Flexibility in Growth

In Chapter 4, "Continuing Self-improvement: Major Categories of Supervision Models," you were introduced to the three main supervision models: developmental, integrated, and theoretical specific. As you continue to grow, so will your desired supervision model and needs. Continue to be flexible. Continue to engage in your outcome research and be sure to keep up with the latest research on supervision.

The new research will challenge you to stretch and try new ideas. For example, Perera-Diltz and Mason (2012) examined technology-mediated supervision (TMS) among other types of supervision for school counselors. Their results may have great implications on how supervision is conducted using technology. Among benefits and limitations, they found that some benefits of TMS include improved opportunities for case reflection, increased opportunities for feedback from supervisor and peers, more accessible supervisors, and more flexibility of timing of supervision. Many in the helping professions may not believe that technology-mediated supervision is ideal. However, it is now a reality for many counselors and counseling students. Change in you and change in the profession will always keep you active and challenged! Be sure to continue supervision over the life of your counseling career. Be responsible and accountable for your supervision by knowing what your Supervision Question is for your supervisor and team (Russell-Chapin & Chapin, 2012).

As you continue to seek out supervision over the span of your counseling career, use that same process to remind you of the gut/brain connection and the importance of healthy eating over your lifespan. What you eat and do today definitely impacts how you age tomorrow and in the future.

5: Telling the Entire Story

Chapter 5, "Conceptualizing the Client: Diagnosis and Related Issues," introduced you to client conceptualization, related treatment, and diagnosis. You learned the importance of diagnosis using the DSM-5 and that an accurate diagnosis can give you a clearer picture of the client's concerns.

As it is in counseling, looking at the entire picture adds clarity and depth. This skill, too, can generalize to your life. Make sure that you are looking at the big picture of your new professional counseling life and your personal life. Get all the supervision and support to make it work well. While looking at the big picture, continue to exercise knowing how those brain-derived neurotrophic factors (BDNF) assist you in healthy decision making.

6: Universal Communication Skills

"Becoming a Culturally Competent Helping Professional: Appreciation of Diversity" was the theme of Chapter 6. You were introduced to multicultural models and cultural identity development. Remember that the profession of counseling as an organized and standardized organization is still very young throughout the world, but the function of counseling transcends years and years of organizations and cultures.

In a study by Bond and co-workers (2001), who researched the nature of counseling in fifteen countries on every continent, results emphasized that counseling is a socially constructed mechanism. In many of these countries, the term counseling was not even recognized, but what translated throughout the languages were universal and facilitative communication skills that help others to solve relevant cultural problems. The universal skills were those we tend to label as active listening, empathy, and self-empowering skills! More recently, Lorelle et al. (2012) examined globalization and professional issues in counseling. They state that as counselors become more aware of the structural impact of marginalized populations and advocate for social justice in our communities, we are obligated to include systems in the connected world as a whole as well.

The results of research on cultural competence are extremely important for you as a beginning helping professional. You cannot impose your cultural values on others, but you can listen and work within the client's framework wherever you end up working.

As you encounter others with differing views and values, practice the self-regulation skill of peripheral skin temperature control to help in responding with calmness and respect.

7: Risk Management and the World of Counseling

In Chapter 7, "Working with Ethics, Laws, and Professionalism: Best Practice Standards," you read about the ethical guidelines that assist us professionally. Landmark case law and skills necessary to be successful in counseling practice, such as record keeping, case notes, and referral procedures, were also emphasized. The HIPAA regulations were discussed with practical suggestions for implementation.

You are beginning to understand that it is your job as a counselor to advocate for all your clients. As counselors and helping professionals, you continually strive to affect human welfare in a positive manner (Montgomery, Cupit, & Wimberley, 1999). With advocacy and counseling come risks. That is why you must continue to be supervised, maintain your professional licenses and certifications, hold memberships in professional organizations, and obtain excellent malpractice insurance. In a survey exploring professional issues and personal experiences related to malpractice, the authors were surprised that the threat of malpractice actually has resulted in better informed helping professionals and increased attention to best practice activities (Montgomery et al., 1999).

As Carl Jung (1954) so aptly stated, "Small and invisible as the contribution may be, it is still a magnum opus. . . . The ultimate questions of psychotherapy are not a private matter—they represent a supreme responsibility."

The supreme responsibility of counseling can be enhanced with the self-regulation skill of heart rate variability. All these regulation skills calm the central nervous system, making you a more effective and efficient counselor.

8: Evidence-based Best Practice

Chapter 8, "Counseling Research Outcomes: Discovering What Works," offered material about the efficacy of counseling. You were encouraged to ask three essential questions about your counseling effectiveness. You were also asked to make a commitment to conducting your personal research to advance the field of counseling. Different research designs were reviewed and explored. Evaluating your individual and group counseling sessions, skills, counseling styles, and programs on a consistent basis was encouraged and recommended.

Another self-regulation skill, neurofeedback (NFB), was described in this chapter. Adding this noninvasive technique to your referral base offers you more resources for clients who have chronic concerns.

9: Helping Self and Others

Chapter 9, "Staying Well: Guidelines for Responsible Living," presented information about the importance of keeping well as a helping professional.

The chapter offered you an opportunity to consider balance from a viewpoint of proportion as opposed to equity. You were able to assess your wellness lifestyle and set several personal wellness goals.

One of many things you can do to ensure your professional balance is to join professional associations that will assist you in keeping in touch with the latest advances in your specialties or the counseling profession in general. Another excellent way to ensure professional health is to present or teach the material that you believe others need to know. In other words, be an active member of the profession. As you network with others, your knowledge seems to grow exponentially. Remaining current by continuing education, attending conferences, and reading professional journals will be vital to your wellness.

Review your old goals and evaluate your success. If all your goals were achieved, select three new measurable goals to assist you in this transition between ending your graduate career and beginning a new job. You may want to continue one of your previous goals as well.

Review your scores on the Lifestyle Assessment Survey and the Therapeutic Lifestyle Change Inventory to observe your needs and wants. Remember the availability of harmonic music and instruments to help the brain entrain with the world around it.

Practical Reflection 4: Writing New Goals for Your Professional Life

Several times throughout this text, you had an opportunity to assess your counseling skills, supervision style, and wellness philosophy. You were asked to set personal goals for this class and for creating a balanced lifestyle. Go back to those goals to reassess how you are doing in your counseling goals and personal life. It may be time to set new goals. Write down at least one new measurable goal.

_____

_____

_____

_____

10: Where Am I Now and Where Do I Need to Go?

In Chapter 10, "Becoming a Professional Helper: Advocacy for Clients, Self, and the Profession," you reviewed all ten chapters of this text. Chapter 10 encourages you to be an advocate for your clients, yourself, and the counseling profession. Advocacy promotes and moves forward a certain effort, person, or organization. We are using the term here to request that you assert your thoughts, actions, and deeds concerning the complementary and unique skills that professional helpers demonstrate. There are many advocacy resources available, but you must recognize that you and your skills as a professional counselor are some of the best resources offered for you, your clients, and the general population (Kiselica & Robinson, 2001).

Each helping discipline has guidelines and plans for advocating for clients, individuals, and the profession. A professional counseling organization that promotes and advocates for the profession is Chi Sigma Iota, Counseling Academic & Professional Honor Society International. Leaders in Chi Sigma Iota have been identifying components of professional advocacy and presenting these to members of the counseling profession. Resource Z lists professional advocacy themes from Chi Sigma Iota. The American Counseling Association has a variety of resources related to advocacy as well. Resource Z.1 lists ACA's Advocacy Competencies adopted in 2003. You can locate additional advocacy resources at http://www.csi-net.org and http://www.counseling.org/knowledge-center/center-for-counseling-practice-policy-and-research.

Continue to practice your mindfulness techniques along with the other nine self-regulation skills to help you be as healthy a practitioner as possible.

As you look back on your practicum and internship, reflect on all that you have gained. Remember your fears, insecurities, and joys, and those of your clients. Your counseling career is just beginning, and you will continue to grow with every new client. As you grow, so does the counseling profession. Continue to be flexible and find "within the narrative of psychological healing a place for tools plundered from related disciplines" (Simon, 2002, p. 45).

We hope your field experience journey has been an adventure filled with joys, challenges, and fears. You have entered an exciting profession, especially now in this era of neurocounseling. May it bring you a lifetime of satisfaction and growth! Be sure to fill out the evaluation at the end of this book giving us feedback about your journey!

Summary and Personal Integration

Chapter 10 began the integration efforts from your practicum and internship experiences.

- Chapters 1 through 10 were summarized, emphasizing self-regulation skills and neurocounseling.
- You were requested to make new goals for your future.
- The importance of advocating and being smart for your client, yourself, and the profession was emphasized.

Practical Reflection 5: Integration and Lessons Learned

This is your final reflection question, and it may be the most important one. What has been the biggest lesson you have learned during your field experiences? Was it an advocacy lesson for your client, yourself, or the profession? Share with your colleagues as a closing exercise.

_____

_____

_____

_____

Resource Z

Chi Sigma Iota Advocacy Themes

THEME A: COUNSELOR EDUCATION

GOAL: To ensure that all counselor education students graduate with a clear identity and sense of pride as professional counselors.

THEME B: INTRA-PROFESSIONAL RELATIONS

GOAL: To develop and implement a unified, collaborative advocacy plan for the advancement of counselors and those whom they serve.

THEME C: MARKETPLACE RECOGNITION

GOAL: To ensure that professional counselors in all settings are suitably compensated for their services and free to provide service to the public within all areas of their competence.

THEME D: INTER-PROFESSIONAL ISSUES

GOAL: To establish collaborative working relationships with other organizations, groups, and disciplines on matters of mutual interest and concern to achieve our advocacy goals for both counselors and their clients.

THEME E: RESEARCH

GOAL: To promote professional counselors and the services they provide based on scientifically sound research.

THEME F: PREVENTION/WELLNESS

GOAL: To promote optimum human development across the lifespan through prevention and wellness.

Resource Z.1

ADVOCACY COMPETENCIES: Lewis, Arnold, House, & Toporek (2002)

Endorsed by the ACA Governing Council, March 20–22, 2003.

CLIENT/STUDENT EMPOWERMENT

- An advocacy orientation involves not only systems change interventions but also the implementation of empowerment strategies in direct counseling.
- Advocacy-oriented counselors recognize the impact of social, political, economic, and cultural factors on human development.
- They also help their clients and students understand their own lives in context. This lays the groundwork for self-advocacy.

EMPOWERMENT COUNSELOR COMPETENCIES

In direct interventions, the counselor is able to:

1. Identify strengths and resources of clients and students.
2. Identify the social, political, economic, and cultural factors that affect the client/student.

3. Recognize the signs indicating that an individual's behaviors and concerns reflect responses to systemic or internalized oppression.
4. At an appropriate development level, help the individual identify the external barriers that affect his or her development.
5. Train students and clients in self-advocacy skills.
6. Help students and clients develop self-advocacy action plans.
7. Assist students and clients in carrying out action plans.

CLIENT/STUDENT ADVOCACY

8. When counselors become aware of external factors that act as barriers to an individual's development, they may choose to respond through advocacy.
9. The client/student advocate role is especially significant when individuals or vulnerable groups lack access to needed services.

CLIENT/STUDENT ADVOCACY COUNSELOR COMPETENCIES

In environmental interventions on behalf of clients and students, the counselor is able to:

10. Negotiate relevant services and education systems on behalf of clients and students.
11. Help clients and students gain access to needed resources.
12. Identify barriers to the well-being of individuals and vulnerable groups.
13. Develop an initial plan of action for confronting these barriers.
14. Identify potential allies for confronting the barriers.
15. Carry out the plan of action.

COMMUNITY COLLABORATION

16. Their ongoing work with people gives counselors a unique awareness of recurring themes.
17. Counselors are often among the first to become aware of specific difficulties in the environment.
18. Advocacy-oriented counselors often choose to respond to such challenges by alerting existing organizations that are already working for change and that might have an interest in the issue at hand.
19. In these situations, the counselor's primary role is as an ally. Counselors can also be helpful to organizations by making available to them our particular skills: interpersonal relations, communications, training, and research.

COMMUNITY COLLABORATION COUNSELOR COMPETENCIES

20. Identify environmental factors that impinge upon students' and clients' development.
21. Alert community or school groups with common concerns related to the issue.
22. Develop alliances with groups working for change.
23. Use effective listening skills to gain understanding of the group's goals.
24. Identify the strengths and resources that the group members bring to the process of systemic change.
25. Communicate recognition of and respect for these strengths and resources.
26. Identify and offer the skills that the counselor can bring to the collaboration.
27. Assess the effect of the counselor's interaction with the community.

SYSTEMS ADVOCACY

28. When counselors identify systemic factors that act as barriers to their students' or clients' development, they often wish that they could change the environment and prevent some of the problems that they see every day.
29. Regardless of the specific target of change, the processes for altering the status quo have common qualities. Change is a process that requires vision, persistence, leadership, collaboration, systems analysis, and strong data. In many situations, a counselor is the right person to take leadership.

SYSTEMS ADVOCACY COUNSELOR COMPETENCIES

30. In exerting systems-change leadership at the school or community level, the advocacy-oriented counselor is able to identify environmental factors impinging on students' or clients' development.
31. Provide and interpret data to show the urgency for change.
32. In collaboration with other stakeholders, develop a vision to guide change.
33. Analyze the sources of political power and social influence within the system.
34. Develop a step-by-step plan for implementing the change process.
35. Develop a plan for dealing with probable responses to change.
36. Recognize and deal with resistance.
37. Assess the effect of the counselor's advocacy efforts on the system and constituents.

References

Bond, T., Courtland, L., Lowe, A., Malayapillay, M., Wheeler, S., Banks, A., Kurdt, K., Mercado, M., & Smiley, E. (2001). The nature of counselling: An investigation of counselling activity in selected countries. *International Journal for the Advancement of Counselling*, 23, 245–60.

Davis, D. & Hayes, J. (2012, July/August). What are the benefits of mindfulness? *Monitor on Psychology*, pp. 64, 66–70.

Hölzel, B., Carmody, J., Vangel, M., Congletona, C., Yerramsetti, S., Gard, T. et al. (2011). Mindfulness practices lead to increases in regional brain gray matter density. *Psychiatric Research: Neuroimaging*, 191, 36–43.

Ivey, A.E., Ivey, M.B., & Zalaquett, C.P. (2014). *Intentional Interviewing and Counseling: Facilitating Client Development in a Multicultural Society*. Belmont, CA: Cengage Learning.

Jung, C.G. (1954). *The Practice of Psychotherapy*, vol. 16. London: Routledge & Kegan Paul.

Kiselica, M. & Robinson, M. (2001). Bringing advocacy counseling to life: The history, issues, and human drama of social justice in counseling. *Journal of Counseling and Development*, 79, 387–97.

Lewis, J., Arnold, M.S., House, R., & Toporek, R.L. (2002). ACA Advocacy Competencies. Retrieved from http://www.counseling.org/Resources/Competencies/Advocacy_Compe tencies.pdf

Lorelle, S., Byrd, R., & Crockett, S. (July, 2012). Globalization and professional issues in counseling. *The Professional Counselor*, 2, 115–23. http://tpcjournal.nbcc.org

Montgomery, L.M., Cupit, B.E., & Wimberley, T.K. (1999). Complaints, malpractice, and risk management: Professional issues and personal experiences. *Professional Psychology: Research and Practice*, 30, 402–10.

Perera-Diltz, D.M. & Mason, K.L. (2012). A national survey of school counselor supervision practices: Administrative, clinical, peer, and technology mediated supervision. *Journal of School Counseling*, 10(4). Retrieved from http://files.eric.ed.gov/fulltext/EJ978860.pdf

Russell-Chapin, L.A. (2016, in press). The power of neurocounseling and self-regulation. In J. Edwards, S. Young, & H. Nickels (eds.). *Handbook of Strengths-based Clinical Practices: Finding Common Factors*. New York: Routledge.

Russell-Chapin, L. & Chapin, T. (2012). *Clinical Supervision*. Belmont, CA: Cengage.

Siegal, J. (2010). *The Mindful Therapist: A Clinician's Guide to Mindsight and Neural Integration*. New York, NY: W.W. Norton & Co.

Simon, R. (2002, June). The larger story. *Psychotherapy Networker*, pp. 45–6. Washington, DC.

Williams, M., Teasdale, J., Segal, Z., & Kabat-Zinn, J. (2007). *The Mindful Way Through Depression: Freeing Yourself from Chronic Unhappiness*. New York, NY: Guilford Press.

INDEX OF NAMES

INDEX OF SUBJECTS

References to figures are in *italics*. References to tables are in **bold**.